M000036056

BERNARDO BERTOLUCCI

INTERVIEWS

CONVERSATIONS WITH FILMMAKERS SERIES

PETER BRUNETTE, GENERAL EDITOR

Alessia Bulgari

BERNARDO BERTOLUCCI

INTERVIEWS

EDITED BY FABIEN S. GERARD,
T. JEFFERSON KLINE AND
BRUCE SKLAREW

UNIVERSITY PRESS OF MISSISSIPPI / JACKSON

http://www.upress.state.ms.us

Copyright © 2000 by University Press of Mississippi
All rights reserved
Manufactured in the United States of America

08   07   06   05   04   03   02   01   00   4   3   2   1

∞

Library of Congress Cataloging-in-Publication Data

Bertolucci, Bernardo.
    Bernardo Bertolucci : Interviews / edited by Fabien Gerard,
T. Jefferson Kline, and Bruce Sklarew.
        p.   cm. — (Conversations with filmmakers series)
    Filmography: p.
    Includes index.
    ISBN 1-57806-204-7 (cloth : alk. paper). — ISBN 1-57806-205-5
(pbk. : alk. paper)
    1. Bertolucci, Bernardo Interviews.   2. Motion picture producers
and directors—Italy Interviews.   I. Gerard, Fabien S., 1956–   .
II. Kline, T. Jefferson (Thomas Jefferson), 1942–   .   III. Sklarew,
Bruce H.   IV. Title.   V. Series.
PN1998.3.B48A5   2000
791.43'0233'092—dc21   99-31087
                                                              CIP

British Library Cataloging-in-Publication data available

CONTENTS

INTRODUCTION

"I LOVE THE SHADOW with her light step...she is always at my side," writes Bernardo Bertolucci prophetically at age eleven in a youthful poem (Leoncini). "I want to make a film in which shadows will have a special importance," he will tell Gian Luighi Rondi thirty years later; "the more important the shadows are, the more value and meaning the film will have." Certainly one of the values of a set of interviews such as we have gathered here, must be the opportunity it affords to discover the deep resonances that run, like buried cables, throughout Bertolucci's work and thought. He notes the primary importance accorded Proust on his father's bookshelf, (Nowell-Smith and Halberstadt) and himself claims, "The poet whom I like most is Proust. When I wrote poetry," he tells John Bragin, "it was poetry entirely based on remembrance of the past. On the other hand, film has made me discover that there is a future." And, like Proust, who spends his life attempting to overcome the intermittences of time through the discovery of involuntary memory and metaphor, Bertolucci is always looking for elements that connect various scenes within his own films and that connect his films with the whole history of cinema.

What we have attempted to connect, then, in this volume, are a series of threads in the career of a man considered by many to be the preeminent Italian film director of his generation. From *The Grim Reaper* (1962), his first full-length feature based on an idea by Pasolini, to his most recent film, *Besieged* (1998), Bertolucci has succeeded like no other European director in uniting a radically experimental vision of film with a broad appeal to American audiences that won him nine Academy Awards for *The Last*

Emperor in China (1987). From among the hundreds of interviews Bertolucci gave, beginning in 1952 when he was eleven and including an interview he gave forty-six years later in 1998, we have selected conversations that we feel meet a wide variety of objectives: as autobiography, as psycho-history (for he is remarkably candid about his years in analysis), as a production journal of each of his films, as a lament for projects never completed, as a portrait gallery of his contemporaries, as a compendium of film theory and an ABC of ideas on actors, auteur theory, Bazin, the camera, color, dance, dreams, editing, French cinema, Godard, Italian cinema, right on through to Zavattini and Zen. Perhaps most importantly to English-speaking audiences is the fact that over half of the interviews in the volume appear here for the first time in English.

Of course one of the most fascinating aspects of such a collection is the glimpse it affords of the evolution of a man and of a mind. Sally Quinn notes, for example, that in the five years that she has known Bertolucci, his earlier "arrogance camouflaging insecurity" has become "a humility based on self-assurance." Bertolucci himself stops here and there in his later interviews to reflect on the changes in his attitudes. But the interested reader will be able to chart these changes as they happen and enjoy the contradictions that they produce in Bertolucci's thinking. Indeed, contradiction, ambiguity, and paradox are far from negative assessments for Bertolucci, who several times claims that he loves contradictions!

The collection provides something of a psycho-history of Bertolucci as well: of his relations to his father and mother, to psychoanalysis itself, to the psychological reasons that give rise to his poetry and his film. Of his own place in the world, Bernardo remembers a childhood and adolescence full of great serenity, happiness and magic. One particularly revealing memory of this period occurs when the family had fled the city during the fascist years and had found refuge in the country in very primitive conditions. Since there was neither running water nor a toilet, whenever little Bernardo had to "do his business" his father would make him squat over a waterproofed map. When his son had finished, Attilio would toss his contributions into the fields. Such a scene cannot fail to evoke the scene of little Pu Yi's chamber pot in *The Last Emperor,* another moment of childhood omnipotence, and it nicely anticipates Bernardo's other "offering" to his father: his poetry.

Of his father, Bertolucci has good and bad things to say—a cloud of ambivalence and ambiguity that begins in adoration and ends in a series of fantasized murders! His first impression of his father, related in an interview with Maraini, was that he was perfect, "equal only to himself" but "more than handsome, he was irreplaceable." The most pervasive influence of Attilio Bertolucci in his son's life was his voice. The father managed to transform the most routine events into poetry and ritual, so that his son's first encounter with poetry was not garnered from school books but experienced as an essential quality of his childhood landscape. And so the usual father-son rivalry evolved into a full-scale competition as Bernardo began writing his own poetry. Of course, the Oedipal rivalry existed as well: "My father was an extension of my penis," Bertolucci tells Dacia Maraini, "For me it was as if it was I who engendered my father and not the other way around." Little wonder, psychologically speaking, Bernardo competed poetically with his father throughout his adolescence, but when he was finally forced to realize who had engendered whom, he was impelled to strike out in a new direction. And later when he showed his first major cinematic success to a group of friends in Parma, he admitted that he was reliving an adolescent experience and that he'd really come back to Parma to show his father's friends that he was capable of doing something on his own. And what he was to do, indeed, was to make a series of films in which the father is revealed as traitor and hero (*Spider's Stratagem*), or knifed (*The Conformist*), shot (*Last Tango*), butchered with a pitchfork (*1900*) or, at the very least, betrayed (*Tragedy of a Ridiculous Man*), before being merged with the figure of the analyst (*Last Emperor*) and finally revered (*Little Buddha*).

The interviews in this volume reveal Bertolucci's mother to have been likewise the object of a series of ambivalent fantasies. He frequently associates her with the moon and explores the various faces of that identity in *Luna*. Another version of his personal mythology about her has it that, as a child, on her way from Sydney to Parma, someone had substituted an Indian girl for her—an identity that may explain why Jesse, his alter ego in *Little Buddha*, leaves his Caucasian parents to seek his "original" family in Tibet, in a very Indian yet uniquely Bertoluccian version of Freud's "family romance."

Should these interpretations seem too arcane, one need only refer to the numerous references Bertolucci himself makes throughout these pages to the role of psychoanalysis in his life and films. At various moments he credits psychoanalysis as the inspiration for his films. Of *Spider's Stratagem* he talks about the parallels between his own experience in psychoanalysis and the itinerary of his character, Athos Magnani. Elsewhere he confesses that he is a repressed person and that his work often serves as an outlet for his energies, aggressions and libido. "We know our ghosts," he tells Sally Quinn, "and we don't tell anybody, not even our partners, about our ghosts. We live with our ghosts. We keep the ghosts inside in our life. . . . [But] I can put my ghosts on the screen. I think I have understood this through psychoanalysis." Indeed, he will argue, psychoanalysis was to become a feature of his cinematography. Comparing the first several months of analysis to the discovery of a new universe, Bertolucci claims that he had to find a whole new vocabulary to navigate this new territory. And because psychoanalysis had caused such a profound change in his personal orientation, it was to become one of the most important elements of his films: "For each film," he tells Jean Gili, "I go through an elaboration, a plumbing, a perverse simplification that is created through the working through of Freudian analysis." More than just background work, "psychoanalysis," Bertolucci continues, "is like having an additional lens on my camera, or an instrument that would be at once a lens, a dolly, a tracking shot, truly a tool of the trade that would combine all of these aspects together."

This analogy between psychoanalysis and film quite naturally evoked in its turn an association between film and dreams that, over time, becomes a richly complex metaphor for Bertolucci. Believing dreams and films to originate from the same psychological material, Bertolucci shared with Jean Gili his belief that cinema is "woven on a dream loom."

And it is precisely through this metaphor of dreaming that we can measure the distance traveled in his basic orientation to his films and to the very ontology of film. When he first began making films, Bertolucci was pulled in two very different directions: his first master was Pasolini, who initiated him to the act of creating not just *a* film, but of inventing the language of film. But, as he was to discover, Pasolini's milieu (the *ragazzi* of Rome) and his basic orientation (cinema as a sacred passion) were unappealing to his disciple. Instead, once initiated, Bertolucci turned to France. Indeed, in the sixties he was so convinced of the importance of the French New Wave that he began speaking French with his interviewers, proclaiming that French was the language of cinema. Later he would understand that his own origins had somewhat predisposed him for this obsession, for the French occupation of Parma had everywhere left its residues in the city's dialect, architecture, furniture and cuisine. Whatever its origins, this fascination with France, soon turned into a fascination with Jean-Luc Godard's New Wave extremism, his spirit of improvisation, his Marxist politics and Brechtian style, which his younger Italian disciple saw as a kind of cinematic terrorism, comparing Godard's radical jump-cuts to throwing a bomb.

Bertolucci's own political education had long prepared him for such radicalism. He recalls that as a child playing in a tomato field on his father's farm near Baccanelli, he heard the word "communism" for the first time from the peasants there who were organizing a demonstration to protest the death of Alberti. In that moment, he tells Jean Gili, he connected communism with heroism and became a communist, though he didn't join the Communist Party until much later. His first films express much more the confusions and ambiguities of growing up in a bourgeois household while adhering to Marxist ideology, but when *Before the Revolution* incited violent anti-communist reactions at its release in Paris, Bertolucci joined the Party. As his career evolved, however, he would argue that the most important politics of all is to remain true to oneself and he eventually admitted to Marilyn Goldin that "the most important discovery I made after the events of May 1968 was that I wanted the revolution not to help the poor but for myself . . . I discovered the individual level in political revolution."

Such a personal view of politics may explain Bertolucci's fascination with Godard, for Godard more than any other director connects radical politics with avant-garde aesthetics. The French director represented above all an unflinching search for the answer to André Bazin's famous question, "Qu'est-ce que le cinéma? [What is cinema?]" Bertolucci took up this question in his turn as a kind of aesthetic talisman. In his early films, especially *Before the Revolution* and *Partner,* all that mattered was technique and the search for a language that was specific to film. From France Bertolucci also borrowed the idea of *auteur* cinema which he associated with radical extremism and this search for a new aesthetics. Films must become conscious of what they are, he would proclaim, and cinema must speak about cinema challenging all the old traditions of expression and film grammar. As he worked on *Partner,* his most political (and admittedly inaccessible) film, he talked about the necessity of teaching the public what films are and how to read films. This crusade would last well into the seventies, when Berto-lucci would claim that the public was cinematically "illiterate" and needed to be taught how to see. Still later he would look back on the arrogance and militancy of his early years as a kind of blind romantic, even childish notion, joking with Stefano Consiglio and Francesco Dal Bosco that he had been obsessed with making "Miuras'—the name given in bull fights to "the most dangerous, strongest and lithest bulls: even a mosquito couldn't penetrate his asshole." Making a 'Miura' film, he laughed, meant that not a single spectator would enter the theater.

The "truth" was, as Bertolucci would discover, that he needed an audi-ence, and the appreciation of this audience, to survive. In keeping with the preeminence of psychoanalysis in his thinking, then, he instinctively returns to the metaphor of dreaming to describe why his early radicalism couldn't succeed: "It's the thing that annoys the audience the most; they'll accept anything except to be awakened from the dream they're having in the movie theater. Within this dream you can make them swallow anything, but if you tell them that the dream they're experiencing has a speed of 24 frames a second and that it comes out of an acid bath and Technicolor labs down the street, then they get angry and won't go along with it." (Adriano Aprà, Maurizio Ponzi & Piero Spila).

And so these pages allow a privileged (if often somewhat voyeuristic) view of Bertolucci's career and his gradual evolution from a radical "Miura" filmmaker to the serene elder statesman he is today. We follow his en-thusiasm for each new project—even when these projects never lead to productions, as in the cases of no less than nine of the "films" discussed: a film to be made in Latin about the middle ages; a film based on Goethe's *Wilhelm Meister* to star Adriana Asti in her role as a star of the Italian stage; a project called *Natura contro Natura* conceived as a thinly disguised homage to Pasolini; a film for the Italian Communist Party about working women; a Brazilian musical comedy; a film adaptation of Moravia's *1934* and another of Dashiell Hammett's *Red Harvest*; and finally projects for Malraux's *Man's Estate* and a sequel to his own *1900*.

As these projects are born or die, old attitudes evolve into new ones: Bertolucci's ideas on montage and editing move from an absolute rejection of any editing whatsoever to a complete fascination with montage. Like-wise his relationship to his audience evolves from one of refusal to a great need of affection. In politics, Bertolucci relaxes his militancy of the early years into a more personal and less radical stance. And, as might be expected, these changes give rise to internal contradictions. When discussing *Partner,* with Adriano Aprà, Maurizio Ponzi & Piero Spila, Bertolucci at one point rigidly refuses the idea of cutting, and moments later argues the need to cut "just to deny the continuity of the scene." And yet, as he realizes the contradiction he has just enunciated, Bertolucci makes the first of many *apologia* for contradiction, arguing that, in fact, the artist needs constantly to work against what he has done. Such contradictions build on each other, he argues, and ultimately guarantee not only vitality but inevitably lead the artist beyond facile traditions to his own personal truth.

Indeed, if there is any constant theme in these interviews that runs throughout the volume, it is this insistent apology for contradiction: the new dramaturgy of *Luna* is founded on the contrary of consistency and the need to portray the contradictions in life. *1900,* he argues, is likewise founded on contradictions because the film itself represents a kind of historical compromise. Throughout these interviews the attentive reader will at first believe he has "caught" Bertolucci in a flagrant contradiction only to realize that Bertolucci enjoys such ambiguity and contradictions because, for him, freedom must always be total and absolute even if it leads to apparent incoherence. With such a realization in mind, let us sit back and listen to Bertolucci talk; weaving stories of his life, his films, his contemporaries, especially Pasolini, Rossellini, and Godard — and even of his favorite smells — a sense we had forgotten given the primacy of the image in his art. We shall hear him tell of filming a scene based on Murnau's *Sunrise* without ever having seen that film, and realize how uncannily he intuited what Murnau had included in his film. We shall learn that, years before he ever contemplated *Little Buddha,* he had explored its most fundamental implications in a scene in *Before the Revolution.* We will appreciate the immense importance of chance in his films and, likewise the remarkable freedom he offers his actors. We'll see him anticipate with uncanny clarity Peter Weir's *Truman Show* while discussing the possibilities of video and television with Wim Wenders. We shall learn, not surprisingly, of his love for painting and music — and even of his secret frustration at never having been a composer.

But most of all we will be convinced that Bertolucci was "fated" (since fate and the unconscious are, for him, one) to be a poet of the seventh art.

It is an art he calls a private eye of memory, and it is an art through which he speaks to the child and to the adult in each of us.

Conforming to the policy of the University Press of Mississippi in regard to its interview series, the interviews assembled in this volume have not been edited in any substantive way. While this may result in an occasional repetition in Bertolucci's comments, it offers, we believe, more integrity for the scholarly reader. Perhaps more importantly, such repetitions may reveal the director's continuing obsessions or concerns and are therefore quite revealing.

Finally, the editors wish to thank the Bertolucci archives of PARTNER, asbl for having provided the selection of interviews in this volume. We also gratefully acknowledge the generous contributions of the following: Elena Marco, Nicoletta Billi, Bruna Conti, Cmilla Lazzari-Panni, Julie Anderson, Sevilla Delofski, Jocelyn Cousins, Fabiano Canosa, Venanzio Ciampa, Nicholas Vreeland, Paolo Lagazzi, Marcello Garofalo, and Marizio Schiaretti and Bruce Byall.

CHRONOLOGY

1941   Bernardo Bertolucci is born March 16 at the Bertolucci family farm
        near Parma, Italy, to the half-Irish Ninetta Giovanardi and well-
        known poet Attilio Bertolucci. From an early age, BB accompanies
        his father to the movies in town since Attilio is also the film critic
        for the *Gazzetta di Parma*.

1947   Giuseppe Bertolucci, BB's only brother is born in Parma. He will
        practice poetry and painting for years and later become a filmmaker
        himself in the late '70s—notably developing a close collaboration
        with Roberto Benigni—after having worked on several films as BB's
        assistant and co-writer.

1952   The Bertolucci family moves to Rome.

1956   During the summer and winter vacations back in the Parma coun-
        tryside, the fifteen-year-old BB shoots two fiction home movies with
        a 16mm camera he has been lent by a relative: *La Teleferica (The Cable)*
        and *La morte del maiale (Death of a Pig)*.

1959   As a reward for completing his high school education, BB spends
        one full month in Paris along with his cousin Giovanni Bertolucci
        and eagerly attends Henri Langlois's *Cinémathèque Française*.

1961   BB decides to give up his courses in modern literature at the Univer-
        sity of Rome to assist his father's close friend, the writer and poet,
        Pier Paolo Pasolini, on the set of Pasolini's first feature film, *Accattone*.

1962   BB's first published collection of poetry, *In Cerca del mistero (In Search of Mystery)* wins the prestigious Viareggio Prize.

Meanwhile, BB directs his own first full-length feature, *La Commare secca (The Grim Reaper)*, based on a Pasolini story, especially praised by Richard Roud who will soon invite this "new talent of outstanding promise" to the first New York Film Festival.

1964   A more autobiographical work, *Prima della rivoluzione (Before the Revolution)*, opens at the Cannes Festival. Although BB is immediately considered by *Cahiers du cinéma* the Italian avatar of the "New Wave," this film will not be properly released until 1967. Martin Scorsese would later see it as a model.

1966   BB directs for Italian TV *La Via del petrolio (The Oil Route)*, a meandering documentary divided into three episodes, shot in Iran, Suez, and Switzerland.

Sergio Leone asks BB to co-write the story of *Once Upon a Time in the West*, starring Henry Fonda, Charles Bronson, Jason Robards, and Claudia Cardinale.

BB engages Julian Beck's Living Theatre to play in the kind of experimental episode *Agonia (Agony)* that he contributes to an omnibus film revisiting various parables from the Gospel, eventually released in 1969 as *Amore e rabbia (Love & Anger)*.

1968   The "prophetic" value of *Before the Revolution*—finally released in Paris thanks to Langlois—is acclaimed by the students of the Sorbonne. A few weeks later, the very title of the film is quoted in the headlines of a well-known French newspaper to comment on the May uprising.

BB convinces his cousin Giovanni to produce *Partner*, a modern interpretation of Dostoevsky's *The Double*. Started in early April, the shooting extends until the end of May. In the meantime, BB and his French actor Pierre Clémenti use as their inspiration the actual events taking place in the Paris boulevards.

1969   BB joins the Italian Communist Party and begins Freudian analysis.

During the summer, he directs *Strategia del ragno (The Spider's Stratagem)*, a low-budget film made for Italian TV after Borges's story,

"Theme of the Traitor and the Hero," and by the end of the same year he has begun filming *Il Conformista (The Conformist)*, based on the novel by his old friend Alberto Moravia. Both films deal with the fascist period as well as with Oedipal relationships and will meet with unexpected success at their release, one year later.

1971   As BB co-directs, with his brother Giuseppe and editor Franco "Kim" Arcalli, a militant documentary entitled *La salute è malata o I poveri muoiono prima (Health Is Ill or The Poor Die First)*, *The Conformist* is nominated for an Academy Award for "Best Adapted Screenplay," and Francis F. Coppola declares this film "the first classic of the decade."

1972   *Last Tango in Paris*, written by the same team and produced by Alberto Grimaldi, opens at the New York Film Festival. Pauline Kael's review in *The New Yorker* helps the film become a landmark in film history. BB, Marlon Brando, and debutante Maria Schneider make the covers of *Time* and *Newsweek*: a modern legend is born.

1974   BB begins the year-long filming of *Novecento (1900)*, again teaming up with his brother Giuseppe, Franco Arcalli, and Alberto Grimaldi. Financed by Warner Bros., Fox and Paramount, the film is shot in the Parma countryside, casting Hollywood icons such as Burt Lancaster, Sterling Hayden, and Donald Sutherland, but also newcomers named Robert De Niro and Gérard Depardieu, not to mention a group of genuine Emilian peasants BB had known as a child.

1976   The full-version of *1900*—5 hours 30 minutes—opens at the Cannes Festival. Encouraged by the huge success of the film in Europe, BB agrees to spend another year working on a shorter version—4 hours— especially made for the U.S. market. American audiences will have to wait until 1990 to see the director's cut.

1979   Jill Clayburgh plays the part of an opera singer in *Luna*. Although French critics consider the film a masterpiece, the American press fiercely attacks the director's so called "New Dramaturgy"—a mix of Douglas Sirk and Lubitsch touches, using gorgeous operatic back-drops to depict the last taboo of incest between a drug addicted teenager and his whimsical mother.

1981   Ugo Tognazzi wins the "Best Actor" award at Cannes for his role in *La Tragedia di un uomo ridicolo (Tragedy of a Ridiculous Man)*, perhaps BB's most underrated work which revisits Oedipal themes in the context of the nightmarish years of Italian terrorism.

1984   BB eventually decides to abandon the cherished project of filming Dashiell Hammett's *Red Harvest* because of serious differences with his former producer, Alberto Grimaldi.

1987   BB begins a new collaboration with his brother-in-law, writer Mark Peploe, and the independent British producer, Jeremy Thomas. This new team gives birth to the spectacular biopic *The Last Emperor,* shot on location in the Forbidden City in Beijing, which will be released throughout the world with striking success. The following spring, the film wins no less than nine Academy Awards, including "Best Film" and "Best Director."

1990   The acclaimed "Signor Oscar" (according to *Time* magazine) directs Debra Winger and John Malkovich as Kit and Port Moresby, the seasoned travelers of *The Sheltering Sky,* adapted from the 1949 cult novel by Paul Bowles, set in the Sahara.

1993   *Little Buddha,* a very unpredictable approach to Eastern philosophy, mostly shot in the Himalayas, completes BB's "oriental trilogy." Keanu Reeves plays Prince Siddhartha in this film clearly intended as a modern fairy tale. Bridget Fonda and Chris Isaak are the parents of a Seattle boy believed to be a reincarnated Tibetan Lama.

1996   BB makes a return to Italy with *Stealing Beauty,* co-written by Susan Minot. The film, set in Tuscany and introducing Liv Tyler to co-star Jeremy Irons, centers on the summer vacation of a nineteen-year-old American virgin growing up in a time of AIDS awareness.

1998   During the long preparation of a new project focusing on the life of the sixteenth-century composer Carlo Gesualdo, BB directs *Besieged,* a low-budget film produced by his brother for Italian TV. Based on a short story by John Lasdun, BB co-signs the screenplay with his wife and closest collaborator on the set, Clare Peploe.

FILMOGRAPHY

1956
The Cable (La Teleferica), home movie
Director: **Bernardo Bertolucci**
Screenplay: **Bernardo Bertolucci**
Cast: Giuseppe Bertolucci, Marta Galeazzi, Galeazzina Galeazzi
16mm, B&W
About 10 minutes

1956
Death of a Pig (La Morte del maiale), home movie
Director: **Bernardo Bertolucci**
Screenplay: **Bernardo Bertolucci**
16mm, B&W
About 10 minutes

1962
The Grim Reaper (La Commare secca)
Compagnia Cinematografica Cervi SpA
Producer: Tonino Cervi
Director: **Bernardo Bertolucci**
Screenplay: **Bernardo Bertolucci,** Sergio Citti (from a story by P. P. Pasolini)
Cinematography: Gianni Narzisi
Production and Costume Design: Adriana Spadaro

Sound: Sandro Fortini
Editing: Nino Baragli
Music: Piero Piccioni (from a Renaissance theme composed by Santino Garsi); songs "Addio, addio" by Claudio Villa, "Come nasce un'amore" by Nico Fidenco
Cast: Francesco Ruiu (Canticchia), Giancarlo De Rosa (Nino), Vincenzo Ciccora (Sindaco), Alvaro D'Ercole (Francolicchio), Romano Labate (Pipito), Lorenza Benedetti (Milly), Emi Rocci (Domenica), Erina Torelli (Mariella), Renato Troiani (Natalino), Marisa Solinas (Bruna), Wanda Rocci (the prostitute), Alfredo Leggi (Bustelli), Carlotta Barilli (Bustelli's girlfriend), Gabriella Giorgelli (Esperia), Santina Lisio (Esperia's mother), Clorinda Celani (Soraya), Ada Peragostini (Maria), Silvio Laurenzi (homosexual), Allen Midgette (Costantino Teodoro), Gianni Bonagura (police inspector's voice off), Nadia Bonafede, Ugo Santucci, Santina Fioravanti, Elena Fontana, and Maria Fontana
35mm, B&W
100 minutes

1964
Before the Revolution (Prima della rivoluzione)
Iride Cinematografica
Producer: Mario Bernocchi
Director: **Bernardo Bertolucci**
Screenplay: **Bernardo Bertolucci**, with Gianni Amico
Cinematography: Aldo Scavarda
Costume Design: Federico Forquet
Sound: Romano Pampaloni
Editing: Roberto Perpignani
Music: Ennio Morricone; "Walking with G. A." and "Invention for Fabrizio & Gina" by Gato Barbieri; excerpts from Giuseppe Verdi's "Macbeth;" songs "Ricordati" and "Vivere ancora" by Gino Paoli, "Avevo 15 anni" by Ennio Ferrari
Cast: Francesco Barilli (Fabrizio), Adriana Asti (Gina), Allen Midgette (Agostino), Morando Morandini (Cesare), Cristina Pariset (Clelia), Domenico Alpi (Fabrizio's father), Emilia Borghi (Fabrizio's mother), Giuseppe Meghenzani (Fabrizio's brother), Iole Lunardi (Fabrizio's grand-

mother), Ida Pellegri (Clelia's mother), Gianni Amico (filmbuff), Cecrope Barilli (Puck), Goliardo Padova (painter), Guido Fanti (Enore), Evelina Alpi (little girl), Salvatore Enrico (priest)
35mm, B&W
112 minutes (Italian version: 100 minutes)

1967
The Oil Route (La Via del petrolio)
Documentary in three episodes: I. *The Origins (Le Origini)*, II. *The Travel (Il Viaggio)*, III. *Across Europe (Attraverso l'Europa)*
RAI-Radiotelevisione italiana / ENI
Producer: Giorgio Patara
Director: **Bernardo Bertolucci**
Screenplay: **Bernardo Bertolucci**
Narrators: Nino Castelnuovo, Mario Feliciani, Giulio Bosetti, Nino Dal Fabbro, and Riccardo Cucciolla
Cinematography: Ugo Piccone (I, II), Maurizio Salvadori (II), Luis Saldanha (II), and Giorgio Pelloni (III)
Sound: Giorgio Pelloni
Editing: Roberto Perpignani
Music: Egisto Macchi; excerpts from Giuseppe Verdi's "La Traviata," Miles Davis, etc.
Cast: Mario Trejo, as the "Patagonian journalist" in the 3rd episode
16mm, B&W
48 minutes (I), 40 minutes (II), 45 minutes (III)

1967
The Canal (Il Canale)
Documentary filmed in Suez during the shooting of *The Oil Route*
Patara Films srl
Producer: Giorgio Patara
Director: **Bernardo Bertolucci**
Screenplay: **Bernardo Bertolucci**
Cinematography: Ugo Piccone and Maurizio Salvadori
Sound: Giorgio Pelloni
Editing: Roberto Perpignani
Music: Egisto Macchi

16mm, color (Eastmancolor)
About 12 minutes

1967–69
Agony (Agonia)
Episode of *Love & Anger (Amore e rabbia),* also known as *Vangelo 70*
Castoro Film srl (Rome)/Anouchka Film (Paris)
Producer: Carlo Lizzani
Director: **Bernardo Bertolucci**
Screenplay: **Bernardo Bertolucci** (based on the Parable of the Barren Fig
Tree, Luke 12:6–9)
Cinematography: Ugo Piccone
Production Design: Lorenzo Tornabuoni
Editing: Roberto Perpignani
Sound: Manlio Magara
Cast: Julian Beck (the dying man) and the twenty-four members of the
Living Theatre (the visitors), Milena Vukotic (nurse), Giulio Cesare
Castello, Adriano Aprà, and Romano Costa (priests)
35mm, color (Eastmancolor)
28 minutes

1968
Partner
Red Film srl
Producer: Giovanni Bertolucci
Director: **Bernardo Bertolucci**
Screenplay: **Bernardo Bertolucci,** Gianni Amico (based on "The Double"
by F. Dostoevsky)
Cinematography: Ugo Piccone
Production Design: Jean-Robert Marquis (Francesco Tullio Altan)
Costume Design: Nicoletta Sivieri
Sound: Manlio Magara
Editing: Roberto Perpignani
Music: Ennio Morricone; song "Splash," performed by Peter Boom
Cast: Pierre Clémenti (Jacob), Stefania Sandrelli (Clara), Sergio Tofano
(Petrushka), Tina Aumont (salesgirl), Giulio Cesare Castello, Romano
Costa, Antonio Maestri, and Mario Venturini (teachers), John Ohettplace

(piano player), Ninetto Davoli, Jean-Robert Marquis, Nicole Laguiné, Sybilla Sedat, Gianpaolo Capovilla, Umberto Silva, Giuseppe Mangano, Sandro Bernardone, David Grieco, Rochelle Barbieri, Antonio Guerra, Alessandro Cane, Vittorio Fanfoni, Giancarlo Nanni, Salvatore Samperi, and Stefano Oppedisano (students), Stanko Molnar (man with hat in the street)
35mm, color (Technicolor, Techniscope)
105 minutes

1970
The Spider's Stratagem (Strategia del ragno)
Red Film srl/RAI-TV
Producer: Giovanni Bertolucci
Director: **Bernardo Bertolucci**
Screenplay: **Bernardo Bertolucci**, Eduardo De Gregorio and Marilù Parolini (based on "Theme of the Traitor and the Hero" by Jorge Luis Borges)
Cinematography: Vittorio Storaro and Franco Di Giacomo
Production and Costume Design: Maria Paola Maino
Sound: Giorgio Pelloni
Editing: Roberto Perpignani
Music: excerpts from Giuseppe Verdi's "Rigoletto" and "Attila" and from Arnold Schoenberg's "Chamber Symphony n.2, op. 32;" song "Il Conformista" by Mina; "Usignolo," "Germana" and "Giovinezza," performed by the Cantoni band from Colorno
Cast: Giulio Brogi (Athos Magnani), Alida Valli (Draifa), Tino Scotti (Costa), Pippo Campanini (Gaibazzi), Franco Giovannelli (Rasori), Allen Midgette (sailor), Attilio Viti (lion tamer), Giuseppe Bertolucci (lion's head carrier)
35mm, color (Eastmancolor)
110 minutes
Award: "Prix Luis Buñuel" (France, 1970)

1971
The Conformist (Il Conformista)
Mars Film (Rome)/Marianne Productions (Paris)/Maran Film GmbH (Münich)

Producer: Maurizio Lodi-Fè
Director: **Bernardo Bertolucci**
Screenplay: **Bernardo Bertolucci** (based on the novel by Alberto Moravia)
Cinematography: Vittorio Storaro
Production Design: Ferdinando Scarfiotti
Costume Design: Gitt Magrini
Sound: Massimo Dallimonti
Editing: Franco Arcalli
Music: Georges Delerue; songs "Chi è più felice di me?" by Cesare Andrea
Bixio, "Tornerai" by Olivieri
Cast: Jean-Louis Trintignant (Marcello Clerici), Stefania Sandrelli (Giulia),
Gastone Moschin (Manganiello), Dominique Sanda (Anna Quadri), Enzo
Tarascio (Professor Quadri), Pierre Clémenti (Lino), José Quaglio (Italo),
Milly (Marcello's mother), Giuseppe Addobato (Marcello's father), Yvonne
Sanson (Giulia's mother), Fosco Giachetti (fascist colonel), Benedetto
Benedetti (fascist Minister), Christian Alégny (Mr. Raoul), Marilyn Goldin
(flower girl), Romano Costa (Prof. Quadri's student in Paris), Antonio
Maestri (confessor), Pierangelo Civera (nurse), Pasquale Fortunato
(Marcello aged 11), Christian Belègne (gipsy), Gino Vagni Luca (fascist sec-
retary), Marta Lado (Marcello's daughter), Carlo Gaddi, Franco Pellerani,
Claudio Carpelli, and Umberto Silvestri (killers), Alessandro Haber and
Massimo Sarchielli (two blind men in the restored version)
35mm, color (Technicolor)
110 minutes (restored version: 116 minutes)
Awards: "BFI Award" (London, 1971), "Grand Prix de l'UCC" (Brussels,
1971), Academy Awards nomination for "Best Adapted Screenplay"
(Hollywood, 1971)

1971
Health Is Ill or The Poor Die First (La Salute è malata o I poveri muoiono prima)
Documentary about the situation of Roman hospitals
ARCI/Unitelefilm
Director: **Bernardo Bertolucci**
Cinematography: Elio Bisignani and Renato Tafuri
Editing: Franco Arcalli
16mm, B&W
35 minutes

1972
Last Tango in Paris (Ultimo Tango a Parigi)
PEA Cinematografica (Rome)/Artistes Associés (Paris)
Producer: Alberto Grimaldi
Director: **Bernardo Bertolucci**
Screenplay: **Bernardo Bertolucci**, Franco Arcalli (from a story by **BB**,
Giuseppe Bertolucci, and Franco Arcalli); collaboration to the dialogues:
Alberto Moravia
Cinematography: Vittorio Storaro
Production Design: Ferdinando Scarfiotti
Costume Design: Gitt Magrini
Sound: Antoine Bonfanti
Editing: Franco Arcalli and Roberto Perpignani
Music: Gato Barbieri
Cast: Marlon Brando (Paul), Maria Schneider (Jeanne), Jean-Pierre Léaud
(Tom), Veronica Lazar (Rosa), Maria Michi (Rosa's mother), Massimo
Girotti (Rosa's lover), Luce Marquand (Jeanne's nanny), Gitt Magrini
(Jeanne's mother), Catherine Allégret (girl washing the bathtub), Giovanna
Galletti (old prostitute), Armand Ablanalp (old prostitute's client), Darling
Legitimus (black concierge), Catherine Breillat (Mouchette), Marie-Hélène
Breillat (Mouchette's sister), Catherine Sola (TV script-girl), Mauro
Marchetti (TV cameraman), Dan Diament (TV boom operator), Peter
Schommer (TV assistant director), Mimi Pinson (tango contest jury),
Ramon Mendizabal (conductor), Stéphane Kosiak and Gérard Lepennec
(dancers), Rachel Kesterber (Christine); actors in scenes cut from the final
version: Michel Delahaye (Bible salesman), Laura Betti (Miss Blandish),
Jean-Luc Bideau (sailor on the barge)
35mm, color (Eastmancolor)
126 minutes
Awards: "Prix Raoul Lévy" (Paris, 1972), "Nastro d'Argento" for Best
Director (Rome, 1973), Academy Awards nominations for "Best Actor" and
"Best Director" (Hollywood, 1974)

1976
1900 (Novecento)
PEA (Rome)/Artistes Associés (Paris)/Artemis Film (Berlin)
Producer: Alberto Grimaldi

Director: **Bernardo Bertolucci**
Screenplay: **Bernardo Bertolucci**, Giuseppe Bertolucci, and Franco Arcalli
Cinematography: Vittorio Storaro
Production Design: Ezio Frigerio
Costume Design: Gitt Magrini
Sound: Claudio Maielli
Editing: Franco Arcalli
Music: Ennio Morricone; songs "Era di maggio" by Mirna Doris, "Chi è più felice di me?" by Cesare Andrea Bixio; traditional Italian folksongs performed by the Cantoni band from Colorno, Le Ocarine from Budrio, Ocarina solista Rota from Fidenza
Cast: Robert De Niro (Alfredo), Gérard Depardieu (Olmo), Stefania Sandrelli (Anita), Dominque Sanda (Ada), Burt Lancaster (Alfredo Berlinghieri, Sr.), Romolo Valli (Giovanni Berlinghieri), Werner Bruhns (Ottavio Berlinghieri), Francesca Bertini (sister Desolata), Anna Maria Gherardi (Alfredo's mother), Ellen Schwiers (Regina's mother), Sterling Hayden (Leo Dalcò), Maria Monti (Olmo's mother), Antonio Piovanelli (Turo Dalcò), Paolo Branco (Orso Dalcò), Liù Bosisio (Nella Dalcò), Edoardo Dallagio (Oreste Dalcò), Giacomo Rizzo (hunchback), Laura Betti (Regina), Donald Sutherland (Attila), Alida Valli (Mrs. Pioppi), Pietro Longari Ponzoni (Mr. Pioppi), Paolo Pavesi (Alfredo aged 11), Roberto Maccanti (Olmo aged 11), Anna Henkel (Olmo's daughter), Stefania Casini (epileptic girl), Pippo Campanini (priest), Allen Midgette (tramp), José Quaglio (Avanzini), Salvatore Mureddu (cavalry colonel), Gabriella Cristiani (Stella), Carlotta Barilli (peasant), Katerina Kosak (Rondine), Sante Bianchi (Montanaro), Girolamo Lazzari (Tiger), Irene Bianchi (servant), Fabio Garriba
35mm, color (Technicolor)
325 minutes (Cannes version); 245 minutes (U.S. version); 315 minutes (director's cut)

1976
Silence Is Complicity (Il Silenzio è complicità)
Documentary on the assassination of Pier Paolo Pasolini
Produced by the FGCI-Federazione Giovanile Comunista Italiana
Collective direction coordinated by Laura Betti with the collaboration of Bernardo Bertolucci, Mario Monicelli, Marco Bellocchio, Liliana Cavani,

Ettore Scola, Sergio Citti, Franco Arcalli, Dacia Maraini, Enzo Siciliano, and others.
Color
About 60 minutes

1979
Luna (La Luna)
Fiction Cinematografica SpA/20th Century Fox
Producer: Giovanni Bertolucci
Director: **Bernardo Bertolucci**
Screenplay: **Bernardo Bertolucci**, Giuseppe Bertolucci, and Clare Peploe
(from a story by **BB**, Giuseppe Bertolucci, and Franco Arcalli)
Cinematography: Vittorio Storaro
Production Design: Maria Paola Maino and Gianni Silvestri
Costume Design: Lina Nerli Taviani and Pino Lancetti
Sound: Mario Dallimonti
Editing: Gabriella Cristiani
Music: excerpts from Giuseppe Verdi's "Il trovatore," "Rigoletto," "La Traviata" and "Il ballo in maschera;" W. A. Mozart's "Così fan tutte;" songs "Saint Tropez" by Peppino Di Capri, "Saturday Night Fever" by the Bee Gees
Cast: Jill Clayburgh (Caterina Silveri), Matthew Barry (Joe), Tomas Milian (Giuseppe), Alida Valli (Giuseppe's mother), Fred Gwynne (Douglas), Veronica Lazar (Marina), Peter Eyre (Edward), Renato Salvatori (Emilian communist), Pippo Campanini (innkeeper), Franco Citti (homosexual), Elisabetta Campeti (Arianna), Stéphane Barat (Mustapha), Nicola Nicoloso (Manrico in the "Trovatore"), Mario Tocci (count di Luna in the "Trovatore"), Iole Cecchini (hairdresser), Iole Silvani (dresser), Rodolfo Lodi (old music teacher), Liana del Balzo (old Maestro's sister), Franco Magrini (doctor), Roberto Benigni (upholsterer), Julian Adamoli (Julian), Shara Di Nepi (servant), Francesco Mei (barman), Mimmo Poli (furniture mover), Massimiliano Filoni (street boy), Enzo Siciliano (conductor at the Opera House), Alessio Vlad (conductor at Caracalla), Carlo Verdone and Ronaldo Bonacchi (directors at Caracalla); actors in scenes cut from the final version: Laura Betti (Ludovica), Lorenzo Tornabuoni (sidewalk painter)
35mm, color (Technicolor)
116 minutes (U.S. version); 135 minutes (European version)

1981

Tragedy of a Ridiculous Man (La Tragedia di un uomo ridicolo)
Fiction Cinematografica SpA/The Ladd Company
Producer: Giovanni Bertolucci
Director: **Bernardo Bertolucci**
Screenplay: **Bernardo Bertolucci**
Cinematography: Carlo Di Palma
Production Design: Gianni Silvestri
Costume Design: Lina Nerli Taviani
Sound: Mario Dallimonti
Editing: Gabriella Cristiani
Music: Ennio Morricone; songs "Rock 'n' Roll Is Good for the Soul" by
The Boppers, "Horror Movies" by Linda & the Dark
Cast: Ugo Tognazzi (Primo Spaggiari), Anouk Aimée (Barbara Spaggiari),
Laura Morante (Laura), Victor Cavallo (Adelfo), Ricky Tognazzi (Giovanni
Spaggiari), Vittorio Caprioli (Marshal Angrisani), Renato Salvatori (Colonel
Macchi), Olimpia Carlisi (numerologist), Margherita Chiari (servant),
Gaetano Ferrari (gardener), Pietro Longari Ponzoni, Gianni Migliavacca,
Ennio Ferrari, and Angelo Novi (usurers), Antonio Trevisi (bank manager),
Giuseppe Calzolari (man with Bogie's hat)
35mm, color (Technicolor)
110 minutes
Award: "Grand Prix d'interprétation masculine" to Ugo Tognazzi (Cannes
Film Festival, 1981)

1985
Postcard from China (Cartolina dalla Cina)
Video documentary filmed by **BB** and his assistants, as they were scouting
locations for *The Last Emperor.*
Director and Narrator: **Bernardo Bertolucci**
Editing: Gabriella Cristiani
First shown on Italian TV: December, 1985
color
About 10 minutes

1987
The Last Emperor (L'ultimo imperatore)
The Recorded Picture Company Ltd. (London)/Tao Film srl (Rome), in
association with the China Film Coproduction Corporation (Beijing)

Producer: Jeremy Thomas
Director: **Bernardo Bertolucci**
Screenplay: **Bernardo Bertolucci** and Mark Peploe with Enzo Ungari
(based on the book *From Emperor to Citizen* by Aisin-Gioro Pu Yi)
Cinematography: Vittorio Storaro
Production Design: Ferdinando Scarfiotti
Costume Design: James Acheson
Sound: Ivan Sharrock
Editing: Gabriella Cristiani
Music: Ryuichi Sakamoto, David Byrne, and Su Cong; excerpt from Johann
Strauss's "Kaizer Waltz;" song "Am I Blue?" by Harry Akst & Grant Clarke
Cast: John Lone (Emperor Pu Yi), Joan Chen (Empress Wang Jung), Peter
O'Toole (Reginald F. Johnston), Ying Ruocheng (Pu Yi's reeducator), Dennis
Dun (Big Li), Victor Wong (Chen Pao-shen), Ryuichi Sakamoto (Mr.
Amakasu), Maggie Han (Eastern Jewel), Ric Young (interrogator), Wu Jun
Mei (Wen Hsiu), Cary Hiroyuki Tagawa (Chief Eunuch), Jade Go (Pu Yi's
wetnurse), Fimihiko Ikeda (Colonel Yoshioka), Richard Vuu (Pu Yi aged 3),
Tijger Tsou (Pu Yi aged 8), Wu Tao (Pu Yi aged 15), Fan Guang (Pu Chieh),
Henry Kyi (Pu Chieh aged 7), Alvin Riley, Jr. (Pu Chieh aged 14), Lisa Lu
(Empress Dowager Tzu Hsi), Hideo Takamatsu (Japanese General), Basil Pao
(Pu Yi's father), Liang Dong (Pu Yi's mother), Jiang Xiren (Lord
Chamberlain), Chen Shu (Minister of Trade), Chen Kaige (chief of the
imperial guards), Zhang Liangbin (Big Foot), Huang Wenjie (hunchback),
Constantine Gregory (occulist), Madame Soong (Empress Dowager Lung
Yu), Michael Vermaaten (American dancer), Matthew Spender
(Englishman), Xu Chunqing (Manchukuo officer), Gu Junguo (Johnston's
driver), Yang Hongchang (prison clerk), Wang Biao (prisoner), Akira Ikuta
(Japanese doctor)
35mm, color (Technicolor, CinemaScope)
158 minutes (director's cut: 218 minutes)
Awards: four "Nastri d'Argento" (Rome, 1987); eight "David di Donatello"
(Rome, 1987); "César du Meilleur Film Etranger" (Paris, 1988); four "Golden
Globes;" and nine Academy Awards, including "Best Film" and "Best
Director" (Hollywood, 1988)

1990
Bologna
Subliminal essay made on occasion of the World Cup

Istituto Luce
Director: **Bernardo Bertolucci**
Editing: Gabriella Cristiani
Music: Nicola Piovani
Color
30 seconds

1990
The Sheltering Sky (Il Té nel deserto)
The Sahara Company Ltd. (London)/Tao Film srl (Rome), in association
with The Aldrich Group
Producer: Jeremy Thomas
Director: **Bernardo Bertolucci**
Screenplay: **Bernardo Bertolucci** and Mark Peploe (based on the novel by
Paul Bowles)
Cinematography: Vittorio Storaro
Production Design: Gianni Silvestri and Ferdinando Scarfiotti
Costume Design: James Acheson
Sound: Ivan Sharrock
Editing: Gabriella Cristiani
Music: Ryuichi Sakamoto; Arab music: Richard Horrowitz; "Jewal" by
Bachir Attar & the Master Musicians of Jajouka; "Gnawa Drums" by
Ibrahim Kebir; "Midnight Sun" by Lionel Hampton; songs "Je chante" by
Charles Trenet, "Those Who Are in the Grave" by Mohammed Abdel-
wahab, "Dalili Ethar" and "Sharan Liwahdi" by Om Kalsoum; "The Sacred
Koran" and "Han el wid" by Simone Shaheen; "Ameur" by The Ouled-Nail,
"Vocal Solo" by Mustapha Choki
Cast: Debra Winger (Kit Moresby), John Malkovich (Port Moresby),
Campbell Scott (Tunner), Jill Bennett (Mrs. Lyle), Timothy Spall (Eric Lyle),
Eric Vu-An (Belqassim), Amina Annabi (Marhnia), Sotigui Kouyate (Abdel
Kader), Philippe Morier-Genoud (Captain Broussard), Ben Smail (Smail),
Brahim Oubana (young Arab), Menouer Samiri (bus driver), Kamel Cherif
(ticket seller), Mohammed Ixa (caravan leader), Ahmed Azdum, Alghabid
Kanakan, Gambo Alkabous, and Sidi Kasko (young Tuaregs), Azahra
Atamout, Marhnia Mohammed, and Oumou Alghabid (Belqassim's wives),
Sidi Alkhadar (Little Sidi), Keltoum Aloui (woman at the Hotel du Ksar),
Tom Novembre (French immigration officer), Carolyn de Fonseca (Miss
Ferry), Veronica Lazar (nurse), Nicoletta Braschi (young woman at the

café), Paul Bowles (the Narrator)
35mm, color (Technicolor)
132 minutes

1993
Little Buddha (Piccolo Buddha)
The Sahara Company Ltd. (London)/CiBy 2000 (Paris)
Producer: Jeremy Thomas
Director: **Bernardo Bertolucci**
Screenplay: **Bernardo Bertolucci,** Rudy Wurlitzer, and Mark Peploe (from
a story by **BB,** with Fabien Gerard, and Giovanni Mastrangelo)
Cinematography: Vittorio Storaro
Production and Costume Design: James Acheson
Special FX: Richard Conway and Val Wardlaw
Sound: Ivan Sharrock
Editing: Pietro Scalìa
Music: Ryuichi Sakamoto; songs "Let the Mystery Be" by Iris Dement,
"Chandranandan" by Ali Akbar Khan, "Raga Jog" by Shiv Kumar Sharma
Cast: Ying Ruocheng (Lama Norbu), Bridget Fonda (Lisa Conrad), Chris
Isaak (Dean Conrad), Alex Wiesendanger (Jesse Conrad), Sogyal Rinpoché
(Kenpo Tenzin), Jigme Kunzang (Chompa), Raju Lal (Raju), Greishma
Makar Singh (Gita), T. K. Lama (Sangay), Jo Champa (Maria), Khyongla
Rato Rinpoche (Abbott), Dzongsar Khyentse Rinpoche (young Lama),
Surehka Sikri (Gita's mother), Doma Tshomo (Ani-La), Rinzin Dakpa
(oracle), Mantu Lal (Mantu); ancient part: Keanu Reeves (Siddhartha),
Rudraprasad Sengupta (King Suddhodana), Kanika Panday (Queen Maya),
Madhu Mathur (Prajapathi), Rajeshwaree (Yasodhara), Bhisham Sahni
(Asita), Santosh Bangera (Channa), Vijay Kashyap (vizir), Anupam Shyam
(Mara), Anu Ehetri, Kavita Hahat, Tarana Ramakrishnan, Saddiya Siddiqui,
and Anita Takhur (Mara's daughters), Rashid Mastaan (beggar), Nagabab
Shyam, Chritra Mandal, Kumar Lingeshewer, Mahana Amar, and
Narmadapuree (ascetics), Nirmala (shepherd girl)
35mm (ancient part filmed in 75mm); color (Technicolor, Technovision)
117 minutes (U.S. version); 137 minutes (European version)

1996
Stealing Beauty (Io Ballo da sola)
The Recorded Picture Company Ltd. (London)/UGC Images

(Paris)/Fiction srl (Rome), in association with Fox Searchlight
Producer: Jeremy Thomas
Director: **Bernardo Bertolucci**
Screenplay: **Bernardo Bertolucci** and Susan Minot (from a story by **BB**)
Cinematography: Darius Khondji
Production Design: Gianni Silvestri
Costume Design: Louise Stjernsward and Giorgio Armani
Sound: Ivan Sharrock
Editing: Pietro Scalìa
Music: Richard Hartley; songs "2 Wicky" by Hoover, "Glory Box" by
Portishead, "If 6 Was 9" by Axiom Funk, "Annie Mae" by John Lee Hooker,
"Rocket Boy" by Liz Phair, "Superstition" by Stevie Wonder, "My Baby Just
Cares for Me" by Nina Simone, "I'll Be Seeing You" by Billie Holiday,
"Rhymes of an Hour" by Mazzy Star, "Alice" by Cocteau Twins, "You
Won't Fall" by Lori Carson, "I Need Love" by Sam Philipps
Sculptures made by Matthew Spender; paintings by Bernardo Siciliano
Cast: Liv Tyler (Lucy Harmon), Jeremy Irons (Alex Parish), Sinead Cusack
(Diana Grayson), Donal McCann (Ian Grayson), Carlo Cecchi (Carlo
Lisca), Stefania Sandrelli (Noemi), Jean Marais (Mr. Guillaume), D. W.
Moffett (Richard), Rachel Weisz (Miranda), Joseph Fiennes (Christopher),
Roberto Zibetti (Niccolò), Ignazio Oliva (Osvaldo), Leonardo Treviglio
(lieutenant), Francesco Siciliano (Michele), Anna Maria Gherardi (Chiarella
Donati), Jason Fleming (Gregory), Rebecca Valpy (Daisy), Daria Nicolodi
(Marta)
35mm, color (Technicolor, Technovision)
118 minutes

1998
Besieged (L'Assedio)
Fiction Films srl (Rome)/Navert Film (Milan), in association with Mediaset
Producer: Massimo Cortesi
Director: **Bernardo Bertolucci**
Screenplay: Clare Peploe and **Bernardo Bertolucci** (based on the short
story "The Siege" by James Lasdun)
Cinematography: Fabio Cianchetti
Production Design: Gianni Silvestri
Costume Design: Metka Kosak

Sound: Maurizio Argentieri
Editing: Jacopo Quadri
Music: Alessio Vlad; excerpts from A. Scriabine's "Study op. 8 n.12 in D sharp major," E. V. Grieg's "Sonata op.7 in E minor" (2nd movement), L. Van Beethoven's "32 Variations in C minor" and W. A. Mozart's "Fantasy in D minor, K 397," arranged and performed by Stefano Arnaldi; Rodgers & Hammerstein's "My Favourite Things" by Jimmy Coltrane, "Diaraby" by Ry Coodder & Ali Farka Toure; songs "Maria Valencia" and "Le Voyageur" by Papa Wemba, "Sina" by Salif Keita, "Africa" and "Nyumbani" by J. C. Ojwang, "Mambote na nje" by the Bondeko chorus, "Full Option" by Pépé Kalle, "Cuore matto" by Little Tony
Cast: Thandie Newton (Shandurai), David Thewlis (Mr. Kinsky), Claudio Santamaria (Agostino), Cyril Nri (African priest), Massimo De Rossi (usurer), Veronica Lazar (university professor), Mario Mazzetti di Pietralata (hospital professor), Veronica Visentin, Andrea Quercia, Lorenzo Mollica, Naralia Mignosa, Elena Perino, Fernando Trombetti, and Alexander Menis (children at the party), J. C. Ojwang (African singer), Paul Osul (Shandurai's husband)
35mm, color (Technicolor)
90 minutes

BERNARDO BERTOLUCCI

INTERVIEWS

Flowers in the Shadow of the Indian Hut

LEONIDA LEONCINI/1952

IN THE FRESHNESS OF his eleven years, the child is reflected in a bubble of poetry.

Among the most beautiful poems of *The Indian Hut* are three that Attilio Bertolucci wrote for his children, Giuseppe and Bernardo. Giuseppe, the younger brother, is presented, one might even say photographed, as he walks with uncertain steps through the calm of an October afternoon on a path yellowed by fallen leaves. Bernardo, the older brother, is portrayed as he launches a small paper airplane, which, as it disappears into the dusk, will never reappear in the images of the days of our lives. Bernardo reappears again as he is coming home from school along a road bordered by wilting violets.

In these poems, as in the ensemble of the anthology, the motif of a tranquil and melancholy nature persists, an autumnal nature which communicates the fleeting quality of life and all beautiful things. Here we must add a delicate observation—one so exact that it is transformed into a plastic representation of the gestures of his children who move about under the watchful eye of their father whose heart is overflowing with trepidation and paternal adoration.

I think that when Attilio Bertolucci offers us his next edition of poetry he will be able to capture once again in his older son a new attitude: the attitude of a child who abruptly quits his games to take up his pen with

From *Giornale dell'Emilia* (Bologna), 24 March 1952. Reprinted by permission. Translated by Fabien Gerard and T. Jefferson Kline.

great concentration in order to fix in verse some image which has just unexpectedly and with great luminosity united his heart and mind. Indeed, Bernardo is also a poet. And, let it be said immediately, it's not a question of imitating his father and even less of letting his father serve as his guide. Doubt arises obviously when one learns that this son of a Poet also writes beautiful poetry. When I carefully read his verses, which are not without errors or even stylistic problems, but are which already genuine poetry, I became absolutely convinced that the son had inherited from his father this precious spark of inspiration.

Since I hadn't met Bernardo, I went to wait for him at the Baccanelli school where he is in fifth grade. He's a relaxed and talkative child and yet quite modest for all that. His teacher tells me that he is a very good boy, of an exceptional generosity that has won the affections of all his school-mates, whom he is always ready to help or excuse if necessary.

We spent a long time together strolling around the courtyard of the school, occasionally reading the little notebook in which he has composed his poetry. He hasn't written many poems, but almost all of them are beautiful, spontaneous and original. The little poet has just celebrated his eleventh birthday; the first poems were written when he was seven. At that age, he was writing verses like this:

> I once went into a little house
> It was on a morning jellied with white frost
> I saw a very beautiful fairy
> (Perhaps she possessed the clarity of a star)
> She asked me if I wanted to stay with her
> I told her no, for I wanted to be near my own kind . . .

In addition to his unusual intelligence, Bernardo displays an exceptional degree of sensitivity and versatility, a breadth of knowledge and capacity for judgment which are well beyond his years. I asked him which he liked better: seeing movies or reading adventure stories. In fact, he reads a bit of everything he can find that gives free rein to his imagination. In a school assignment entitled "My House," he wrote, "My house has eight eyes and two mouths." His most recent poems reveal a progressive interest in images and feelings and a constant improvement of form and stylistic fluidity. I reproduce here a poem entitled *The Shadow,* which seems to me among the most significant of his recent efforts. As we read it together, I feel moved to ask suddenly, "But where did you get this idea of writing a poem about shadows?" Bernardo answers without hesitating, "I was alone in my room; the sun was streaming through the window and the shadow of the dresser was projected onto the floor; I thought about it a little, and then..."

> I love the shadow with her light step,
> She follows me everywhere and is always at my side.
> She is black, even when there is snow
> Which covers the fields with its white coat,
> And you'd think she was angry when I'm not there.
> She wants to show me what I look like
>
> Am I walking straight? Am I bent over? Am I dragging
>   my feet or jumping?
>
> I love the shadow but her finesse
> Which makes me feel all high and mighty
> Deep deep down makes me sad
> But I know she works hard
> She runs through the meadows, through the mountains
>   and sometimes too in a very dense wood
>
> I love the shadow with her light step
> She is black, very black, even when there is snow.

Making Movies? It's Like Writing Poetry

ALFREDO BARBERIS/1962

WHEN YOU TELL HIM he gets angry. And yet Bernardo Bertolucci, a twenty-one-year-old student of letters from Parma who has taken only one of the exams necessary for his degree, a film director who had his first film at Cannes this year with *The Grim Reaper,* and also a candidate for the Viareggio Prize for his collection of poetry *In Search of Mystery,* looks a lot like Vittorio Gassman. Only he looks a little sweeter, a little nicer because in his eyes and in the lines of his mouth there's a kind of residual shadow of adolescence.

"I've been coming here every summer since I was a kid; I can no longer do without it," he says leading me through a little door into the courtyard of his house at Casarola. To get here, I had to take a mule path, accompanied by a herd of cows and by the lengthy curious stares of the peasants. On the stone archway of the entryway is engraved in stone 1791, the year this ancient seat of the Bertolucci family, who came to Emilia from Toscanella, was rebuilt. On one of the walls, Bernardo's brother Giuseppe has drawn in charcoal a procession of cows full of the movement of the Lascaux cave paintings. I enter a huge room with a low ceiling supported by beams, suspended over a very rustic wooden floor grayed by dust. The furniture in this room is reduced to the bare essentials reminiscent of certain hilltop convents which are an antique dealer's dream. "In these woods," he says, pointing out the window at a spot of green way across the lush fields, "I

From *Il Giorno* (Milan), 19 August 1962. Reprinted by permission. Translated by Fabien Gerard and T. Jefferson Kline.

shot my first film. I was fifteen at the time. Some cousins had brought me a 16mm camera to the village and asked if I didn't want to try it out. So I wrote a rudimentary little script, chose as actors my nine-year-old brother and two of my girl cousins who were younger than I was, and I shot the film in the middle of this stand of chestnut trees. It was about three children who try to uncover the cable of an old cable car which they had played with in previous summers. They waste a lot of time looking for this cable and finally they find it, but they're disappointed because it's completely covered with grass and moss. It was a minor subject with not much, to be sure, but it contained a concept I care a lot about: the fact that nothing is repeatable and the past is irretrievable. In any case, I have remained very attached to these woods. I insisted on shooting the opening sequence of my first feature film, *The Grim Reaper,* in a little wood near the EUR (Esposizione Universale Romana, which is the name given since the time of Mr. Mussolini to this park which was built in the '30s) especially for the Exposition, because I felt more at ease with this kind of space around me. I remember that when I shot the first interior scene I was seized with panic. The room I'd chosen was quite small and I literally didn't understand how to work in such a limited space. Luckily this uneasiness lasted only a day and I learned very quickly. In any case what counts in film making isn't technique or experience: all you need is to have enough inner maturity."

Bernardo Bertolucci leaves the window, lights a cigarette. "You see, making movies is like writing poetry. I believe much more in this equation than in the equation that one usually makes between films and novels. I felt these things in a confused way when I was fifteen and making this little film on a cable. I remember that I wrote some of the explanatory titles in poetry. I recopied them as carefully as I could, filmed them and inserted them in the editing. Now I believe that to edit a sequence of a film is like placing words in a poem. There's the same tension and the same liberty of expression."

"Pasolini wrote the first treatment of *The Grim Reaper.* You were his assistant for *Accattone*; do you think that as a director you were influenced by Pasolini?"

"No. We have entirely different styles. Pasolini's style can be defined as Romanesque, a frontal style that has a kind of primitive essentialism. His tracking shots resemble the first tracking shots in the history of cinema. His close ups resemble the invention of the close-up. My style is more impressionistic. I approach things much more gently and don't see them from an entirely frontal position. I try to move around my subject. As for actors, like Pasolini, I don't like professionals and prefer people I've found in the street. Of course I made an exception of Adriana Asti, but she's the woman to whom I dedicated my book of poetry, *In Search of Mystery*. I have a very intense and direct relationship with her and she has none of the faults of professional actors who are already trapped in their professional tics and who scare me because you always have to start over at zero. I wasn't trained as a theater director. Theater interests me only as a writer and for the moment I'm too involved in directing films. After *The Grim Reaper,* which I agreed to do because it allowed me to debut as a director, I wanted to shoot only subjects I'd written myself."

"Did you ever think of making films for television?"

"Well, they offered me work and told me I could do any thing I wanted, but since I know that certain things that mean very much to me simply can't be expressed in video, I always refused their offers. I prefer the cinema. I'm preparing a film which will be called *Before the Revolution* which is based on a quote from Talleyrand. In fact I'm not such a careful reader and confess that I didn't discover this quote myself; someone else quoted it to me. The quote is more or less, 'Anyone who didn't know France before the revolution could never know how sweet life can be.' I've made good progress on the script. It will be the story of the sweet death of the bourgeoisie, the story of two crises: one concerning a young man who, after having been a Stalinist, will end up marrying an industrialist's daughter; the other concerning a woman who loves him to the degree that she is neurotic but who manages to distance herself from him as she grows more healthy. I hope to make an unusual film which will be the first Italian film to talk directly about politics."

Behind the door I catch sight of the profile of Attilio Bertolucci, and his son immediately falls silent, made shy by the massive presence of his father as if he were a child who had been caught telling forbidden things. Bertolucci senior, a discrete gentleman farmer, disappears again. I ask Bernardo what he thinks of the rumor that he will win the Viareggio Prize awarded for a first work of literature. His embarrassment grows, and he says he knows nothing about it and that in this little mountain village he doesn't even get the newspapers. "I would be devilishly happy to win this prize," he admits. "It's worth a million lire, but please don't write that! And then, of course, the publicity generated by such a prize is the only way to get your poetry read by the public."

We leave the house, crossing the little courtyard. I catch sight of Giuseppe, Bernardo's strapping fifteen-year-old younger brother, leaning against a window quietly painting.

"And the air has the smell of cows—which smell like grass."

Interview with Bernardo Bertolucci

LOUIS MARCORELLES AND

JACQUES BONTEMPS/1965

c c : *What were your first films?*

B B : My first films were 16 mm films, of course. One was called *The Death of a Pig*. I was fifteen and the subject had the value of a myth for me. I shot the film near my country house in Parma. I also made a film using my little brother and my girl cousins called *The Cable*. Then I was Pasolini's assistant for *Accattone*, which I believe to be a very important film for Italian cinema. I would have liked to continue working with Pasolini, but this producer asked me to write a screenplay based on a subject Pasolini had written but didn't want to film. And that's how I wrote *La Commare Secca* (*The Grim Reaper*). The producer was the same one who had done *Boccaccio '70*, so he was a producer of commercial films, but he had confidence in young directors. He liked my script and wanted me to direct it. I found myself face to face with a film I hadn't written for myself but for someone else. I discovered the brutal truth — that it's no good writing screenplays, even if they're yours, because when you begin shooting, they belong to someone else.

The film was presented for the first time at the Venice film festival in the "section informative" where it was very well received by certain critics and very badly by others. I think it's a film that doesn't try to say much — or rather it tries to express one thing modestly. It tries to communicate

From *Cahiers du cinéma*, March 1965. Reprinted by permission. Translated by T. Jefferson Kline.

through images the basic idea of all poets: time passing, the flow of the hours. It's a very modest idea, I think. I'd written some poetry, but I'd never made any films, so I needed one guiding idea in order to make this film. It was the restitution of the quiet flow of the minutes throughout a day.

c c : *Is there any relationship between this idea and Antonioni's work?*
B B : In Antonioni's work, the passage of time takes much more grandiose dimensions. He's really an epic poet. This is the unique overriding dimension of his work. It is the most hidden aspect of my film—the thing so hard to discover that few have noticed it. So there's no connection with Antonioni.

c c : *So you've written poetry.*
B B : Yes, I wrote a collection of poems over a period of seven years—from age fourteen to twenty-one—which was published in Italy (*In Search of Mystery*, Longanesi, Milano, 1962) and won a prize before my film opened in Venice. So I arrived with this fairly important Italian prize, the Viareggio Prize which a lot of people resented. To have just won a prize and to go to Venice with a film was just too much. It seemed like a publicity campaign, and it caused some antipathy. Looking at it from others' points of view, I might have shared this impression, but as I was at the center of this story, I just had to deal with the consequences. Unfortunately in this way I learned a lot of quite important things the hard way.

c c : *How did you move from poetry to the cinema? Was it a long-standing desire or just an accident?*
B B : As I've already said on several occasions, I don't see any difference between cinema and poetry. What I mean is that from the idea to the poem there is no mediation, just as there isn't any between an idea and a film. If the idea isn't already poetic, there's no chance it will become so. I followed the same process in writing my poems and making my films. The connections between poetry and film are infinite. I believe, to sum this up in a general way, that there are semantic values in poetry that you can also find in cinema. Certain critics, whom I trust, have discovered a certain lyricism in my films, which is, I believe, the thing my poetry and my films share. But I don't believe it's a very important thing.

c c : *Do you intend to continue your writing?*

b b : I'd like to write some more poems, and I was writing poetry up until last year. Unfortunately, making films completely takes over my life. It's something so invasive that it makes it difficult to succeed at two occupations at once; but I'll write more poems. And especially even when I'm making films, I have to keep reading. A lot of film directors I know let themselves be taken over so completely by cinema that they no longer have time for anything else—for literature for example—and it's a shame. But cinema does that to you, and you have to be very strong to avoid letting it happen.

c c : *Who are the poets you read?*

b b : In my literary education just as in my cinematic education, there's an infantile stage, and then comes maturity—at, say, about thirty. I began like everyone else reading Garcia-Lorca, Dylan Thomas, T. S. Eliot. Then I loved reading Emily Dickinson and afterwards I picked up Rimbaud and Baudelaire. Right now I'm rediscovering some enthusiasm in rereading authors I discovered several years ago. Maybe they are the true, the most important writers. I also enjoy new American poetry which is full of experimentation—but the great poets are the ones I mentioned—and also Brecht, though he's a playwright.

c c : *And what sort of cinematic culture do you have?*

b b : I went to the movies a lot. I saw four films a day for years and I still love seeing films. But I have a lot of trouble talking about films because I'll defend a film even if I liked only one minute of it—so there are a lot of films I like. But the thing that's touched me most in recent years was seeing Dreyer's *Joan of Arc* after seeing Godard's *Vivre sa vie*. It was weird but I felt that Dreyer owed something to Godard.

c c : *In* Before the Revolution *you quote* Une Femme est une femme. *Is it an important film for you now?*

b b : Not very. It appeals to my least profound side—my music-hall side. It's a film I understood better when, two years ago in Venice, I saw some films by Lubitsch which I hadn't seen before. I think all of Godard's quotations, all his homages, are not, as Benayoun argues, signs of his lack of culture or attempts to shore up his films, but instead reveal his true culture.

They're the result of thoughtful choices which have nothing to do with playfulness or snobbism.

c c : *What do you think of the American cinema?*
b b : To be honest, certain films that I like a lot are not appreciated here at *Cahiers* and vice versa. For example, I love *The Maltese Falcon* but not *Cleopatra*. Unlike some of you, I don't love *all* of the American cinema. For me it's a cinema that, even though it has nothing to say, nevertheless manages to say some important things and to enjoy some success thanks to certain *auteurs*. Sometimes though, the same director can make horrible films and then extraordinary ones. Unlike you, I didn't like *Hatari!* but I admire some of Hawks's films, like his latest one, *Man's Favorite Sport*. It's a film made by an old sage and consequently is full of youth and grace. But Hollywood's economic structure is not so ideal as *Cahiers* sometimes seems to believe.

c c : *Among Italian directors, whom do you admire the most?*
b b : Rossellini is the greatest, and I only learned to appreciate him, I'm ashamed to say, thanks to *Cahiers*. I began reading *Cahiers* which I found lying around the house because my father was a film critic, and I've continued to read it ever since. So that's how I discovered Rossellini. I haven't seen his last film since I don't know him personally—and I hope we don't meet because too often our myths are destroyed when they encounter reality.

c c : *You were born in Parma, and in your second film, which takes place in Parma, the characters bear the same names as those in Stendhal's* Charterhouse of Parma.
b b : I don't think there are any very obvious Stendhalian elements in *Before the Revolution*. If my characters are named after those in *The Charterhouse*, it's because, as soon as I thought about making this film, I thought about a film-novel and since the greatest novel ever written is *The Charterhouse of Parma*, I thought I'd use the characters' names in my first film as a kind of homage that anyone who tries to write a novel should make to the greatest writer who ever lived.

c c : *But it's more than that. Your hero is in love with his aunt.*
b b : Yes, there are some coincidences like that. You know how things work in film: in the beginning you have an idea, but this idea changes

completely when you start shooting, because there's a beat and some time has elapsed. At first my story was a modern *Charterhouse*, but then it gradually developed into *The Sentimental Education*. As it was transformed, some residues remained from what was once *The Charterhouse of Parma*, then *Sentimental Education* and, no doubt, the film is full of these residues and these memories.

C C : *Did you follow a detailed screenplay or did you change it as you went?*
B B : I had to change it because when I began shooting, as I read it, I wondered who had written it. It was long and detailed, it was a novel that contained all my faults, all my literary quirks. I had the feeling I was reading a screenplay that wasn't mine, so I changed a lot of things. I felt very far away from what I'd started out to do, so much so that my next film won't have a detailed screenplay.

C C : *Tell us about that project.*
B B : Well, I have two of them. One will be difficult to do because it takes place in 500 A.D., and the dialogue will be half in Latin and half in a barbarian dialect. It will cost a lot because I want to use stars, color and cinemascope. I've still got to find a producer for it. That's why I'm thinking of doing a small 16 mm film on the theater with Adriana Asti, the actress in *Before the Revolution*. She has done a lot of work in the theater, especially at the Piccolo Teatro in Milan, and she was very helpful in *Before the Revolution*. To thank her, I'd like to do a film with her which would really be dedicated to her. It will be a film about an actress during the '30s in Italy at a time when fascism had quietly become accepted by many people. I wanted to make this film after reading Goethe's *Wilhelm Meister*. Once again the names are borrowed from the novel: Wilhelm and Marianne. I'll improvise everything. What I've written won't become a screenplay—it's just notes on certain characters and certain phrases from the novel. I think it will be a very free film.

C C : *Freedom already characterizes* Before the Revolution.
B B : To my mind the most extraordinary example of improvisation is *Vivre sa vie*. I don't know if the film was partly improvised or entirely written; however that may be, it has a spirit of improvisation and very masterful improvisation at that. For example, the scene where Anna Karina

dances around the billiard table is one of the most moving I've ever seen in the cinema, and it appears to be improvised or at least to belong in the category of things that are not important in the screenplay and only become so when they are shot and are the most charming moments in all of cinema. There's only one line in the screenplay but when it's shot, it becomes essential to the film and the rest of the page is forgotten.

c c : *What importance do you ascribe to the character of Agostino and the bicycle scene?*
b b : In the screenplay I wrote, "Agostino does a little show on his bike to get Fabrizio to forgive him for what he'd said before." But the American actor, Allen Midgette, whose face I find very moving, didn't know how to ride a bike too well, and when I asked him to do certain things, he kept desperately falling off but never confessed he didn't know how to ride a bike. And all these falls were so much sadder than the scene I'd written that I decided to change everything around and do something I don't normally like to do: to show a person's state of mind by means of a very precise action. I generally prefer to cover what is most important with other voices, other actions. But these falls were so important that I just had to shoot them.

c c : *Your film talks about both love and politics. How did you come to invent this character who is tempted by communism but never becomes a communist and who ends up in such a cowardly fashion?*
b b : It's a very personal, very subjective question and one which like all subjective things has a tendency to become typical and general. Fabrizio's character is entirely fictional, absolutely lyrical and totally poetic. He is the incarnation of an exorcism. I needed to exorcise certain fears. I was a Marxist with all the love, all the passion, and all the despair one can expect from a bourgeois who chooses Marxism. Naturally in every bourgeois Marxist, who is *consciously* Marxist, I should say, there is always the fear of being sucked back into the milieu he came out of, because he's born into it and the roots are so deep that a young bourgeois finds it very hard to be a Marxist. So I had—and still have—a terrible fear that I tried to exorcise in this character. All the Stendhalian parts of him—the references to Fabrice del Dongo, to his ideological and political evolution, are purely literary allusions which on a superficial level might seem important but which only

play on the most external chords of my sensibilities. This is a film which disappointed the Italian Marxists who saw it. They expected a very negative, desperate film. I used a phrase from Talleyrand as an epigraph to the film: "Those who did not live before the revolution cannot know the sweetness of life." If I had put this phrase at the end, the meaning of the film would have been simpler because the counterpoint between the aunt in tears and Fabrizio who is getting married would have been clear. But, as I said, clarity isn't my cup of tea so I preferred to put this phrase at the beginning of the film. He who lives before the revolution doesn't feel, in my view, the sweetness, but instead the anguish of life—and almost no Italian critic understood this.

c c : *Why did you choose for* Before the Revolution *a cameraman as famous as Scavarda?*

B B : The film's photography isn't as I imagined it would be when I started out, but I like it a lot. My dream was to have Raoul Coutard, but he was scheduled to do *Farenheit 451* with Truffaut. I wrote to Agnès Varda about this, and she suggested I try the young cameraman who did *The Grim Reaper*, Gianni Narzisi, who had only done two films. But of the three or four Italian directors of photography I could have accepted, Scavarda was the only one who was free. Di Venanzo would have cost too much. Scavarda was Antonioni's age and had never worked with a young director. At first he didn't seem to understand what I wanted, but in the end he used his fine sensitivity to lead me to where we could find common ground. We each made some compromises and ended up agreeing on the fairly white photography of the film.

A Conversation with Bernardo Bertolucci

JOHN BRAGIN/1966

THE FOLLOWING CONVERSATION, OR *happening,*
as Bertolucci prefers to call it, took place in the middle of June
when he was just beginning work on the script for his new film.
It is translated, slightly condensed, from a tape in Italian.

Did the style, half interview and half detective story, of La Commare Secca
come directly from the screenplay, or later, during shooting?
It came to me at the moment of shooting, this manner, vaguely *cinéma
vérité,* of the Police Commissioner's interrogation of the various characters
of the film. Many things came to me at the moment of shooting that were
different in the script. This happened because, when I wrote the script of
the film, I did not know that I would direct it—another director was supposed to do it. I was hired only as scriptwriter; afterwards, the producer
was very satisfied, and got the idea of having me direct. Thus, for me it was
a question of taking in hand this script that I had written without going
into the real problems, which I had left to the director who would have
shot it. I had a great problem which was to bring this story, these characters (not originally mine because the treatment, two or three pages of the
treatment, were Pasolini's), to bring them close to me, close to my sensibility. This explains how many things changed in the film. In the film there
is this effort, that perhaps one senses, to adapt some characters, in the

From *Film Quarterly,* Vol. 20/No. 1, Fall 1966. © 1966 by The Regents of the University of
California. Reprinted by permission.

beginning not created by me—because the environment of the Roman proletariat is not an environment which I come from, but is Pasolini's. In fact, one episode is shot in one way, and another in a different way. Really, there is this continuous stylistic effort, still rather ingenuous, because I had never shot anything before this film. It seems to me a rather naïve film, and at the same time rather refined, because—having gone to films a lot, having dreamed a lot about films—I had some ideas about how films are made. Naturally, these ideas afterwards, in the concrete realization, changed or did not come out the way I had planned.

Anyhow, it is a first film, and that device of the interviews came absolutely at the moment of shooting. The Commissioner and all the particulars of his environment were described in the script: a typewriter, a desk—but at the moment of shooting I was in such an environment and didn't like it. I wanted this interrogation to be less realistic. In fact, the Commissioner is never seen, only his voice is heard. Why? Because I was a bit afraid of the mechanism of the detective story, the thriller; and, more than that, it did not interest me. The thing that interested me in the film was and is the thing I discovered shooting it: the thing that interested me was to render the passing of the hours, the passage of time, the sense of the day that goes by, as a poetic fact, rather tragic, through some locations and some characters. This idea, the sense of time passing, is very simple, it is an idea which is at the base of much poetry. (I had written poetry before this.) It is the thing that I felt in this story, the element that I felt the most.

Inasmuch as the subject of La Commare Secca *was not your own, did you have in mind another story to do as a first film, and, if so, was this* Prima della Rivoluzione *or a film much like it?*
I didn't expect to begin to make films so quickly. I had begun as assistant to Pasolini on *Accattone*. It was very interesting and very important. I was not one of those fellows who have a script ready and waiting to be shot. I used to tell myself: "The day when I can do a film the story will come to mind."

In fact, after *La Commare Secca* I wanted to do a film of my own and thought of a story. Perhaps I already had the story inside, the idea of the film was inside me for a long time. It comes from a statement of Talleyrand that was put as an epigraph to the film, which says: "Qui n'a pas connu la vie avant la Révolution ne sait pas ce que c'est la douceur de vivre."

The idea of the film came from this statement, that is it came from the need to contradict this statement, which is true, but whose contrary is also true.

I set myself to work and wrote a story with characters. I worked a bit to find the producer, and then made it.

The things which you did shooting La Commare Secca, *did they influence* Prima della Rivoluzione, *or did you try to begin again from the beginning?* La Commare Secca was certainly of use to me. The new thing for me in *Prima della Rivoluzione* was my relation to the story, since in *La Commare Secca,* chiefly the style was my own, the major effort was stylistic, that is to render the film *mine* through the style.

Pasolini saw this world of the Roman proletariat in a primitive style— of fixed compositions, close-ups like the paintings of Masaccio; as he says himself he had looked at more paintings than films, with a few basic movies: *Joan of Arc. . . .* On the other hand I was much more of a cinephile, I had seen many films and had different ideas. In *Prima della Rivoluzione* the difficult problems were problems of story, characters, and structure. Also, because the film was "very much mine," I had written a huge script, three hundred pages, almost a novel, which at the moment of shooting, as perhaps must always happen, I no longer felt to be my own: it seemed to me to have been written by someone else.

Every day there was the problem of inventing new things, because, really, in film, in my experience, it is impossible to see ahead, it is impossible to write beforehand. It is necessary to make, at bottom, only sketches to be thrown away, and afterwards to leave oneself very free. Films must be open, even at the moment of creating them. For example, how can one say: "In this street or in this room these things happen." At the moment one is in that street that has been chosen, in that room in which one shoots, everything may happen outside of what was thought of. I leave myself very free, or at least I try to do so. . . .

I was told that you were working on a documentary for Radio-Televisione Italiana. They are three programs of about three quarters of an hour each, on petroleum. I was asked by the large Italian petroleum industry, ENI, and they proposed this trip for a film that would be called *La Via del Petrolio,* and I accepted and made the trip.

The first program is on the origins of the petroleum that arrives here in Italy, from Persia, and the second is on the trip from Persia to Genoa, on the oil-tanker. The third is on a pipe line from Genoa to Germany.

What style did you shoot them in?
It was interesting because I had never made documentaries and thus it was, in a certain sense, the discovery of a way of filmmaking. I shot according to concrete demands; having very little time at my disposition, I would shoot whatever hit my eye. Thus such films have a very aboriginal aspect, they have the aspect of the discovery of a country; they have a style, also, because the style is born in the editing. I have spent four months in cutting these three films. It was a very interesting experience because I would shoot, in the Orient, without knowing what I was getting. It is not like filmmaking where every day one sees rushes.

I tried to create a rapport with the photographer, leaving him very free. It is very difficult to talk about this experience, because it is not yet digested enough, because I am finishing the cutting right now. The crew was very small. Practically there were three of us — myself, a cameraman, and an assistant cameraman who also did the sound, and also a production organizer. The wonderful thing, the most poetic, was, at bottom, this small troupe that would shoot in the deserts with its small 16mm camera with a great deal of freedom.

Did you have a large shooting ratio?
I shot a lot, I would shoot all the time without stopping, and thus had about 12 hours of projection which I cut to 2½ hours.

After this, what are your plans?
I should do — it is very difficult now in Italy — a feature in September, or, better, begin shooting in September; I am writing it now. The title is *Natura contro Natura.* The story of three young fellows who live in Rome. All three are foreigners. They are three foreigners not because I wanted to do a film about characters who were foreign but because, having chosen three foreign actors, and wanting to shoot in sync sound, automatically the characters will speak Italian with a foreign accent. That is, sync sound has conditioned me in the creation of the characters. One is Allen Midgette, who is the young fellow in *La Commare Secca,* an American, who will play the part

of the soldier. The other is Jean-Pierre Léaud who has just done Godard's film, and the third is Lou Castel, the one who did *I Pugni in Tasca*.

Did you have this in mind before doing the documentaries?
The idea came to mind a few days ago, travelling by car from Cannes to Rome.

When you shoot, will you use a fairly free system as with the documentaries?
It was very useful for me to shoot those documentaries, precisely to discover what is possible, even necessary, in shooting in sync. In Italy this is not usually done—everything is dubbed here, the talkies have not been discovered yet. But I think that shooting in sync is very important, and I don't believe that it will prevent me from having the same freedom I had making the documentaries, because I want to shoot with a very small crew this time also. I will work with the same cameraman who shot the documentaries. In Italy there is a mania for virtuoso sound created in the dubbing room, an absurd perfectionism. Godard said, and rightly, that, if two people are speaking and a truck or very loud car passes, it is right that one cannot hear what the two of them are saying.

When you write, do you describe the locations in detail?
Very little, very vaguely. That is I see the places then write, or first I write then I look for them, and if the locations are different I change the screenplay. It is the same thing that happens with the actors. One writes, and after having written looks for the actor. I find it very important to change the written character to fit the actor, not to try to have the actor become the written character. Generally they say to the actor: "Read this character to yourself and try to enter into him." I do the opposite, that is, I change the written character, I even have him become the opposite of what he was, to adapt him around the actor like a suit.

Do you work a lot with the actors?
It depends on the case. For example, in my first film no one was an actor, except for one or two very small parts (the soldier had been an actor before) and so my work reduced itself to this: having seen that actor, at dinner, laugh in a way that I liked, I would say to him: "Try to laugh as you did last night." That is, to refer the performance always to something of their

own, never to something abstract. To always take, as a point of reference, their way of moving, of laughing, of speaking.

Do you prefer nonprofessionals, then?
When I was doing the first film, yes. In the second he was a nonprofessional actor, she was a theater actress—thus really professional down to the last drop of blood. In the next, all three are actors—however, they are film actors and also have done few films. They are rather virginal. Also, there is something that will help me: all three speak a language that is not their own. This is, already, a great help in eliminating the defects, the bad habits, the virtuosities that all actors have and that are so ugly. The fact of their speaking in Italian will cancel, brutally, all the artificial, forced intonations.

To return to present-day Italian filmmaking. Of those directors who have made their first feature in the last few years, such as Pasolini, De Seta, Brass, Rosi, Olmi, are there any that you prefer?
All those you have mentioned are directors I value. The one I value most is Pasolini; he seems to me to be the most interesting director in Italy, the most important. I learned from him one thing that seems very important to me, that is that films are always being invented, and rediscovered. I would watch him work, watch him invent his film day by day, invent his filmic style, do his tracking shots or closeups, and I seemed to be present at the birth of the cinema. The fundamental thing in films is to continually re-invent them and re-discover them. In other words to do a tracking shot as if it were the first tracking shot, and a stylistic solution as if it were always new, as if it were the first time it was used even if there have been thousands before you who have done the same things. This is very important, this sense of discovery—it should always be this way.

But I must tell you that the Italian films I love most are those of Rossellini. I like the French cinema as well—above all, Godard. Fellini, Antonioni, and Visconti are great personalities, but Rossellini is the greatest of them all. Regarding Rossellini's style there is this capacity of having things never too far away and never too close, the ideal distance that his camera has from things and from characters. It is one of the first cases of a truly open cinema. The best critical judgment of Rossellini I heard was given by Henri Langlois, Director of the *Cinémathèque Française.* One time

I was at the Palais de Chaillot, and since the screen is very large (it takes up the entire back wall of the theater without borders). I asked him why the screen was so large. He answered: "It is a screen for the films of Rossellini," and I replied: "But it is very large, that is, the picture area is very small." "Yes, because Rossellini's compositions can really continue to the right, left, above and below." It is a very just definition, it is precisely that way.

Do any other arts influence you particularly? Do you feel yourself close to any contemporary movements?
It seems to me that the cinema has been influenced by everything and since films look at reality, and music, painting, literature are all part of reality, the film must be interested in these also. I am evading, for a moment, the question that you asked me: A film director must begin to take a position not only in confronting the world that he describes and the society that he describes, but, also, in confronting the art he creates. It would be good to see films becoming conscious of what they are, as music has done, as literature has done, that is that there might be a cinema that looks at itself, a cinema that speaks about cinema. In the films that I will do, and, also, at bottom, in the films that I have done, especially in the second, above all in those that I will do, I wish that I might take a position in confronting the language that has been chosen. It is very useful as well because the public does not know what films are, it is necessary to teach them. This is the thing that interests me most at this time. I like poetry very much, I don't have other specific interests, only poetry. I also look at much painting, listen to music, but poetry interests me very much. I wrote poetry for years; afterwards I stopped because, since I would have said the same things in poetry and in films, it would have been a repetition, so I stopped writing poetry. There is no movement, however, at this time of which I feel a part.

Pasolini told me that he had felt, when he started making films, that he was only changing techniques, but later realized that he had changed languages. How do you see your change from writing to filmmaking?
No, Pasolini, remember, is a philologist, a critic of style, thus he posed philologic problems to himself, linguistic problems; he has written several studies of philology. For me, instead, the change was very natural, it was a passage without problems. For example, experiences as a poet were very

useful to me in doing *La Commare Secca*—precisely the experience of putting one verse after the other. Now I know that all this is quite different, that films are rather a long way from poetry.... But at that time I saw films very much as music, rhythmic, made up of slowness, acceleration, of contrasting rhythms.

When you wrote the screenplay of La Commare Secca *did you feel influenced by this?*
No, it seemed to me that I was doing literature. While doing the film *La Commare Secca* it seemed to me that I was doing poetry, writing the script it seemed to be literature. In fact, as far as I am concerned, a film is much closer to poetry than to a novel.

And with Prima della Rivoluzione?
No, partly because some time had already passed, partly because with *Prima della Rivoluzione* I came out of a kind of idyllic state, a state of unconscious creativity in which I made *La Commare Secca*. I came out of this rather false kind of state and found myself face to face with very deep problems, very intimate ones. In *Prima della Rivoluzione* it was a question on my part of exorcising the fear, of clarifying my ideological position. The film is the story of the ideological experiences of a young fellow who believes himself to be a Marxist and later discovers that he is not. Now, this has nothing to do with my personal history, however, it was a film that allowed me to clarify many things, to clarify my position, and above all to put certain fears at a distance. Thus, poetry was very far away....

And with Natura contro Natura? *If you can say anything this early.*
I know that it is a film that will cost me a lot, as *Prima della Rivoluzione* cost me. I feel that already there is a kind of struggle inside of me, because it is a film about sexuality, about eroticism as a painful fact, as a tragic fact and thus it is a film in front of which I am already inhibited—I have created characters before whom I am already inhibited. It also is a rather moral film, I hope, having real problems.

With Prima della Rivoluzione, *do you think you clarified to a great extent, your ideological conflicts?*

Yes, but one is never content with what one does, on the contrary I am in general always profoundly discontent, that is, I do not succeed in being objective in the face of what I do. Also, the past interests me little, I am always interested in what is before me; it is this which films have helped me to discover. When I wrote poetry it was poetry entirely based on remembrance, on the past. On the other hand, film has made me discover that there is the future, where poetry is always a reconstruction of past moments. The poet (one can call him a poet as well) whom I like most is Proust. On the other hand, film has given me a different solidity, humanly as well; it has made me discover a new dimension, has made me leave an adolescence too prolonged, carried on too far ahead in years.

Could one call this discovery hope?
No, the hope of hope. Certainly, when one does his first film everything is easier because films are still something mythic. That is, one leaves behind, by degrees, with the first, with the second, this myth. I have gotten out of the mythology of filmmaking. Now it has become something more normal, that is more a part of me. I think, also, that films have remained rather static, that it is necessary to move them forward. At bottom, the film, since it was invented, has not moved very far forward, it has remained rather static, with a few exceptions. At first I thought that it might be the style, the technique that must move film forward. Now I no longer know. Perhaps, instead, it is the narrative forms. It is very difficult, at this time, to speak about films. Very difficult.

Do you have more ideas, stories?
Yes, I have many stories, and it would be fine for me if films became a way of life, as is writing for a poet, for a novelist; painting for a painter. Unfortunately, there is still a kind of barrier of ice, of glass to break.

What is that? The public, producers?
Everything, everything that is not the filmmaker. I said glass because behind it everything moves as in another world; one passes into it and then turns back out, it is always like this. Godard makes two or three films a year. So he lives films. This is something that I dream about: to live films, to arrive at the point at which one can live for films, can think cinemato-

graphically, eat cinematographically, sleep cinematographically, as a poet, a painter, lives eat sleeps painting.

Given this, how does the present situation of film appear to you in Italy?
It seems to me that films—but not only in Italy, almost everywhere in the world at this moment—are persecuted, hated, given kicks in the face. I was first at Cannes, and after at the Festival of Pesaro where a group of people who love films had come together. In general, at festivals one finds people who hate the cinema, who want to destroy it. In Italy, in France, as well, it is very difficult. This is a very sad subject. In Italy there is a great danger: that is of compromise. Even the best directors, even the best of the young directors, fall very easily into making films they believe in only half-way. I am making these documentaries precisely in order not to be forced to make such compromises. I believe that, as a novelist like Moravia in order to live writes articles on trips that he has made to India, or Egypt, or Cuba, it is right for a director to make documentaries in order to live—but not westerns he doesn't believe in. Instead, here in Italy there is this alibi of "the life that must be lived" with which many try to justify themselves. But there is television, documentaries, there are many possibilities to work. It is necessary that every Italian director, I mean those who have something to say (not the others, because it is right they make the films they do), should refuse to do those films.

Is your intention only to describe, or do you have, as well, some moral or message?
I cannot say it of myself, but it appears to me that all poets, from the moment they are real, are also moral: from the moment they speak about reality. It is very difficult to say what reality is, I don't know if you know Zen: when they asked the wise men what was reality the answers were many, for example, a very fine answer is a slap from the teacher, or a kick...at any rate I do not pose myself such problems. I pose myself moral problems in the style.

What is the thing that, above all, I do not like in films? In general? A style that is amoral, devoid of morals, downright immoral. The films of Jacopetti, those like *Africa Addio*. It is an immoral film for its racism, but beyond that it is also immoral because of how it is made, how he uses the lenses, how he uses the camera. Perhaps still more immoral than for its racism that, at bottom, is so obvious, hysterical, and fanatic. There is an amorality in the composition.

For La Commare Secca *and* Prima della Rivoluzione*?*
There is a search, but I don't know if this morality follows from it. Sometimes, perhaps. The style of Rossellini, for example, is a profoundly moral style; a style with its own ethic. An angle, a shot in a film is already a world. Every shot has its own story, its own atmosphere, and has its own poetry as well as its own moral. A tracking shot, for example, may be moral or not moral. It is difficult to define all the cases in which it is moral and it is difficult as well to give a single definition, because a definition does not exist which says that this is moral and that not. But, there is an ethic in the style of many directors; for example, for Godard the style is already a way of seeing the world, for Rossellini as well. They would be able, at bottom, to relate nothing, or to tell stories which were absolutely not interesting or not important, or not to tell stories. But, their style is so profoundly moral that their films would be quite valid. In this discussion someone could contradict me by saying: "But that tracking shot is functional because in that moment of the film, of that given story, it works like that." But the story is only important up to a certain point, because in a film the relation between shots is independent of the needs of the story; because it is enough to put one shot in the middle, one first and another after, and already there is a relation between the shots, whatever it might be. It is for this reason that every angle has its own particular value.

These things that I am saying are so confused that I don't know what will come of them, but I am not a scholar, they are things that I think on my own.

In Refusing to Make Westerns Bertolucci Has Come to the Gospel

MORANDO MORANDINI/1967

I MEET BERNARDO BERTOLUCCI at the door of the editing
room where he is doing the last phases of the montage of the episode he
made for *Vangelo '70 (The Gospel '70)*. Having grown accustomed to working
in the dark these past few weeks, he squints as he emerges into the blind-
ing Roman sun. I immediately engage him in talking about his "Fico" (Fig
Tree). *Vangelo '70* is a collective film composed of five episodes. Jean-Luc
Godard has been involved in the project, with the particular cinematic
language which characterizes his work, presenting the story of the Prodigal
Son, interpreted by Nino Castelnuovo (the actor from *The Umbrellas of
Cherbourg*); Carlo Lizzani has discovered the Good Samaritan in the figure
of a gangster fleeing through the streets of Manhattan; Pier Paolo Pasolini
has again focused on the theme of eschatology that had become his trade-
mark in *The Gospel According to St. Matthew*; Valerio Zurlini went to Africa
to shoot an episode on the Good Thief, starring Woody Strode and Franco
Citti among others. As for Bertolucci, I'd heard he'd chosen the "Fico
Infruttuoso" (The Barren Fig Tree), and for the past several days I'd been
struggling to understand why this story would have interested him and
how he'd managed to find cinematic images to illustrate the episode of the
Accursed Tree: "Now in the morning as he returned into the city, he hun-
gered. And when he saw a fig tree in the way, he came to it, and found
nothing thereon, but leaves only and said unto it, Let no fruit grow on thee

From *Il Giorno* (Milan), 22 September 1967. Reprinted by permission. Translated by Fabien
Gerard and T. Jefferson Kline.

henceforward for ever." (Matthew XXI, 18–19). A parable that represents, at least for me, one of the most mysterious passages of the entire New Testament...

Bertolucci immediately smiles, shaking his head, "No, no, you're wrong: it's not the 'Accursed Tree' but the 'Barren Fig Tree.' It's in Luke's gospel, not in Matthew's! Here, to the landowner who has ordered a fig tree chopped down which had not borne fruit for three years, the peasant answers, 'Lord let it alone this year also, till I shall dig about it and dung it and it bear fruit, well; and if not, then after that thou shalt cut it down.' "

And he continues: "I was led to choose this parable in an unusual way. For a long time I've had the idea of filming a man who is dying. Twenty five minutes of agony, and then death: it's difficult to find a more absolute subject for a short film. Once I'd found the beginning, the middle and the end, I noticed that this subject corresponded completely to my interpretation of the parable of the fig tree."

I confess that I don't understand this very well: how could the agony of a human being illustrate this parable?
"The theme of the parable is cowardice," he says. "Just like the fig tree, the man who is dying has sinned by his aridity, his sterility. In other words, he has never done anything really wrong, but he hasn't done any good either—though he could have and should have. Although still alive, he was already a dead man among the living. Just as in the parable, a last chance will be given to him. But the fertilizer evoked by St. Luke is in this case a kind of human fertilizer; it is reality that this man has spent his entire life trying to flee, and now reality gradually invades the space of his room as he lies in agony,—the air, the floor, the walls, the curtains, his very body—until he suffocates from it. That's how the man's cowardice connects in some way with the sterility of the tree in the Gospel story."

Why did you use the actors from the Living Theatre in your film? Because they're all the rage now in Italy?
"This question of being in vogue strikes me as a bit off the mark; if that was what I was after I would have been better off by calling on Mastroianni or Vittorio Gassman, who are much more "the rage" than Julian Beck and the Living Theatre! In fact I've wanted to work with the Living Theatre ever since the day I was lucky enough to attend the premiere of *Mysteries*,

in 1964 and I remember it as producing the deepest, perhaps the only real emotion I've ever felt in the theater. When I met Julian, I was immediately, I'd even say irresistibly seduced by his extraordinary intelligence as well as a kind of spirituality that he exudes physically. And then, when last year I reread the Third Canto of Dante's *Inferno,* I was also struck by the descriptions of torture that were inflicted on those whose sin was cowardice: condemned to run without rest, constantly harassed by a swarm of hornets and wasps, while at their feet an army of disgusting worms suck the blood from their wounds ... A description worthy of Antonin Artaud, a sort of anticipation of "the theater of cruelty." The Living Theatre, as you know, is derived from Artaud, and Julian Beck is probably Artaud's most faithful disciple."

What kind of rapport did you develop working with the members of The Living Theatre?
"A rapport that was both exciting and anxiety provoking. And yet the reasons for the excitement are identical to those that produced the anxiety; theater is theater and cinema is cinema, and when you mix the two genres, the two languages—two realities that are not just very distant from each other but diametrically opposed—you've opted for danger over security, risk rather than tranquillity. Another source of anxiety and excitement for me was the occasion I had to experiment with a type of dramatic improvisation where the words 'cool', 'trip,' 'feeling,' and 'square,' miraculously sufficed to express everything we needed to say. It was also my first encounter with the systematic use of color, cinemascope, as well as Electrovoice, this incredible microphone capable of picking up every sign of an actor, the least little crack of his joints."

To provoke Bernardo, I object that there are plenty of films that are adapted from the theater, and are played by actors from the stage.
"I'm acutely aware," he responds, "that the pseudo-theater works perfectly well with a conventional cinema that is easily digestible—not to say predigested. Indeed, Robert Bresson claims that ninety percent of the films distributed today are nothing more than filmed theater. The difference is that the Living Theatre does theater in its deepest, most revolutionary sense, a theater irreducible to words, whose gestures and cries strip traditional theater of its bourgeois traditions. Since the kind of cinema that I'm

trying to do also aspires to a kind of "rigor" (which, by the way, prevented me from working for several years,) I feel that our meeting was quite explosive. I don't yet know what the product of that meeting will look like; all I can say is that for ten days the Living Theatre and I burned with the same fire."

This idea of a film which returned to the Gospels with a modern twist comes from two journalists from catholic newspapers, Puccio Pucci and Piero Badalassi. It took some courage for them to propose this project to directors who were "not typically catholic" as has been pointed out. The executive producer of Vangelo 70 *is Carlo Lizzani, who coordinated the production for Italnoleggio, the new distributing company created by the Italian State. I ask Bertolucci if there is any connection between the five episodes of the film, or if, instead, the choice of the parables and the selection of the filmmakers was more the result of chance.*
"Aside from the common reference to the Gospel, a text from which we could continue to draw inspiration until the end of time without ever losing our grounding in reality, I don't see any other connection. As for the five film makers, it's true that none of us is really a believer in the strict sense of the word. That's probably the best approach if you want to interpret the Gospel with honesty and a real sense of awe—and maybe to obtain an unpredictable and fresh inspiration."

Three years of inactivity is a lot for a film director, and it's even more for a director as young as Bernardo Bertolucci. We remember that in 1962, thanks to Pasolini, he made his directorial debut at the age of only twenty-one, with The Grim Reaper. *In 1964 he made* Before the Revolution. *Ignored by the public, and, with but few exceptions, rather badly treated by the Italian press, the film was rediscovered in France and became one of the principal symbols of the New Wave in Italy. After which, a long silence, aside from a documentary broadcast on television last January, and today this little film on the parable of the fig tree . . . How do you explain this situation?*
"For some time in Italy, there hasn't been any money except to make Westerns which are shot in Spain. As a director, I've spent the last three years turning down such proposals!"

Bernardo Bertolucci: *Before the Revolution, Parma, Poetry and Ideology*

JEAN-ANDRÉ FIESCHI/1968

BERNARDO BERTOLUCCI IS DOUBTLESS, with Marco Bellochio (*Fists in their Pockets*) one of the most talked about young Italian directors of these last few years. Although it was an important discovery, his film *Before the Revolution* was only known in France by a happy few: it was shown two years ago during the "Week of the *Cahiers du cinéma*." This film opened last week in Paris in a small art cinema. The author's words explain the film's genesis and intent.

J F : *Let's begin at the beginning: I'd like you to talk about how you came to film* The Grim Reaper *based on a scenario by Pasolini?*
B B : In 1961, Pasolini was making *Accattone*. I'd known him since I was a child, since he was a friend of my father's, and I got to be his assistant on *Accattone*. Pasolini, who at that time knew nothing about cinematic technique, was shooting his film as if in a dream: it was the dream of the Roman suburbs, based on realistic elements (costumes and dialect) but ultimately quite fantasmagoric. Now, *Accattone*, which played roughly the role in Italian film of the '60s that *Breathless* played in French film of the same period, was a huge popular success. You know the originality of the typical producer: they say, "let's make a Pasolini-esque film," i.e., a film about Rome, in Roman dialect, etc. One of Pasolini's stories, *The Grim*

From *Les Lettres Françaises* (Paris), 10 January 1968. Reprinted by permission. Translated by T. Jefferson Kline.

Reaper, was lying around in a producer's office. They asked him to direct it, but he refused since he was already planning *Mamma Roma*. So they asked him to designate someone to work on the screenplay, so the film could be shot by someone else. Pier Paolo suggested my name and I got right to work. It was a curious sort of work for me: I had to write a script with a commercial film in mind but for another director, and my biggest problem was trying to imitate *Accattone*. I was supposed to deliver a product of a certain type, as requested by the producer. When the producer, a pretty young guy, read the script, he said to me, "Why don't you direct this yourself?" I was twenty-one and simply a poet who had published a little collection of poems, and I knew practically nothing about film. I went to the movies for fun, and as for serving as Pasolini's assistant, if it taught me an enormous amount on the human level, it left me pretty much a virgin on the level of technical competence. But I was pretty bold, quite imprudent, and in a moment of madness, a kind of vertigo, I accepted this crazy proposal. I set out doubly handicapped—on the one hand by my lack of cinematic knowledge, and on the other by the fact that the story wasn't mine and wasn't even very close to my personal sensibilities. It was set in a specifically Pasolini-esque milieu which was pretty unfamiliar to me: the Roman underclass of pimps and prostitutes and delinquents. So I told myself that I would have to work hard to make this completely foreign story closer to my own sensibilities, and I think that if there's anything capable of touching the audience in this film it's this effort at poetic appropriation. In any case, I can never think about the first day on the set without getting cold shivers in my back: when the cameraman ceremoniously asked me where to set up the camera, I experienced one of the most anxious moments of my life. After that I got caught up in the flow of things; it was almost like sleep-walking and I just let the film carry me along. I asked myself all the most important questions: What's the ideology of this film? What does it mean? I ingeniously connected my poetry and my filmmaking by telling myself that it was a film about the passage of time, about the flow of time. This was my way of transforming a fairly naturalist subject into a purely poetic idea. And I made a lot of absolute statements: I said I'd never work with professional actors who are just robots; all you have to do is push a button to get them to act #3 (comedy) or #7 (pathos) or #11 (tender), etc. I was delighted, on the contrary, to see this kid act, maybe maladroitly, but so poetically. Obviously, when later I made *Before the Revolution* with a real actress who was famous for her work in the theater, I changed my mind on this subject, and my "bressonism" had been tempered a lot. But *Before the Revolution* was different. I had written it, I'd shot it in my own hometown of Parma, and I was much more at ease. My ideas on the cinema change constantly, but the idea I've held onto on actors is to leave completely open-ended the characters when I write the screenplay so that the chosen actor can bend the role to his own sensibilities. That's another way of saying that it isn't the actors who must enter into the written roles, but the characters as written who must conform to the actors.

J F : Before the Revolution *develops on several levels, poetic, sentimental, political. . . . Let's begin with the political.*
B B : The Italian left and right both attacked the film for ideological reasons. It was really a generational question. We belonged to the generation that was too young to have participated in the resistance against Fascism and too old to belong to the generation of '68. And we really discovered politics at the end of the period of commitment. It was an empty, really hollow moment and that explains the ambiguity of my film and why I'm not afraid to name it. It's even doubly ambiguous: both on the level of a certain political discourse and on the level of aesthetics, of the language of film. I think film directors, especially young directors, those who are still training, should just try to define themselves in relation to the world, or society or History, but also vis a vis cinema itself. You have to ask tirelessly "what is cinema?" even if you can't give a dogmatic answer. What's wonderful is to see a film and to discover the cinema through this film.

J F : *Asking this question another way, what are your connections with the central character of the film, Fabrizio?*
B B : I wanted to describe a character who is defeated, impotent, who thinks he's something that he isn't at all. At another level, Fabrizio is me, just as Gina is me, Puck is me, and Cesare is me. I am fond of all these characters—that's something that jumped out at me when I saw the film again two years after making it. All the characters are loved by the director. If I had to make a film about really negative characters, I have no idea how I'd go about it. Fabrizio represents the impossibility for a bourgeois to be a Marxist. He is the crystallization of all that I was afraid of when I was mak-

ing the film: my own inability to be a Marxist, being bourgeois. It's a problem I haven't resolved yet: the only way I know to be a Marxist is to grab on to the dynamism, to the incredible vitality of the proletariat, of the people who are the real revolutionary force in the world. I've grabbed hold of this movement, and I let myself get dragged along since I don't seem to be able to be pushed ahead.

That's pretty much what I mean by ambiguity. It's important to look one's ambiguity straight in the eye and to try to get beyond it. I occupy an ambiguous position because I am a bourgeois, like Fabrizio in the film, and I make films to keep away dangers and fears, my fear of weakness, of cowardice. For I come from a bourgeois milieu which is terrible because it's so crafty, because it has anticipated everything and accepted (or coopted) realism and communism with open arms. And this liberalism is obviously the mask of its essential hypocrisy.

And since we're talking about realism, I'd like to add that what I don't like about Italian cinema is that it's not a realist cinema but instead a naturalist one. That's a very equivocal position: they insist on naming realism what is really its caricature. Whereas Godard's cinema, for example, is realist. And the only true realist in Italy is Rossellini.

J F : *Let's come back to the sentimental and poetic aspects of* Before the Revolution.

B B : There is both a kind of courage and a kind of complacency in my film: courage because the film is a kind of exorcism by which I try to burn the bridges with my childhood and adolescence; and a complacency because this voluntary break with my past produced a few tears on my part. I was twenty-three and I'd never known this "sweetness of life." Hence the quote by Talleyrand used as an epigraph. I thought of putting this quote at the end of the film where it would have had a much more forceful meaning after all that happens in the film, but maybe too powerful a meaning, in fact, and so that's why it's placed at the beginning to announce the complexion of the film.

J F : *Is the poetics of the film tightly linked to the bleached quality of the photography?*

B B : Yes, I've always been struck by the fact that we remember much more about the lighting of the films we love that about the story line. For instance, there's a *Rules of the Game* lighting, which is an absolutely prophetic light-ing, which foretells the coming war. And there's a *Voyage in Italy* lighting, which is not the conventional light of Southern Italy that you find in *Salvatore Giuliano*, for example, but which is a light "invented" by Rossellini. Then there's the lighting of *Breathless*, which remains for our generation the most characteristic lighting of the '60s. Maybe now there's a *Before the Revolution* lighting.

J F : *The film is constructed around several literary allusions, Stendhal most obviously.*
B B : Of course, especially in the sense that Parma is a dreamscape of Parma. Stendhal's descriptions of Parma don't correspond in the least to the real Parma, and in his travel diaries, he states simply, "it's a pretty bor-ing town," before moving on to something else. I think he situated his novel *The Charterhouse of Parma* there uniquely because of his passion for Correggio. And as everyone knows, there's never been a Charterhouse in Parma!

J F : *Parma is also Verdi's birthplace.*
B B : Yes, and that plays a very specific role in this film. Verdi, who at the end of the nineteenth century represented the spirit of the revolution, today incarnates the spirit of the bourgeoisie. The long scene in the Parma Opera House with Verdi's *Macbeth* is really there to display this grandiose and ridiculous bourgeois temple.

J F : *Isn't the connection between the poems of your youth (*In Search of Mystery*) and* Before the Revolution *a certain metaphorical attitude?*
B B : You're always trying to make metaphors in the cinema, but it's almost not worth all the trouble since they are born of themselves. What I don't really like are "intentional" metaphors like the big fish at the end of *La Dolce Vita*. But the minute you put one shot next to another, you find metaphors. It's strange because the cinema isn't essentially metaphorical: images are absolute; it's words that are metaphorical. If you write the word "tree" the reader can imagine all the trees in the world, words are symbols of other things, but when you film a tree, it's that particular tree and no other. It's not absolutely symbolic of other trees. The strange thing is, given the absolute character of the image, that you can't avoid creating metaphors

the minute you make one image follow another. Until I made *Before the Revolution*, I thought poetry and cinema were the same thing. After *Before the Revolution* I changed my mind. The only thing I would still maintain is that cinema is closer to poetry than to the novel or the theater. Not because of some illusory community of language, but simply because you discover in making a film the same degree of liberty you have writing a poem. The novelist is, in my view, less free.

J F : *Your father is, with Montale, Ungaretti, Pasolini and Penna, one of the great Italian poets of today. Did he influence you?*

B B : I owe him everything. He's the one who introduced me to poetry, not by teaching me theories or dogmas, but by making me sensitive to a kind of generalized poetry of life. I began to write poetry at the age of six to imitate him, and I stopped writing verse later in order not to imitate him any longer, because it was becoming paradoxical that all my life I would imitate him! He was also a film critic; we lived in the countryside near Parma, and he would take me into the city once or twice a week to see movies. That's how I got to know John Ford and the others. So he initiated me to cinema as well as poetry.

J F : *What cinema counts the most for you today?*

B B : The directors I prefer are Pasolini and Godard. I adore both of them. They're both great minds and great poets and that's why I want to make films against Pasolini and against Godard, because in order to make any headway, to succeed in giving something to others, I think you always have to be doing battle with those you love the most.

Bernardo Bertolucci: *Partner*

ADRIANO APRÁ, MAURIZIO PONZI AND PIERO SPILA/1968

B B : The behavior of the spectator of *Partner* should be that of the ideal
spectator, i.e., a very passive spectator who succeeds in finding in the one
hour and forty-five minutes of the screening enough time to sleep at least
ten minutes and during these ten minutes to dream, thus overcoming his
own passivity. I think that should be every spectator's normal behavior in
the cinema.

A , P & S : *At a certain moment of the film doesn't Clémenti address the film's
spectator and invite him to look around, claiming that in the movie theater he's
in, everyone can find his own double two rows in front of him or two rows in
back of him?*
B B : Yes, but if you think about it for a moment, which audience is
Clémenti addressing? He's addressing an audience that doesn't interest us.
In reality, Clémenti here is creating a fiction: he's playing at being an actor
who is addressing the audience. Also, not only does Clémenti address an
audience who hasn't understood him, but the things he says are lies; he's
pretending that the problem of the film is that of doubling, that "you
should also find your double," etc. All of that is supposed to be very un-
realistic because it is voluntarily reductive. However that may be, I'd like to
add something about this sequence. The speech you hear from Clémenti
was added during the Italian dubbing. In the original French version, it is

From *Cinema e film* (Rome), Nos. 7–8, Spring 1968. Reprinted by permission. Translated by
Fabien Gerard and T. Jefferson Kline.

quite different: when I was shooting the film, Clémenti was doing his mad discourse on ways of opposing American imperialism. Let's see if I can remember it. He said something like, "The number one enemy in the world today is American imperialism. If the fishermen in the Gulf of Naples blew up an American aircraft carrier, if the whores in Genoa spread syphilis every night to twenty U.S. Marines, if everyone behaved like this, then maybe we could do something positive and have a permanent spectacle." When I was editing the film, this speech seemed too moralistic, so in the Italian version, I dubbed in an completely different text.

A , P & S : *When you made* Before the Revolution, *did you pose the same problems for yourself as you did in* Partner, *or did the passage of the four years in between change your relationship to the audience? We ask this because when we look at* Partner *we see that you still love* Before the Revolution, *and you can understand this very well when you look at certain scenes....*
B B : I think that the two films are very close. As close as the "me" who made *Partner* is to that other "me" who made *Before the Revolution*. After that film four years passed during which I did almost nothing. It's as if after four years you were seeing me for the first time today. I'm the same as then, but it's four years later. It's the same for my life; it's the same as then, but four years have passed. I didn't do any special preparation for the spectator, unlike, for example, Godard who makes three films a year and so you aren't aware of the changes he might undergo between *My Life to Live* and *Made in U.S.A.* although in reality there are enormous changes. There is this enormous problem concerning the private relationship, the personal relationship with one's films. In my case, now, I know for example, that I should make another film immediately, that I should make films more and more often because you can't just make films every four years. You completely lose the easy relationship you have to filming, you start attributing too much importance to every little thing. At times, I've found myself agonizing over every scene I've shot as if my life depended on it. That's not right. And then, during all those years when I wasn't filming I did almost nothing but think about film, about cinematic style, I don't know, about the fact that some shots are completely autonomous and that every shot is a film. Now all that weighed me as I was making *Partner*. I tried as often as possible to do shots that would be autonomous. Another idea in this vein is that I was obsessed for two or three years by the idea

that it's during the editing that every film loses its stylistic violence, the moment when, cutting the stylistic "misfits," the whole film becomes leveled out. I think editing is the moment which stopped the history of the evolution of the cinema. Because shooting, even though you have to see things through the lens and tripod, the cameramen, etc., is a gestual and instinctive act which produces moments of authentic stylistic liberty. Editing was invented by the *auteurs* and instrumentalized by the production studios precisely to eliminate this freedom, to level everything. The American studios, in fact, retained by contract the right to modify the editing of their films. They even invented a term to designate this process: the final cut. At a certain point, I found myself almost paralyzed by these ideas: my uncut scene or death! etc. And in my films you can sense my desire to abolish editing, reducing it, when there is any editing at all, to its most elementary form. For example, in the scene of the party, I used editing but it's a very primary kind of editing, a Chaplinesque editing.

A , P & S :   *In the scene of the party, indeed, you do use a very simple form of editing. In the establishing shot, the camera doesn't favor Stefania Sandrelli: she's placed in the shadows, under a staircase her back to the camera, despite the fact that she's the most important character in the scene. But immediately you insert an isolated closeup which is sufficiently long to eliminate this strange effect and then you come back to the view of the whole room.*
B B :   Yes. This is very elementary editing. In only two or three scenes does the montage have an expressive function: at the party, in the scene in Jacob's room when the two exchange clothes, etc.

A , P & S :   *The typical scene of this desire to overcome montage is the scene where the two meet in the public urinal and at a certain moment when they're talking about nature and you use a dolly shot to capture the cityscape and then you come back to a frame of the urinal.*
B B :   Yes, but in fact the thing I've never understood is why at a certain moment you have to cut. When? Why?

A , P & S :   *The ideal would be an infinite scene. On the other hand, Ophüls's* The Earrings of Madame de *doesn't give the impression of having been edited. Or else you'd have to make a whole bunch of little films and run them one after the other.*

B B :   That's it! During all these years of inactivity I've probably thought too much about such things. That's why I was saying that I'd felt a loss of my natural approach to things. I think *Partner* is not a very natural film.

A , P & S :   *Let's just say that reflection is all well and good, but that it's better to make your reflections while making a film.*
B B :   That's the criticism I make of myself, but it's a criticism not of the film but of my personal situation.

A , P & S :   *The people who ask questions about the vitality and the autonomy of a single frame have an enormous problem cutting: why? where? how? You, for example, why do you cut sequences that could just as well have been made in a single shot? To interrupt a scene, if it isn't crazy, always has some significance.*
B B :   Often I am tempted to cut my scenes. In *Partner* there are some very long shots interrupted by an insert, for example. In those cases, the insert becomes microscopic. Often I cut precisely to deny the continuity of the scene. Ultimately I don't do this critically. I do the shot and then I cut it because I feel in general that we ought to work against what we have done. You do something, then contradict it, then contradict the contradiction and so on. Vitality is precisely due to the ability to contradict oneself constantly, to deny oneself and eventually you discover that you haven't contradicted yourself but rather followed your very own truth.

In *Weekend* Godard cut a very long tracking shot of the line of cars. He cuts a perfect tracking shot where all the actors are in place, where all the cars are moving in just the right way, where everything is perfect. I think that he made this cut just to destroy something that was working too well. It's as if someone came to Siena, or on the Grand Canal in Venice, and realizes that everything is too well preserved and throws a bomb and blows up some of the buildings.

A , P & S :   *The film's titles are in a perfectly continuous sequence, though.*
B B :   It's true. In *Partner* I did the titles very simply.

A , P & S :   *Did you use Nicholas Ray's colors?*
B B :   The colors of Viet Nam. The Vietnamese flag is a recurring motif in the film and the number of flags is always increasing, until the Vietnamese

flag becomes a decorative element, the molotov cocktail which explodes only once in five tries.

A, P & S: *Our impression is that in* Partner *you accumulated all the films you weren't able to do during those four years. Every shot of the film seems to be the result of ten other shots together, it seems to us that you meant to do this. When you could have chosen to eliminate all that you left behind, you didn't, and instead of burning it inside you, you burned it by exteriorizing it in your film. Indeed, in this sense,* Partner *doesn't even seem to be a film but rather a kind of bonfire, an accumulation of material.*
B B: That's all due to the fact that by nature I work by addition rather than subtraction.

A, P & S: *In* Before the Revolution *we could recognize ourselves in every aspect of the film, characters, story, the savor of the city. In* Partner, *on the other hand, it's the opposite, one is only moved if one thinks about the cinematics of it. And yet, at the same time, we refuse to define* Partner *as an intellectualist film.*
B B: In *Before the Revolution* the point of departure was life, but in addition there was the cinema, and more specifically the mythological idea of cinema. Here the inspiration is partly life and partly cinema. When I'm asked what the film means, I always answer, "Nothing: the film means the film and that's all."

A, P & S: *Which is true of all films.*
B B: Certainly. But we have to begin to say this.

A, P & S: *It's strange that the film comes down ultimately to a very simple nucleus; it speaks elementary truths which already belong to us. The most characteristic thing about this film is its simplicity, despite the fact that everything seems to indicate the opposite. For example, the part on the revolution which takes off from the great thunderbolt from false clouds to end up in two or three shots. It's at this moment that the entire film gets its meaning, and since these images are so powerful that they can hold the whole thing up, it means the film is a success. It's the point of maximum risk.*
B B: The revolution is seen from a very particular point of view, of course. There is the student movement represented by a kind of will of the wisp that runs up a staircase with torches of different colors. The spectacle is

only a baby carriage with a bomb inside rolling down a staircase, but there's no bomb in the carriage, there's no baby, there would only be one if there were a film school that had its primer, starting with the sequence on the staircase from *Potemkin*. The simplicity of it is evident: a = airplane, a = ambulance, etc.

A , P & S : *Ideally, your film could be a film about the theater, but in fact it's a film about life, about the present (Viet Nam, advertising, television, etc.) All of life's a stage is the cliché you hear often enough, but in your film, life is against theater, prevents theater, your film could be the story of a failed attempt to do theater.*

B B : I agree, *Partner* is a film about the present. That is to say that all films are about the present. Even when you do a flashback, you are only filming the present of the past.

A , P & S : *There are also utopic films, films which burn all the bridges behind them.*

B B : I, on the other hand, try to see things amid the total confusion that we find ourselves in. The most important thing is to remain true to oneself. It's also the most important thing in politics. Straub told me a very interesting thing in this respect. He told me that he'd seen documentaries on the events in France of May 1968, and within two or three minutes of seeing these films the police had lost their credibility, whereas this idea of repression was better rendered in forty seconds of shots of police in my film than in the French documentaries.

A , P & S : *It's the power of imagination. Fiction has a indestructible power. What Straub said confirms one of the most important limitations of documentary films, i.e., the fact of never sufficiently accounting for the power of the images that are being filmed, images that are wiped out in a matter of seconds.*

B B : The image is a shadow, you have to catch it.

A , P & S : *And there is nothing more dangerous than shadows that resemble reality. Illusion is a terrible thing and includes practically eighty percent of all so-called political films.*

B B : There is a huge risk that the cops on the Boulevard St. Germain in Paris might not communicate the idea of repression. Because while the author of those documentaries was shooting with his 16mm camera, he probably wasn't thinking about making a film about repression, but only wanted a simple document about what was happening.

A, P & S: *Can you say something about the different interpretations of your film.*
B B: The film is full of keys, of quotations, of references. While the double, for example, is telling about his criminal record, he mentions one of his convictions for corruption of "miners" at Marcinelle (a mining town in Belgium where practically all the workers were killed in 1956), and the camera shows a painting on the wall by Paul Delvaux, a Belgian surrealist with the same family name as André Delvaux, in which we see a night train, hence the title: "One night a train." But it's a quotation that I alone appreciate, and it's strange that a cultivated reader of books will always get all the cultural references right away whereas the film spectator never seems quite able to get the same kind of allusions.

A, P & S: *Maybe the most characteristic thing about your style is the way you move the camera.*
B B: But in *Partner* the camera doesn't move very much, and it doesn't move the way Arriflex usually moves but rather more like a Mitchell does, and it's a very different kind of mobility.

A, P & S: *In any case, one feels that you're always thinking behind the camera. It could just as well be a single frame or a tracking shot. Which is a negation of the frame, of the painting, from a privileged point of view.*
B B: There is always a reason for each shot, though. In the example I gave a moment ago, when the double is talking about his prison record, the movement of the camera is like a stage direction.

A, P & S: *Yes, but when you see it on the screen, a movement of this type is much bigger. Often it takes on too much importance.*
B B: The space of the film is always extremely tight. The camera moves only to follow a sort of musical movement. The musicality is perhaps the most important aspect of *Partner*.

A, P & S: *In the film the way you film Rome is very beautiful. Whether it's the Rome of the ruins and the ancient monuments, or even a completely unrecognizable Rome, in any case it's always a Rome we've never seen in film before.*

B B : I didn't want you to recognize Rome. I only wanted to communicate the presence of a city the way certain surrealist paintings do, or like the way Cocteau or Breton do. . . .

A , P & S : *A question about magic realism in the cinema and the way it goes beyond realism. Your film is violently anti-naturalistic. Aside from the fact that the cinema should be realistic by definition because it's based on photography and recorded sound, there's more and more a desire to make films that are increasingly oneiric where the masters would no longer be Griffith, or Lumière, or Rossellini, or Flaherty, but Sternberg, Murnau, Lang, Ophüls, Cocteau. Why this need to reevaluate the oneiric power of the cinema?*
B B : First of all because there has been a surfeit of naturalistic cinema.

A , P & S : *For example?*
B B : All of the Italian neo-realism, with the exception of Rossellini, the entire French cinema with the exception of Bresson. Naturalism goes from the grand naturalism of Kazan or the petit-bourgeois naturalism of Truffaut to that of Forman. Now the curious thing is that the American cinema I was thinking about when I made *Partner* is in fact a cinema I don't really know. I haven't referenced Sternberg or Murnau so much as the idea that I got of their work just from seeing Murnau's *The Last Man* or very few of Sternberg's films. For example, the scene of the pianist at the beginning of *Partner* is very Sternbergian. The scene has no meaning; it's really nonsense, a sort of musical prologue, a homage to Sternberg, or rather to the idea I have of his films: a search for atmosphere through the use of shadow and light. In fact, Lotte Eisner, who witnessed this period of the cinema, wrote me that she liked the film a lot with "its beautiful undulating shadows."

A , P & S : *There was the German Expressionist school of cinema with all of its American followers, and then the cinema that came as a reaction to oneiric films. This is already the third phase. We could say that Godard and a great part of the new cinema have made a new point of departure. So now we seem to be returning to a new surrealism. Already* Weekend *is a surrealist film, for we have to see it as a kind of extended dream.*
B B : Oneirism ought not be only in the things we film. It should come especially from the way we use the camera. For example, in the film *The Visionaries*, oneirism can be found in the way you get to the dissolves. The

scene in which Jean-Marc Bory leaves the theater and begins to walk is filmed from the rear, which is clearly derived from a naturalistic style, but little by little the street becomes something else. The walls of the houses seem as if they were constructed in a studio. Bory himself changes. What happens is that the continuity of the sequence lifts it right out of its naturalism and makes into something different.

A, P & S: *We're sure that many critics will discuss the "distancing" in your film. For example the love scene between Clémenti and Sandrelli in the car, with Sergio Tofano in the front seat pretending to drive, would be considered very Brechtian. It seems to us, however, that it's only in theory that the scene would be "distanced" but in the universe of the film, the scene would only seem so if it* hadn't *been shot in that way, because it would have seemed too realistic.*
B B: If I'd wanted to do distancing of the type Godard does, it would have been impossible with Clémenti, with all I allowed him to do. His involvement in the film is entirely against Brecht, it's very classical. And this may confuse many of the critics, that is, that the film refers constantly to classical models and then directly contradicts them.

A, P & S: *To come back to the discussion of quotations in your film, especially in the character of Tina Aumont, there are two quotes: the detergents/Godard, the eyes/Cocteau; to which we could add Aumont's memorization of a section of Barthes's* Mythologies. *All this accumulation of quotes is countered by Tina's voice, which, at least in the French version, is terribly pathetic. Her performance practically wipes out all these other elements to get to a level of truth which is what your film is really all about.*
B B: When you get behind the camera, you establish a relationship which can wipe out everything that you thought or wrote beforehand. I had thought about the role of Tina Aumont as a kind of robot-woman characterized by the mechanical gestures of a marionette. When I was shooting the film, however, I ended up contradicting these ideas. I had Tina walk on literally hidden by the packages of detergent she was carrying and which at a certain moment inexplicably caused her to start a spinning movement and forced her to collapse on a chair as if she had just fainted. At this moment Aumont became a representation of humanity. There is a contradiction between her humanity and the "eyes" painted on her eyelids which makes her into a kind of prophet of the world of advertising and

consumerism. It's only when she opens her eyes, that her real eyes appear. There is also an obvious sort of doubling here—none of the characters in this film enjoys any credibility.

A , P & S : *This is true not only for the characters but also for the decors in which you filmed them, for the situations, and indeed the whole world of the film. We're thinking of the scene in which Clémenti kills Sandrelli in the bus which seems to us so eloquent.*

B B : It was precisely about this scene that Jean Narboni told me that it reminded him of the scene in Murnau's *Sunrise*, when the husband and wife come to the town in the streetcar. I've never seen *Sunrise*, but my father has been telling me about it for years, saying that it was a film that literally gave him the chills. He told me about the extraordinary presence of this streetcar. So I thought that Jacob should kill Clara in a streetcar. But then for logistic reasons I had to settle for a double-decker bus. In any case, I conceived and filmed all of that thinking about *Sunrise*, a film I'd never seen, and the amazing thing is that somebody actually recognized this.

A , P & S : *The only difference between the two scenes is that in* Sunrise *the streetcar sequence begins in the woods and ends in the city. In your film the whole thing takes place in the city.*

B B : But they're still very similar. The bus in *Partner* like the streetcar in *Sunrise* was a lyrical and poetic place where in the background the façades change constantly as if they were slides, but in fact they are real. And in this setting the characters don't behave as if they were at home, but with circumspection as if they were in a magic place. In this sense the streetcar becomes a veritable magic carpet. The magic carpet of Murnau's *Faust*.

A , P & S : *You made* Before the Revolution, *which is perhaps an idealistic film given the age you were when you made it. Then you went through the huge disillusionment of not being able to make a film for such a long time. Finally you find yourself making films which could be called "films on demand":* The Oil Route (La Via del petrolio) *for TV and also* Agony. *How did you get to* Partner *through these other films?*

B B : *The Oil Route* was certainly a commercial film and had all the limitations of such a film. You could even say it had greater limitations than are normal because you constantly feel all the effects I created to go against the grain of a commercial film. It was a big mistake because a commercial film ought to be just that, a commercial film. Pasolini would say that I did an amphibiological film, neither fish nor fowl.

Partner, on the other hand, is the direct consequence of having made *The Barren Fig Tree (Agony).* The relationship I managed to attain with Clémenti was directly inspired by my formative experience with the Living Theatre. Whether it's with the The Living Theatre or with Clémenti, we were able to get on the same wave lengths. The Living Theatre gave me a sense of the sacredness of theater and of theatrical recitation that I rediscovered a bit in Clémenti. The scene where Clémenti is hidden behind a wall of books and begins his monologue, cries, sings the *Marseillaise,* etc. is a scene based on my position as voyeur, the camera with Clémenti in front as a reality where something happens. Even the instrument by which we managed to capture such intensity is the instrument typical of all the rites of the Living Theatre. In this rite, Clémenti is the Priest and the incense is provided by drugs. That is the zero degree we took off from to make this scene.

A, P & S: *In what way did The Living Theatre and Clémenti rebel against your film?*
B B: They were never opposed to the film because the film exists only as an idea not as a story. They accept the idea though they may not accept the structure or some other aspect of it. Then you have to follow them. In this sense my film is very close to a form of *"cinéma vérité."* Like Straub's film on Bach.

A, P & S: *Did you omit any scenes from the film?*
B B: I took out a very important scene where Clémenti is on his way to the school for the first time and finds the classroom completely deserted. Refusing to admit that his students have deserted him, he gives his lecture to the empty seats and reads a passage from Lautréamont.

I also cut a ten-minute scene where Jacob was spying on two of his students, Jean-Robert Marquis and Sibyl Sedat, who were making another film on the great white staircase of the Valle Giulia, taken from a short story by Norman Mailer entitled *Block Notes.* And I cut a scene which completely demystified the cinematic illusion, showing that the film is merely an object made with a camera and film. It's the thing that annoys the audience the most; they'll accept anything except to be awakened from the dream they're having in the movie theater. Within this dream you can make them swallow anything, but if you tell them that the dream they're experiencing has a speed of 24 frames a second and that it comes out of an acid bath and the Technicolor labs of the Via Tiburtina, then they get angry and won't go along with it.

A , P & S : *Does the film have its own construction? Because given the fact that it resembles a series of isolated scenes, the relation of one scene to another doesn't seem to exist.*
B B : You're right. At the first editing, the film was completely different; it was another film altogether. Then I redid the editing because the film was about to be released and needed a more conventional architecture. I shot the film with a maximum of freedom, without any concerns for the screenplay, and I only discovered its architecture during the editing a bit to please the producer and also for myself. I think that the various scenes of the film are completely autonomous, isolated one from the next, and in any case it makes no difference to me what order they're shown in.

A , P & S : *To pursue an earlier discussion, it seems to us that your method of cutting the images, of breaking the continuity of the scenes, is a kind of violence inflicted on yourself with great sangfroid.*
B B : This is what makes me hated by everyone who otherwise might love me for someone I'm not. The need for rigor that I didn't feel when I was making *Before the Revolution* has grown immensely over these last few years and may soon disappear.

Now I cut constantly to kill any possibility of the kind of passionate relationship between spectator and film you find in *Before the Revolution*, from which I developed a huge guilt complex. Now I believe that in making that film I let myself go too much. This naturally had consequences, for example, in the screenplay for *Natura contro natura*, which was a film with three characters—a poet, a politician and a homosexual—and was divided into three parts. In the first part entitled "Problems," the problem of the poet is to get his poems read by Pasolini, the poet laureate whose verses he carries under his shirt next to his heart. He's unable to meet Pasolini because he's too shy and he doesn't want to run the risk of being disappointed. His problem gets resolved by the homosexual, who says, "Let's wait for the first windy night, go to Pasolini's house, and I'll help you climb over the garden wall, and then you can let the wind carry your pages throughout the garden. Lots will be lost, but many will be caught in the branches of the trees and in the grass and among the roses. In the morning Pasolini will read your poems. If I'd thought of this scene while filming *Before the Revolution,* I would have eventually tried to visualize it with flash forwards because it could only be a scene with a spectacular effect. But if I were to film *Natura contro Natura* today, none of that would be visualized, only the idea would remain recounted by the homosexual. I realized at some point that rather than showing things you have to show the idea of things. To show things is ultimately a way of making us not see them, a way of losing their reality, because often to visualize means merely to furnish a quantity of sensations which distance us from the idea which is the most important esthetic sensation.

A, P & S: *What do you think of recent Italian cinema?*

BB: The only Italian films I like are not Italian. One is Brazilian, *The Tropics* by Gianni Amico; and another is Danish, *The Visionaries* by Maurizio Ponzi; and a Martian film, *The Harem* by Marco Ferreri. In any case the most Italian films of the last few years are those of Milos Forman!

A Conversation with Bertolucci

ELIAS CHALUJA, SEBASTIAN
SCHADHAUSER AND GIANNA
MINGRONE/1970

F C : Spider's Stratagem *was inspired by a story by Borges . . .*
B B : I find that it's a very mysterious film that resembles a psychoanalytic therapy. The Borges story entitled "The Theme of the Traitor and the Hero" in the anthology *Fictions* was what, in some sense, inspired me. I took these three pages of Borges maintaining most of all the mechanism. In Borges, the story takes place in Ireland in the nineteenth century and the discourse of Borges is a very cultural discourse. The story goes as follows: A young Irish man investigates a crime that had been committed many years before, a crime in which a hero of the revolution, one Kilpatrick, had been assassinated in unusually curious circumstances. The assassination, committed during a performance of a Shakespeare play, was linked to a number of very strange things. For example, in the dead man's pocket was found a letter that he'd been given as he entered the theater but that he hadn't had time to read, just like *Julius Caesar*. And then there was a prophecy of a witch which predicted his death just like *Macbeth*. Then the young man continues to investigate this crime committed so many years before, and he discovers there was a political conspiracy whose leader was this great hero who had been assassinated. At the same time he discovers that in this conspiracy there had been a traitor.

This retrospective investigation is pursued until the discovery of a strange coincidence of this crime with *Macbeth* and *Julius Caesar*. At this

From *Filmcritica*, No. 209 (Rome), October 1970. Reprinted by permission. Translated by Fabien Gerard and T. Jefferson Kline.

point the young man feels desperate because, as he says, "It's possible that history could imitate history (i.e. *Julius Caesar*) but it's impossible that history could imitate literature (i.e. *Macbeth*)." He starts all over again and discovers the truth: the traitor of the conspiracy was none other than the chief conspirator, i.e., the man who had been assassinated, the great hero.

Once the conspirators had discovered the betrayal and its author, had decided with his assent that the Irish cause needed a hero and not a traitor, they decided to kill him (making the English appear to be responsible) and thus transforming him into a great hero.

At the moment the young man discovers the truth, he finds himself faced with a doubt as to whether or not he should reveal the truth—i.e., the same doubt that had troubled the conspirators all those years ago. Here the young man understands that the machinery of this conspiracy was so perfect that it predicted his discovery of this same machinery... and so he decides to keep it quiet, to say nothing.... So there it is. I decided to keep only the structure of Borges's story. My film centers on a young man who goes to Emilia, invited there by a mysterious woman named Draifa to investigate the murder of his father, an antifascist hero who had been killed in the theater during a performance of *Rigoletto.*

The mechanism is very similar to that used by Borges but I'm not so focused in his very Borgesian reflection on the cyclical nature of things. The theme of the film is this sort of voyage into the realm of the dead.

In fact, this town where everything takes place and where the young man had never been because his mother had taken him away right after he was born, this town to which he returns after so many years is a kind of kingdom of the dead.

The investigation that the young man is pursuing is a kind of voyage through atavistic memory, through the preconscious. He is, in fact, in search of the figure of his father in his investigation and discovers a maternal figure represented by this woman, Draifa,—who was the lover of his father and who had invited him here. In this sense I would say that it's a film which pursues the itinerary of a psychoanalytic therapy precisely because this town named "Tara" is like the unconscious, or the preconscious.

FC: *Why the Ligabue paintings during the film's credits?*
BB: My choice of Ligabue is due primarily to geographic fidelity. Ligabue painted the same trees and landscapes that you see in the film because he

lived only forty kilometers from the place where I was shooting. Even though he was born in San Gallo in Switzerland, he lived here and really belonged to the Po Valley. Ligabue therefore belongs to the world, to the very circumscribed universe of this valley in which my story takes place. Then on the set I talked a lot with Vittorio Storaro, my director of photography, about the two visual reference points for the film: Magritte and the naive painters. For example, we shot the night scenes, as you remember, in a coloration that is quite unusual for the cinema, that is completely in azure. That is, they are nights in which you can see everything, nights when you can see a house three hundred meters away hidden in the landscape just like in the naive painters' work, and Ligabue is one of these "naive" painters. Also in Magritte's work there is the same type of night "eclairage." There's a painting by Magritte, called "The Empire of Light," in which you can see a rectangular, almost horizontal house, with a tree, and two lighted street lamps just like in the scene at the train station when Athos the son is getting ready to leave at the end of the film.

F C : *Your interest in some of Ligabue's subjects gets transferred directly into the film, especially the lion.*
B B : There are even some dramatic and rather Van Gogh-like portraits and self-portraits of Ligabue which, however, I didn't end up using. I used all the paintings about animals because in the film there is this mythology of the animals, especially of the lion. In fact, the original title of the film was, *The Flight of the Lion through the Poplar Trees*, which I ended up not liking. So the choice of the lion was very important, and with the lion, other animals as well: cats, horses, roosters with big red crests, etc.

F C : *The cats and roosters in this countryside don't surprise us, but the lion. . . .*
B B : The valley is a pretty strange universe. Why the lion? It's the same kind of thing as in Verdi's *Aida* where the Nile is the Po River. I can also imagine lions in the Po Valley.

F C : *The names you chose for your characters—for example, Athos Magnani, Draifa—are not purely fictional names.*
B B : They are fictional in the sense that fiction always imitates reality. Draifa is in reality the name of the wife of one of the three friends of Athos Magnani, the wife of the one who has the tic in his eye . . . so I stole

Alida Valli's name from this lady, whereas Magnani is a name that is common in this region.

F C : *Athos made us think of the sacredness of fathers which must be profaned. . . . And Draifa we associated with "dreifach" (three times) and thus a symbolic connection with numbers.*

B B : It seems to me that you're going a bit far there, though you're on the right road. The film is, of course, a film about fathers and mothers. Probably you're right that I chose these names unconsciously. In any case, in the film Alida Valli explains why she's named Draifa: her father was a fan of Dreyfus and so named his daughter Draifa.

F C : *Tara is the unconscious.*

B B : Yes, perhaps Tara is the unconscious, but Tara is first and foremost the place Scarlet O'Hara returns to after she says, "Tomorrow will be another day." Tara is thus the promised land of *Gone with the Wind*. It's a little private joke, but Tara also has a credible consonance with the names of the villages in the region, for example, Suzzara, Luzzara.

F C : *The interest in the figure of the double, who recognizes himself in another, seems to take on immense proportions here: Athos the son, sees his double in the father, in the mother (and vice versa), in the step-mother, in the child, in the traitor, in the hero.*

B B : I don't know. It seems to me that in general it's a film about the contradictions of demystification—of the myth of the father, of course, and also of the mother at different moments. The moment when the paternal figure is still a myth, when the son profanes the figure of his father and desecrates his father's tomb, right up to the moment when he discovers the truth—everything remains ambiguous. I mean that he discovers that his father is a traitor but he still doesn't know to what extent his father's betrayal was part of a planned series of events. It's a treason that gives to the cause a great hero and therefore a treason that, ultimately, makes a positive contribution to the cause of the resistance against Fascism. The identification that he does with all the characters he meets is a spiritual movement which is quite familiar to me. That is to say that I, too, try to identify quite often with all of the characters in a film.

FC: The Spider's Stratagem *is a film which is entirely about the present, but the flashbacks are the present of the past.*

BB: The past is maybe just the means chosen to make an alibi, a kind of distancing of things in order to talk about them. However, "historical" films simply don't exist since they're always in the present tense. Even *The Conformist*, which is a film which takes place entirely between 1938 and 1943, is a film about the present. The flashbacks in *Spider* are not flashbacks but a representation of what happened. All the characters, with the exception of Athos Magnani, don't get younger in the flashbacks; they're identical to the way they are in the film's present. I did this precisely because I wanted the conventional notions of chronology to be shattered.

FC: *But the research on period costumes seems to be pretty accurate.*

BB: Yes, it's true for the costumes. The costumes in Straub's *Othon* are very accurate, but *Othon* is a film about the present. It's not a film about ancient Rome. Costumes are a convention. Maria Paola Maino was in charge of the costumes in *Spider*, especially for Alida Valli and for the protagonist who wore a pair of shoes that belonged to my grandfather that I had found.

FC: *Alida Valli's hair-dressing seemed a little too perfect.*

BB: She wears her hair like that in real life. And then, I wanted her witch-like nature not to be communicated in any exterior way but remain entirely internal, in her sudden contradictions, in her changes of mood, when she recalls the moment of Athos the father's physical cowardice in their room when he sees the lion that had escaped from the circus. She pretends to faint in the meadow, and then she gets up and is angry with him because he's laughing. She leaves and he follows and she walks away coldly. And then we see her arrive in her garden of what we might call the enchanted castle, where she is the lady and witch of the manor. At this moment, she completely changes moods, tossing her shoes in the air, dancing, and playing. And then she changes again when she pushes him out onto the terrace: "Go, go!" She orders him, chases him out.

I think that for me the film is above all a film parallel to the first three or four months of my psychoanalysis. I began an introspective analysis last February and the film was made in July, so it's a film that I might not have done in the same way if there hadn't been this event in my personal life. And the thing that struck me the most was that, when I was writing the screen play, I was very conscious of all the psychoanalytic elements I was putting into it, even if many were mediated and very indirect. That is to say that psychoanalysis helped me with many of the ideas in the screen-play; later, on the set, all of the self-consciousness had disappeared because film is a gestual and even irrational language, and ultimately I had forgotten all that. I forgot all that because up until twenty days ago I was in Parma with a copy of the film to do a screening of the film for the film's actors, for some friends and some friends of my father's. At the moment, watching the film I realized something—something that maybe I'm the only one to have seen, but which I think is in the film at the level of the unconscious—all the problems of our relationships with our parents.

FC: *Already in another context you defined* Spider *as a psychoanalytic itinerary.*
BB: Yes, but that was more theoretical. I said it rationally but without really feeling it. Now, on the other hand, I've verified this idea. I relived this feeling because this recent showing was quite magical—it was on a Sunday morning in Parma—a little like Sunday morning mass, with these twenty or thirty faces in the theater that I'd known when I was a kid. I hadn't seen them for many years, and so it was a little like reliving feelings from my childhood. Deep down I realized I'd gone there, in front of all my father's friends, to show that I had done something of my very own.

FC: *This film seems to have made you very happy.*
BB: Yes, very happy because *Spider*, as I've maybe already told you, was a film done entirely without any anxiety, I mean without any symptoms of anxiety. I think it's a fairly bitter film, and here and there is quite tragic; in my view the figure of Athos Magnani is tragic enough, but the film as a whole is very serene. The two months that I was making it were two very serene, very quiet months without any stylistic anxiety.

FC: *Maybe to some extent this film represented a kind of psychotherapy for you.*
BB: I'd say yes, definitely. That is to say it was like kind of prolongation of the therapeutic sessions, outside the sessions. But it never would have happened if I hadn't been in analysis; no, I think the experience of analy-

sis is irreplaceable. Nothing else is like it. Perhaps creativity allows us more easily to go beyond certain great oceans of neurosis, but analysis is something much more precise. Outside of psychoanalysis, it's clear that people work, and work because they can channel into their work their libido which would otherwise not find expression. But all that happens at such an unconscious level that, instead of saying "work," we could call it a cry, a gesture or a foot... pressed on the accelerator of a car.

F C :   Spider *is a film which communicates a lot of joy to the audience.*
B B :   Because everything was done on parallel rails: the tracking shots are always lateral, so there are never any violent shocks. You never get too far away; you always remain at a certain distance from the work. Things are almost always followed laterally. Deep down, the film is made exactly like we were on a train, on a local commuter train, which stops at every station. Yes, the style of the film is that of the rural commuter trains.

F C :   *The last shot of the train station leads into something inexorable and transmits a feeling of impossibility.*
B B :   The impossibility of leaving. The train is late, the loudspeaker announces that the train is even later, and then you hear a noise, but it's just three workers who go by on a gang car without stopping. At first the grass is not very thick, but as things go along—and here I can't help being ironic—there is the novel in the novel and there's the railroad in the railroad because it's with a tracking shot that we shoot the railroad and so the tracking shot is of itself because it shows the rails which disappear under the grass which pervades the whole film from the beginning, and that probably means that no more trains will go by for who knows how long.

F C :   *We saw these workers going by as a symbol of life going on; there they are in the sun, moving their arms up and down.*
B B :   I saw them go by and made them come back so we could shoot this scene. They were quite worried because they knew a train was about to arrive. But I really like this gesture: it was like rowing on dry land instead of rowing on the water, pushing their poles. So it seemed to me a kind of premonitory image. I saw it more as a raft than as a gang car, and it seemed to me a kind of premonitory image of the train that would never come.

FC: *So you can't take a train that never comes, just as you can't let go of the fantasies of childhood.*

BB: It's just at this point that he realizes—and he looks at the town which lies there just as immobile as we've always seen it—he realizes that perhaps once you have entered the realm of the dead it's difficult to leave. And this is an extremely pleasurable fear—the terror you feel in the first sessions of psychoanalysis when, after a month or two, you begin to get into the heart of your adolescent relationships and even before puberty to the relationships with your parents in your earliest childhood, you feel that you're entering a very obscure and terrible place, but still you go ahead without knowing whether you'll get out again.

That's why I said that the itinerary of Athos Magnani the son is parallel, as the tracking shots are parallel, to my personal itinerary in the psychoanalytic experience. Of course we can see all this now, and I thought about it before beginning to shoot the film, but it's not the same . . . that is to say, I absolutely refuse to call it a psychoanalytic film because it's impossible to make a psychoanalytic film, because psychoanalysis is psychoanalysis and film is film. I'm not even interested in making a psychoanalytic film in the strict sense of the term.

But I must say that all these observations we're making, we make because it's fun, but in fact they're extremely hidden, they're buried, they're never at the level of conscious thought. The important thing in analysis is to have done it and to realize you've done it. The main thing in analysis is not one's consciousness, not the understanding; the main thing in analysis is the feeling attached to your understanding. Psychoanalysis, for anyone that has never undertaken it, is a kind of discipline that helps you to understand things about yourself. But it's not like that at all: in fact, it helps you understand things about yourself by reliving them. During the sessions it's your unconscious that speaks; during the most important sessions the unconscious expresses itself. Rational understanding doesn't help; it doesn't help you to get beyond anything.

FC: *You wanted to begin analysis after doing* Partner?

BB: Yes. Not right after *Partner* but during the period after I'd done the film. *Partner* is one of the moments, one of the schizoid elements of that period of my life. At a certain point I needed to understand better and to try to see inside myself better.

F C : *You chose to have the child recite Pascoli in the film, given the analogy of*
his poem La Cavallina storna (The Bay Horse) *with the content of the film . . .*
is that also why there's a quotation from Leopardi?

B B : No. I used Pascoli because his poetry was part of my childhood, he's
one of the poets I liked to read as a child, and as you noticed, there's the
identification with the child. Pascoli is the poet par excellence of identification with little children . . . and then, because the kid who was acting in
the film happened to have learned this particular poem by heart. As for
Leopardi, I really like the purity of Leopardi contaminated by the accent of
the child who says: "La donzelletta vien dalla campagna/In sul calar del
sole. . . ."

I think it's really good to have children memorize poetry in school. As a
child I thought it was really idiotic. I was totally against it because I thought
they wanted to make us into parrots: they never explained what poetry was
and just wanted us to photograph it in our minds and repeat it back like
machines. That's why I put up a huge fight against my teachers who wanted
me to learn poems by heart. Now, of course, I'm ashamed of this attitude. I
envy the characters of novels who, at some point, stop everything and quote
a dozen lines from *The Aeneid.* It's wonderful to be able to recite poems
from memory. Maybe you have to be a bit exhibitionist to do it, though.

F C : *What determined a different kind of montage during Athos the son's last*
speech for the final version of the film?

B B : Well, simply, because I wasn't happy with the first montage; but also
there was the fact that I felt the need to go over the film again after six
months. And going over it, I wanted to do something, not just remix it,
but work on it a little bit, so I thought I would integrate into that last
speech scenes of everything we had seen before. But while I was doing this,
I thought, "Look, it looks like the trailer of the film!" In the end, I realized
that if the result was a bit didactic, I nevertheless felt as though I'd made a
generous gesture to the TV audience, which wasn't used to seeing a film as
elliptical as this one, or at any rate as mysterious. It still seems to me that
the new ending helps people understand the heart of the problem, i.e., the
problem of the traitor and the hero.

Before there was the close-up of Athos the son who was giving his
speech and that was all, but it was a bit disappointing. It was disappointing because it felt too much like a minor key. There was a problem of

proportion, given that the ending was in a minor key and that the final scene dies out in the grass of the train station. In terms of tonality it was a bit as if those inserts break the monotony of the scene. Most of the people who saw the film found it was too didactic. As for me, so much the better if it's didactic, if it helps people understand!

F C : *Why did you cut the song "Quando" ("When") by Luigi Tenco from the final version?*

B B : Because the rights to the song were too expensive, so we substituted a song by Mina which she had written for *The Conformist* and that I hadn't been able to use in that film. When we do the editing on the moviola, I always bring in recordings and we try out how they work with the film. "When" worked really well. It's a shame!

Here it's not like in *Partner,* which is full of things that I was never able to combine the way I wanted (maybe precisely because I wasn't really myself when I was shooting *Partner*). I am curious to know what you will think of *The Conformist.* I am tempted to show it to you as soon as possible because it's very different. There's a kind of happiness in *Spider*; it's an entirely closed world. But I'm eager to know what you'll think of *The Conformist,* which is a film entirely without joy, a terrible, even a ferocious film.

F C : *The editing in* Spider *seems essentially to have the function of coordination or association, as if to accentuate the cyclical return of things, which is so Borgesian, though you claim that you weren't especially focused on this . . . whereas in* Partner, *for example, the editing was so elementary, every shot was autonomous.*

B B : Precisely because *Partner* was filmed in a period of neurosis. I had— as one has a persecution complex—I had a single-shot-per-scene complex, but just as like a neurosis, the montage was, as it were, abolished, and ended up as a sequence of shots which I'd conceived of as autonomous and which could be freely interchanged, alternated or combined. By contrast, *The Conformist* is a tightly edited film; there are lots of scenes. There is one five-minute scene in particular which is made up of close to two hundred shots!

F C : *Coming back to* Spider, *when the sailor leaves Tara, the film seems to move from the solid and believable vision of an oneiric reality to one in which pure fantasy gradually takes over.*

B B : They are the same fantasies that we've already seen throughout the film in the town. The town is populated by old men, there are the old men who listen to the opera in the streets, and the shot of the wagon is right out of a vampire film with these old women who seem like vampires with their parchmented faces all colored.

On the one hand, and this is the problem, we enter directly into the loggia where the father had died during the performance of *Rigoletto.* The son walks through the streets where his father had walked before him right up to the theater; he speaks with these old women, so everything is quite realistic. From another point of view, this return to the opera house, with this musical incantation, the music of *Rigoletto* is a kind of magic flute which leads him back; all these people scattered through the streets have the inconsistency of phantoms. In my view of the film they are very real people, but there's this separation between me and the character at this point because I see them as real whereas the character is so completely at the mercy of the suggestion of this mise en scène that he no longer has a connection to reality. At this point his unconscious begins to be flooded with an intuition — the intuition of the truth. That is to say, that the truth is precisely the theatrical mise en scène. This walk from the station to the theater is the beginning of this mise en scène.

F C : *The discovery of the truth seems to coincide with a kind of liberation for the inhabitants of Tara.*
B B : And also with Verdi's music which has a cathartic function. I used *Rigoletto* because this is the land of Rigoletto. Rigoletto is the baritone, Gilda is the soprano, the tenor is the Duke of Mantova, and the story happens in Mantova. Likewise, I shot the film in the province of Mantova. It's music which truly belongs to this region.

F C : Spider *was coproduced by RAI (Italian TV): what possibilities does State Television offer now? What kind of relations did you have with them and how will the film be distributed?*
B B : Once the screenplay was accepted, and it was accepted right away in its first version, RAI never interfered with the production. So I must say to date they're the best producer I've ever worked with. A producer economically present and physically absent amounts to total freedom.

As for the distribution, in Italy it will be limited to television. What happens outside of Italy depends on who purchases the film. Probably some other television company will buy it; it's already been sold in some other countries. Television is the only medium which can respect the film's format (1.33) which is perfect for the TV screen. In Italy it will still be shown in black and white, but maybe that's better. The colors are too beautiful, and I'd like to see whether the film works in black and white.

As for the sound track there's such a terrible problem that it won't be enough just to tinker with it the way they did with *Cinema e Film* or *Filmcritica* or with Straub's films. The only thing is that you have to do your films with direct sound recording, try to get them done with direct sound. I'm very discouraged by current cinematic production methods; it's clear that if I have to fight it's not going to be about direct sound recording. There are too many other battles to be waged first. Which is to say I wouldn't choose to fight over the soundtrack even if it is a fundamental part of the film.

Bertolucci on *The Conformist*

MARILYN GOLDIN/1972

The Conformist is a narrative film, but in it you blend fantasy and reality, you pass from suspense to surrealism to politics. It's as if you were always in the process of exploding the form and then seizing it again.

That's because of the freedom I give myself in shooting. It's only in the actual décor with a precise space, precise lighting, the camera there in front of one, that one discovers and makes the film. In the scenario the film was less varied; it was more of a single colour. But in shooting a great deal depends... For me, actors are very important: they're the ones who make the characters, and the characters in the script disappear before the reality. So a great deal depends on my rapport with the actors. If the actor hasn't slept the night before, the scene will turn out a certain way; another way if he's drunk too much, and so on. And that change is part of my freedom in shooting. If I like a thing I do it, even if it's contradictory to all the rest. At the end, you will see if it was really good. If it doesn't finally enter into the whole, the ensemble, that means it wasn't any good.

There are moments when the actors adopt poses of Thirties stars—for instance, Dominique Sanda leaning against a door with a cigarette in her mouth and her thumbs hooked in her slacks pockets is classically Dietrich... Or Sandrelli, in the scene where she dances to the American record...

·Directing actors means, above all, liking people, liking certain things about people. I looked at Sanda and I imagined her like that, and we tried it and

---

From *Sight & Sound*, Vol. 40/No. 2, Spring 1972. Reprinted by permission.

it worked because it was already in her. It's really a matter of discovering and bringing out of the actors what they really are, and nothing else. Characters must be built on that—on what the actors are in themselves. I never ask them to interpret something pre-existent; except for dialogue and even that changes a lot. You could say I follow the actors like a TV cameraman filming an interview; but the result is very different from television.

That's unexpected because the film is stylishly "acted," not at all like cinéma vérité. *The impression is that Trintignant, for instance, is certainly giving a performance.*
But he *is* acting. Still, I think Trintignant is *that* person, that this is the first film in which he is himself. If he reads this, he's going to be furious. But I chose Trintignant because when I think of him two adjectives immediately come to mind: moving and sinister. And these are qualities of the character. The point of departure is reality, then the actor transcends it. Because there is a camera which moves and which is itself an actor, an actor who makes the others react. The camera is a character like Trintignant, a living presence, not a recording machine.

In Italy, it is well known that Verdi was a revolutionary as well as a composer and now a cultural institution. Were you intending a reference to his politics as well as his music in The Spider's Strategy?
No. It meant a great deal to me that this should be a regional, artisan film. I used many different elements from the crafts of the region and Verdi, the music of the region, is one of them. Of course there is the political significance of Verdi, but that interested me less. Also, Verdi corresponds for me—and thus for the son of Athos Magnani—with a mythic dimension, and that works very well with the mythical stature of the father. Mythic music for a mythic personage.

Your use of colour in the two films is very different. In Spider's Strategy *it is very beautiful, almost lyrical. In* The Conformist *it is as though you were trying to use colour almost cruelly—ugly colours like that harsh neon red in the credits, for instance.*
There is a technical explanation for that. In *Spider's Strategy* we used very little light, whereas *The Conformist* is lighted like a 1930s studio film; even

when we were on location, there were a lot of lights and lighting effects, like that red, or the rays in Sandrelli's apartment, or the blacks when the professor tells the Myth of the Cave.

Even so, you were looking for... For instance, in the sequence when Trintignant goes to the dancing school and takes Sanda into the adjoining room behind the curtains. The lighting there is a kind of sinister blue-green and makes her ugly. It isn't erotic when she undresses, because the colour supplies the emotional tone.

That was an attempt to make the film at given moments more or less impressionistic, like the interior of the dancing school, and at other moments more or less expressionist, like the adjoining room. There was an effort there to violate reality, to do a style of photography that wasn't modern. When she undresses she is going to the slaughterhouse; which is why I used that light. In fact, simply as colours, the tones are much more violent in *The Spider's Strategy*. There, however, they are used in another perspective.

The lighting of The Conformist *is very Sternbergian.*

Yes, indeed. Because in *Strategy* I was more influenced by life, while in *The Conformist* I was more influenced by movies. One could say the point of departure was cinema; and the cinema I like is Sternberg, Ophüls and Welles.

What about your work on the continuous movement and contrast of light within a scene? The ball of the blind, for instance, begins in almost total blackness: then all at once it's lighted, but lighted on blind people who themselves remain in the dark. In effect, there is always a change of lighting during a sequence; and the change is often radical.

You know, this is the first film where I controlled the lighting myself in the old, truly professional classical sense. Most of the young directors reject lighting as something cheap or kitsch; but on this film I really came to understand what you can do with light. You can get unbelievable effects which help the psychology, the narrative, the whole language of the film. When Sandrelli and Marcello see each other for the first time, there are those shuttered windows that refract the light, rays that pass. It helps a lot to establish the atmosphere of the house.

After Before the Revolution *you seemed to leave the bourgeoisie as a subject. Now you take it up again with two bourgeois heroes....*
Yes. One doesn't escape....

And both of them grapple with a Fascist past. That seems to be a theme in your work, that the sins of the father are always visited on the son...Fabrizio, then Athos Magnani fils *and Marcello.*
Yes, Fabrizio...it's true. My own father was anti-Fascist, but obviously I feel that the whole bourgeoisie is my father. And Fascism was invented by the *petit bourgeois*. And there's the fact of having made two films about the past, not having arrived at making films about the present. Or rather, they are two films that arrive at the present by speaking of the past...On top of that, *The Conformist* is a story about me and Godard. When I gave the professor Godard's phone number and address, I did it for a joke, but afterwards I said to myself, "Well, maybe all that has some significance...I'm Marcello and I make Fascist movies and I want to kill Godard who's a revolutionary, who makes revolutionary movies and who was my teacher...."

Do you have perhaps a slightly guilty conscience about having made The Conformist *with Hollywood finance, money from the "American Empire," exactly in the sense that Godard now refuses it?*
No, not at all, not in that sense. I feel ill at ease in the great contradiction of Cinema, which is so difficult to resolve. Jean-Luc's way is *his* way, and that is important, but I don't believe it is the only one or that everybody has to follow it. I think he chose the way he did because he didn't want to be a leader any more. He felt like being left alone.

Throughout The Conformist, *a relation is drawn between politics and sexuality, just as in* Before the Revolution. *In the final analysis Fabrizio's only revolutionary act is to sleep with his aunt. And when Gina leaves him, he leaves the Communist party. So he has acted out the revolution on an emotional level. Marcello's politics seem to derive from the same source. Did you change the motivation from the novel?*
Yes, in the sense that in the book the story of the conformist is a tragedy and, as in the Greek tragedies, everything is related to Fate. Here I substituted Marcello's unconscious—a psychoanalytic explanation, that is—for

the presence of Destiny in the book. And that's also why I changed the end of the story; in the novel Marcello and his wife are killed, and this is presented as God's justice. Marcello is really a very complex character, searching to conform because of his great, violent anti-conformism. A true conformist is someone who has no wish to change: to wish to conform is really to say that the truth is the contrary. But what is tremendous in the novel is the intuition about the character of Marcello: his monstrosity has tragic dimensions. Transforming Destiny into the Unconscious, of course, also affects the rapport between sexuality and politics.

What do you think is the connection between them?
I think the most important discovery I made after the events of May, 1968, was that I wanted the revolution not to help the poor but for myself. I wanted the world to change for me. I discovered the individual level in political revolution. And for me that remains true at the same time that I repeat Sartre's phrase which is quoted in *Spider's Strategy:* "A man is made of all men. He is equal to all of them and all of them equal him." I'm sure that some young occidental Maoists will reproach me for *The Conformist* because it's beautiful to look at and because I mix dirty things like sex with a pure thing like politics. But I think that's Catholic, moralistic reasoning, and I find that the great foolishness of young Maoists in Italy is their slogan, "Serve the People." My slogan is "Serve Myself," because only by serving myself am I able to serve the people—that is, to be a part of the people, not serve them.

To pass to the character played by Sandrelli. She is treated in a comic fashion throughout the film and then, when she speaks at the end about her husband's crime, she suddenly becomes very sinister, a silent conspirator.
Good, because I believe that in the world I present in the film, no one is saved. Not even Sandrelli, who is very appealing and foolish, a cross between a Hollywood character and an Italian *petite bourgeoise.* She is also a part of this monstrous world of bourgeois Fascism. So she becomes like that because I want no one to save himself. And no one does. Not even the professor and his wife. I didn't want to paint a hero's portrait with the professor, as Resnais did for instance with his old Spanish Civil War fighter. For me the professor and his wife were the other side of the medallion of

bourgeois Fascism, linked to it by a chain which is decadence. They are sympathetic, they are on the right side of the barricades, but they are still bourgeois and they are not saved.

It's true that the only relationship you don't illuminate entirely is the one between Anna and the professor.
Because I didn't want to plunge the dagger in even deeper. Otherwise, I would have had to say that the professor knew very well that his wife was a lesbian, and that it gave him pleasure to see her dance with Stefania. It's not very healthy and not important for the story. And people like the professor are really dead, they paid with their lives. It's a bit ferocious to treat them like that.

There is still some nostalgia in Italy for the Fascist period, isn't there?
Yes! That's why I say *The Conformist* is a film on the present. And when I say that I want to make the public leave with a sense of malaise, perhaps feeling the presence of something obscurely sinister, it's because I want them to realise that however the world has changed, feelings have remained the same. Feelings, that is, about normality and abnormality...For Italy, the film is really very savage.

You know, I've done thirty interviews and no one ever asks me why I moved the camera in a particular way, or why I used tracking shots, or how long they were...Take the construction of the *bal populaire*. Giulia dances the tango with Anna with the camera close, and they kiss; then there is a circle of people around them and the camera is high up. They begin to do a sort of farandole and the people follow them, and while the farandole grows the camera descends on a dolly, taking in the orchestra. Then, in the next shot, we see Marcello and the professor watching them, amused. People pass dancing in front of them, and someone takes the professor's hand. Marcello stays alone. Behind him there is a window, and as Giulia passes outside it, leading the dance, the camera leaves Marcello to follow her and to arrive on Manganiello, the professional assassin, who is sitting across the room. Marcello is tapping his cigarette packet on the table, following the rhythm of the dance. When he sees Manganiello he stops, and Manganiello looks at him, and then *he* starts tapping...So, these are the things...*découpage*, camera, technique. It is only through technique that one arrives at doing things.

Do I dare ask a last question on structure? It seems that if one scene is in day-light the next shot will be in darkness; or if a sequence finishes on a close-up, the next will begin in long shot. It is as though you were constantly breaking the atmosphere of the preceding scene, instead of prolonging or varying it. True or not true?

Maybe, but not consciously. I made *The Conformist* very freely, which is why it is an easier film for the public. When I made *Partner* I was obsessed by a kind of neurosis of style, of language.

A Conversation with Bernardo Bertolucci

JOAN MELLEN/1972

Q : *Can you tell me something about your background and education, the peo-ple, experiences and ideas making up your intellectual formation which led to* The Conformist *and* The Spider's Stratagem?

A : My father is a poet. I was born in Parma into a home with many books on poetry. I started to write poems when I was six years old, to imitate my father, I think. I stopped writing poems to finish imitating my father at nineteen or twenty and ended my experience with poetry with a book which created a "tomb" for my poems.

Parma is a town in the north of Italy. There is a melange, a mixture making up a very original culture in Parma because it is a "grand canton," closed off from the rest of Italy, a kind of "capital" with many elements of French culture. Parma is also a "Red Town" — the Communist Party is in the majority in Parma. So the context of my development, politically, was a Communist, a Marxist, context. *The Spider's Stratagem* takes place in this region where I was born. I became interested in cinema very early, and all during my adolescence I was sure that one day I would make movies.

Q : *Were your father and family in the Communist Party?*

A : No, my father was not in the Party, but all my contacts and friends were.

Q : *How did you start in films?*

A : My first work in cinema was as an assistant to Pasolini while he was doing his first film, *Accattone*. I was also doing my first film at that time,

From *Cineaste*, Winter 1972–73. Reprinted by permission.

and neither Pasolini nor I knew the cinema. It was a kind of new birth of cinema because Pasolini, never having made a movie himself before, was inventing the cinema as if for the first time. When he made a close-up, the film, for me, discovered the close-up. It seemed like the first close-up in movie history because it was the first time for Pier Paolo.

Q: *Do you feel that today your films have any resemblance to his?*
A: No, none. I don't think so. He has an idea about "sacerality," a sort of mysticism, and I don't have the same vision of life, of reality. The language of Pasolini's movies is very different from the language of my films.

Q: *Many critics in the U.S. have said about* The Conformist *that it makes too simple an association between homosexuality and fascism. Do you think they are misunderstanding what you intended in the film? They accuse you of saying that all homosexuals become fascists.*
A: Or that all fascists become homosexuals. No. This explanation is too simple. *The Conformist* is first a film about the bourgeoisie, the middle-class, not about fascism. I was speaking about the middle class, and fascism is a moment in the history of the middle-class, a means by which the middle-class protects itself from the working class. Whenever the working class is coming up, up, up, at this moment fascism makes its appearance. In the film there is a fascist and an anti-fascist, but the Professor in Paris, the anti-fascist, is also from the middle-class. We have two faces of the same coin, of the middle-class. One face is fascism, the other is anti-fascism, but not a Marxist anti-fascism, just an idealism. Because he is also in the middle-class, my anti-fascist is not a hero, not a positive man.

In the Moravia novel the presence of "fate" or "destiny" is very important. I read the book in quite a different way. Everything that in the book was attributed to "fate" in the film stems from the subconscious of the character. But I absolutely don't want it to be a question of fascism equalling homosexuality. This is really too simple. Homosexuality is just an element in Marcello's character. Marcello feels himself different because of his secret homosexuality which is never expressed, yet always inside of him. And when you feel "different," you have to make a choice: to act with violence against the existing power or, like most people, to ask for the protection of this power. Marcello chooses to ask for the protection of the power. He becomes a fascist to have this protection that he needs.

Q: *But the system knows that Marcello doesn't believe in fascism. In the first part of the film, the fascist says that people join the party for many reasons, very few because they believe. So Marcello does not join because he believes in fascism.*
A: No, he wants only some protection because he is different, because inside he feels he may be a homosexual. He asks something of the power structure; this power gives him his protection, but asks that Marcello do something in return, that he kill the Professor. It's a contract between the individual and the system.

Q: *Are you interested in the writings of Freud or is this just part of Moravia's treatment?*
A: No, I think that the work I did, the transformation of the novel into a film, was in the sense of Freud. In Moravia everything was determined by "fate" because we never understand why Marcello becomes a fascist. At the end of the book, the night after the 25th of July, Marcello leaves Rome with his wife and they go to the country. A plane flies overhead, killing him. What happens to Marcello is thus caused by a "divine presence." I don't accept this idea. I prefer that the force of the subconscious take the place of "fate."

Q: *At the end it is a psychological fate. Once fascism fails him, Marcello doesn't intellectualize. He feels only that he must accept Lino and return to homosexual feeling.*
A: He understands, he achieves consciousness (*prendere coscienza*), but it's also instinctual, unconscious as well.

Q: *Are you interested in surrealism, in continuing this technique in other films besides* The Conformist? *In that film surrealism expresses something about fascism, about homosexuality and the relation of the son to the mother.*
A: Surrealism was the most important cultural element during the twenties and thirties and *The Conformist* took place at the same time. Actually, *Partner* is my most surrealist film. It's very like Cocteau. I think in *Spider*, too, there is some surrealism because the visual experience is from Magritte.

Q: *Things happen that can't be explained in a practical way, the son gets locked in the barn, etc.*
A: Yes.

Q : *Is there a radical alternative in* The Conformist, *a hint of how to oppose fascism, in the girl who sells flowers and sings "The Internationale," and at the end, after Mussolini has fallen, when the people sing "Bandiera Rosa" in the streets? Doesn't this suggest that another political road might have meant a different experience for Italy and Marcello?*

A : Yes, of course, an indication of something that will come. But in the sense of having any political impact, being truly effective, no. What you change with films is ... nothing.

Q : *Some people did not perceive the criticisms you were making of Professor Quadri in* The Conformist *because they are not accustomed to seeing the social democracy criticized. Would you agree that Anna Quadri was made a lesbian because her decadence was one way of showing the ineffectuality of the social democracy?*

A : I think there is some truth in this, but I am, of course, very interested in homosexuality in general, and therefore also in lesbianism. If this theory were true, I would be very moral, but I am not a moralist.

Q : *Can't you have moral truths in a film if they're expressed in a cinematic way? Then they're not noticed as making a "statement," but become part of the imagery of the film. Otherwise films could not express ideas.*

A : I think film in general expresses "film." I know that's a tautology, but when critics ask me what did you want to say in the film, I say, nothing. With the film I want to say just the film. Because the audiences, the public in general, and critics as well, judge films on the story, the content and not the style.

Q : *Were you interested in Wilhelm Reich's* Mass Psychology of Fascism? *Did that book have any influence in your decision to do Moravia's* Conformist?

A : No, it's not important. I know a little Reich, but on *The Conformist* Reich was not important for me. Freud, however, is very important in my biological-physical life. I think that *Spider's Stratagem*, for instance, was really suggested by my beginning psychoanalysis. I started to do a personal analysis four months before I began to make *Spider's Stratagem*. The relation between father and son is the real point of the film.

Q : *The son wants to become the father?*

A : Yes, all the great problems between father and son are the basis of the film.

Q : *Even the incestuous relation, with Draifa, is present.*

A : Yes, with Draifa.

Q : *I thought you were interested in Reich because he makes the connection between homosexuality and fascism. Have you seen Makavejev's film, W. R.:* Mysteries of the Organism?

A : Although I like Makavejev very much, I haven't seen his latest film. I think in Makavejev one finds the realization of "materialism." He is the one real "materialist" director today in the Marxist sense. His second film, *An Affair of the Heart*, about the killing of a telephone operator, was really a materialist film, very interesting. Nobody else in the socialist countries is making materialist films.

Q : *Some people say that Rossellini is the great materialist filmmaker.*

A : Rossellini is a materialist, but unconsciously. Makavejev is conscious.

Q : *But without hope. He doesn't feel that things can change, that we can make a better society than the fraudulent one we have now. Do you think that the treatment of political ideas in films, the conditions of filmmaking are different for an East European director than those confronting you when you make a film in Italy or in France? That a director like Makavejev faces different problems and therefore makes a different kind of film?*

A : I don't know because I don't know what the conditions are for my fellow socialists in Russia or Yugoslavia. Socialism is in power in the countries of Eastern Europe, so filmmakers don't have to struggle against something as they do here. We want socialism, so it's different.

Q : *Do you believe they have socialism in Yugoslavia or Russia?*

A : Yes, I do. It's not the final stage, but they are countries which are closer to socialism than we are.

Q : *You don't believe that they are in need of a new revolution?*

A : Are you a Trotskyist? I am not a Trotskyist. I am in the Communist Party. The problem of the political film is very difficult. I see a great contradiction in my work when I do political films like *Before the Revolution* and *Partner*, because political films must be popular films, and *Partner*, for example, was anything but popular. So there was a big contradiction. I don't think that *The Conformist* can have a political effect. I think it is just a film about sentiment, and there is a judgment in it about history. But in my country the film cannot have a real political result. And I think the same is true for *Z*, *Investigation of a Citizen above Suspicion*, and the new Petri film, *The Working Class Goes to Heaven*.

Q : *And Godard?*

A : Godard, too. I think that cinema is always political. All films are political, but all films which are made within the system are also exploited by the system. I thought during the sixties that with movies you could make a revolution, but it isn't true. Now I think you can only be at the service of the revolution. Cinema itself cannot be revolutionary—it can only be in opposition (*contestatario*).

Q : *Have you seen* Hour of the Furnaces? *Solanas, of course, had the problem of not being able to show the film to the people he would have liked to have seen it.*

A : When you make revolutionary film in the sense that you and I conceive of a revolutionary film, it never goes into a revolutionary space. It goes into festivals. So you do a revolutionary film for the cinephiles, the people who like movies.

Q : *I was looking back at Borges'* The Myth of the Traitor and the Hero, *upon which* Spider's Stratagem *was based, but your film does not really reflect the sensibility of Borges at all.*

A : In Borges what you have is a "rite," or ritual, a geometric composition around the character of a man who is a traitor and a hero at the same time. As soon as I read the book, I wanted to make a contemporary story of it. Then a very strange thing happened. I wrote the script. The story was about a young man and his grandfather. But the day before we began shooting, I thought that there was something that was not right. And then I understood that for me it is not about the grandfather, but the father.

Q : *Did you intend* The Spider's Stratagem *to make any judgment on the trick of Athos Magnani to have the comrades whom he betrayed kill him and then blame the assassination on the fascists?*

A : Athos Magnani can see in his friends a kind of naiveté. He betrays them. Why? I don't know. Maybe because he thinks it's more important to have an anti-fascist hero, unlike the attempted assassination (*attentat*) of Wallace which was not successful. It's more important to have a dead hero. I don't give any explanation, but I am always thinking within the film about the reason for the treason.

Q: *It's a terrible thing to betray, even if you no longer agree with your comrades.*
A: I don't think it's terrible to betray. It's terrible when an idea needs a hero; to need a hero is terrible.

Q: *You're more sympathetic to Athos the father than I would be.*
A: I am sympathetic, but I killed him.

Q: *If his son hadn't come, he'd still be the great hero, in an absolute sense.*
A: But when the son understands the truth, what does he say? He has to decide whether to tell the truth to the people or not. He doesn't tell the truth. He goes away. But he says. "A man is made by all men . . . he is all the people and all the people are he." It's the last line of Sartre's *Les Mots*. The son during the film, during his one day in Tara, can understand only one thing, the phrase he speaks at the end of the film.

Q: *That is an idea from Borges, too; Borges says, if I speak one line of Shakespeare, at that moment, I am Shakespeare.*
A: Yes, but I took the line from Sartre. Borges speaks about Don Quixote, too, about a second and third Don Quixote made by other possible writers.

Q: *How successful have* The Conformist *and* Spider's Stratagem *been in Italy? Were they popular?*
A: Both films are my most successful. *Spider's Stratagem* was shown on television twice and had an audience of twenty million people. *The Conformist* was not on television, so the films had two different lives. *The Conformist* is popular here, too, but it's impossible to have an audience of twenty million people—no *Dolce vita*, no Sergio Leone film has had this large an audience.

Q: *Could you tell us about your new film,* Last Tango in Paris?
A: The new film is important for me because it is the first time I'm doing something in the present. *The Conformist* is also in the present, but it's the

present dressed as the past. *Last Tango* is really contemporary, the present, the present of "fucking," the "fucking" is just one moment in the present. In *Last Tango* the present is the absolute present as during a moment of love.

Q : *Does* Last Tango *have any historical or political background?*
A : Yes, but sexual as political. Sexuality and politics are very important. But nothing of political events in France.

Q : *What is the context of the film?*
A : It's about a human relationship between a man and a woman in the present. I think it's the most political film I've ever done, but the characters never speak about politics.

Q : *Marlon Brando has lately been choosing films that he feels have a certain political importance, like Pontecorvo's* Burn! *and* The Godfather, *which Brando thought was a criticism of capitalism. But of course it isn't; it's a gangster film. Have you seen it?*
A : I saw it last week. He's incredible, Marlon.

Q : *Brando has said that the two people in the world he'd most like to kill are his father and Gillo Pontecorvo.*
A : I know that Pontecorvo would like to kill Marlon Brando. They had a terrible relationship because of political disagreements. And Marlon felt that *Burn!* was a disappointment.

But *Last Tango* is a sort of tragic *An American in Paris,* because Brando is an American in the film. Do you remember *An American in Paris*? Something like that, but with differences.

Who Were You?

DACIA MARAINI/1973

Q : *Can you tell me when you were born and where?*
A : In Parma, March 16, 1941.

Q : *Tell me something about your family.*
A : My grandfather was the son of a peasant. He belonged to a family of priests and small landowners. When he was a young man, he came down from the mountain into the valley and began to practice horse trading. He was very enterprising and successful at many different things, quite an adventurer. He searched throughout Europe for horses, going as far as Hungary. Then he would come back and resell the horses and set out again. He never stopped. At twenty, he ran off with a Parma landowner's daughter who became my grandmother. Meanwhile with the horse trading he got rich. He bought a property near Parma which is called Baccanelli. It was on this farm that we lived: my father, mother, brother and I during all the years of my youth, until we moved to Rome.

Q : *So your grandfather was a farmer. What about your father?*
A : My father refused any active involvement with the countryside and preferred a more contemplative life. He pursued his studies in the city and became a teacher.

From *E tu chi eri? Interviste sull'infanzia (Interviews on Childhood)*, 1973. Republished in 1998. Reprinted by permission. Translated by Fabien Gerard and T. Jefferson Kline.

Q : *What did he teach?*
A : He taught history of art in a lycee in Parma. Then he became as well the film critic for the *Gazetta di Parma.*

Q : *And your mother, did she work?*
A : Yes. She was a teacher of literature in the middle school.

Q : *How do you remember your father when you were young?*
A : The most important thing I remember about him, before anything else, was butter.

Q : *What was the odor of this, can you give me any idea.*
A : It was a smell of bitter almonds. An intense odor that surrounded him like a kind of halo. An odor that remained in the places he'd passed through, in the objects he had touched. A strong smell and frankly unpleasant, but which I looked for avidly. I had a very well developed sense of smell as a child. I recognized people by their smell. My mother also had her smell. And also my grandfather.

Q : *What was your grandfather's particular odor?*
A : He had the smell of a bald head. The smell of nine o'clock in the evening, a good sweet smell. Every night before going to bed he distributed goodnight kisses to everyone. To kiss my grandfather I had to get up on a chair. His bald head had the same smell as the one I found twenty years later on the head of my analyst.

Q : *Have you been in analysis for a long time?*
A : For four years.

Q : *And you're still in analysis.*
A : Yes.

Q : *What is the most important discovery about yourself that you've made in analysis.*
A : I discovered that I had repressed during many years my aggressivity.

Q: *And now?*

A: The analysis has helped me find a more serene relationship with my unconscious and to accept others, meaning of course myself.

Q: *Let's come back to your father. What was your father like, physically, when he was young?*

A: My father was very dark skinned. He had skin darker than anyone else I knew. I remember an attentive, kind gesture he had: we had fled during the exodus during the war. We were living in a house in the mountains where there was neither bathroom nor running water of any kind. The adults had to go outside to do their business. As for me, since I was little, there was this map. With a slow and very precise gesture, my father opened this map and made me squat over it.

Q: *And why on a map?*

A: I don't know. Maybe because it was made of a waterproof material. I made poops on it. And then my father would throw the waste into the fields.

Q: *Were you more attached to your father or to your mother at this period?*

A: I don't know. But if we move to when I was six years old, I can recall a very important event, the discovery of writing, which I identified with my father. As soon as I learned to write, I began to imitate him. I wrote poetry like he did.

Q: *And did you find your father handsome?*

A: I have always found him equal to himself. More than handsome, he was irreplaceable. But maybe I've repressed in some way the fact of "looking at the father." At first I never looked at him because I was afraid. But then I identified with him, and so even if I looked at him I didn't see him.

Q: *Did this identification with your father last a long time?*

A: Yes, a long time. Until psychoanalysis, meaning about twenty-eight years. From the moment I identified with him, I never judged him. My father was like an extension of my penis.

Q : *Or else you were an extension of his.*
A : No, for me it was as if it was I who engendered my father and not the contrary. Now I've gone beyond this identification, but there are things that belong and have remained glued to me.

Q : *What sort of things?*
A : One of them is nostalgia.

Q : *Nostalgia for what?*
A : The nostalgia for the present which dies in our hands. Another thing is his way of living the present moment in a non-traumatic way, always celebrating life. For us, in the countryside, everything was ritualized, poetic: whether it was the birth of a calf or the burial of a peasant, or even the emergence of glow worms on a summer's night. These things were experienced as a kind of poetic expression before ever being real facts. There was no difference between a "neurotic white rose" that my father described in his poetry and the real white rose which flowered in my garden. I grew up in an earthly paradise where poetic and natural realities were one.

Q : *Didn't your father ever read his poetry out loud?*
A : No, he was too modest to do this. But I snuck off and devoured his poems in secret.

Q : *He didn't read his poetry out loud, but he made you live your life according to his stories. Did he talk to you a lot?*
A : Yes. When I was young, I remember the presence of his voice as a constant in our lives. He spoke to us about everything that happened—but avoided, of course, the things that might have traumatized us.

Q : *And what was your mother's role in all this. Was she active or passive? Did she talk too, or did she merely listen?*
A : My mother was a witness like us. And yet I knew that her presence was necessary and crucial because it was only when she was with us that my father was calm and could tell his stories. If she was outside, bicycling for example, and was late getting home, our entire world began to crack and crumble.

Q : *Was your father an anxious man?*
A : Extremely anxious. His anxiety was maybe the only thing I refused to identify with because I felt it was a kind of obscure and terrible suffering.

Q : *What childhood memories do you have of your mother?*
A : I remember that she was very tanned, that she would go out to the garden in a flowery dress to pick flowers. And then I remember her absences. Sometimes she would remain locked up in her room for several days because she had migraines. When she disappeared from view, I felt abandoned. It was as if she had died. I couldn't see her or hear her anymore. My first memory of my mother is linked to the moon.

Q : *Meaning?*
A : I was very, very little, so little that I was able to sit in the wicker basket that she attached to the handlebars of her bike. Each time she went to visit her relatives several kilometers away, she would take me with her in this basket. When we came back late in the evening, I remember her face in front of me because I was sitting backwards and so I could see her face and behind her face I could see the moon.

Q : *Was your mother also from Parma?*
A : No. She was born in Sydney, and this was an extraordinary thing for me. While she was biking with me, she told me that when she was on her way back from Australia, in Ceylon, someone had substituted an Indian girl for her and I believed her. I marveled at this story and looked at her wide-eyed. I remember her as beautiful, of a beauty that was to be the envy of my school mates for years to come.

Q : *What was the countryside like where you grew up? What are your memories of it?*
A : Baccanelli? Our farm was but three miles from Parma but the countryside was very green and very happy.

Q : *What crops did you grow?*
A : Wheat, tomatoes, potatoes, pears and grapes for wine. There were some cows, some pigs and some chickens.

Q : *And who did the farming?*
A : There was a family of peasants. There were about fifteen of them, quite a large family. They lived in the peasant quarters near our farm. I was great friends with all of them. It was from their mouths that I heard the word communism for the first time. I was playing with the kids in their yard along with a bunch of other kids from around there. My house was a kind of meeting place for all the kids from the area.

Q : *And why did they come there of all places?*
A : The most attractive thing about the place was my bicycle. Right after the war, no one had a bicycle. Mine was red, chrome plated and flamboyant.

Q : *And you loaned it willingly.*
A : I had them all try it out. Other things that attracted all these kids were my toys, my comic strips, my guns and also the fact that we could play with the farm tools. But maybe they were also attracted by me and not just my toys, because I was very good at telling the stories of the films I'd seen, and we made up our games based on these stories.

Q : *What films?*
A : It was the period of American films about the Indians and the war in Japan. We invented real naval battles in the huge wooden vats that were used for irrigation. Some of these vats were used by the peasants to ferment urine for use as fertilizer. We used them for our submarines. Another great game we had was hunting frogs. There was a canal covered with cassis flowers where there were hundreds of frogs. At about three in the afternoon, we would break up into groups of five or ten and go into the water bare legged and stand there like statues until the frogs got up their courage to leave their hiding places. Then we would grab them with our hands and hook them onto wires. The one who caught the most was the winner. Some kids even got a kick out of sticking a straw between the skin and flesh of the frog and blowing up the frog until it exploded.

Q : *And what did you do with all these frogs that you'd stuck on the wires.*
A : We took them to the peasants who ate them. There were also dragonflies along this canal which were of an incredible blue color with enormous

brilliant wings. Each time the ice in the canal melted in the spring and we could see the grass poking through the ice we were ecstatic. When I have kids, I will take them to the countryside.

Q: *Do you want to have children?*
A: Yes, sooner or later I'd like to have some children.

Q: *And what was it like at school?*
A: Things were good. I was a good student. But it wasn't difficult for me since I'd always lived among books. The others were peasant children.

Q: *And you were conscious of this privileged situation?*
A: I felt a certain sense of guilt. But my relationships were pretty easy. Deep down, we were small landowners and there wasn't such a great distance between us and the peasants who worked on the farm. During summer storms, when there was hail, my grandfather and the peasants would all run out together to pull covers over the wheat.

Q: *So you never experienced hunger, even during the war?*
A: No. When we fled to Casarola in 1944, I experienced more fear than hunger.

Q: *Fear of what?*
A: The Germans, the fascists. As soon as we heard them coming, everyone fled into the woods. My father was very brave and didn't run away. I remember once that a boy ran up from the village shouting, "The Germans, the Germans!" There as a general panic and everyone began to run in all directions. My father took a book and sat down on the threshold of our house. We could hear barbarous songs emanating from the road. Then suddenly some boys appeared with helmets covered with leaves. It was the *HitlerJugend.* They were about seventeen or eighteen years old. They stopped in astonishment when they saw my father sitting there quietly reading, and then continued on their way. They could have killed him but they didn't.

Q: *Was this an act of defiance on your father's part or did he trust them?*
A: I don't know. Probably he wanted to express the courage of human dignity as a form of conscientious objection. He simply refused to run and

hide like a mole. After that, though, the situation became too dangerous. In the last months of the war, out of love for us, my father had to flee. It happened in fact that the Germans committed massacres in our village. The only ones left were the old men and women. The Germans had these old people serve them a feast and they ate their fill. Then they set fire to all the houses with the old people still in them.

Q : *Are your father and mother Catholics? What importance did religion have in your family?*
A : My father will never be able to say, "I'm not religious." But in fact he isn't. I've only seen him go to church twice in my whole life.

Q : *But you were baptized?*
A : Yes, apparently our family was a family of practicing Catholics. There are few things more beautiful than going to vespers of a summer evening, carrying lanterns. My mother is not really religious either. They didn't push us to practice religion or prevent us from doing so. They just let things take their natural course.

Q : *But you had some religious feeling?*
A : No. What I felt was more a form of esthetic feeling. I loved the moment that they untied and rang all the bells at Easter. I loved the moment when we knelt to kiss the earth three times. I loved the chants sung by the old villagers. I loved the procession with the statue of the Madonna through the chestnut trees each August 10th. And the moment when the priest arrived with his black mantel to bless the houses just before Christmas. At thirteen I suddenly understood that my emotions weren't religious but esthetic and so I stopped going to church.

Q : *So you didn't experience a loss of faith.*
A : No, since I never had faith. I simply decided coldly to stop going to church after a confession.

Q : *Why after a confession? Did something unusual happen?*
A : No, nothing unusual. It was a typical confession. But when I went to kneel down I was filled with feeling of uneasiness. A feeling of terrible embarrassment and shame.

Q: *And why this shame?*

A: I realized I was reciting a lesson, playing a role. And everything crumbled. I felt I wasn't sincere. Everything was false and unreal. So I left promising never to enter a church again. Maybe this was the most religious moment of my entire life.

Q: *And what place did politics occupy in your family?*

A: My father was a committed antifascist who was opposed to fascism from the outset. But he was not active in politics. He was proud of having had among the twenty-five students in his class at that time fifteen partisans.

Q: *And when did you first begin to get interested in politics?*

A: The revelation of politics came to me in a tomato garden among peasant women. I was about nine at the time. I remember that a peasant arrived shouting, "They killed Attila Alberti!" When one of the peasants asked who Alberti was, they explained to him that he was a worker who had been shot down by the *Celere* (literally The Rapid Ones, the Republican Security Forces) during a demonstration in Parma. At that moment I felt like I'd lost my innocence. I had to take a position with the workers or against them.

Q: *When did you start reading political texts?*

A: At sixteen I read the *Communist Manifesto*. It's a curious thing that I lived in anticipation of this experience that afterward became the sixties' movement. My first film, *Before the Revolution* dates from 1963. It was only released in Paris in '67 and enjoyed a huge success among the students there. The film included a rather scathing criticism of the Italian Communist Party. In fact in Paris the film was successful precisely because it was seen as a criticism of the PCI coming from the left. Then in May '68 when these criticisms exploded into the riots in the streets, I joined the Party. I felt like I had already lived what happened later.

Q: *And were you sexually precocious?*

A: I was too precocious and therefore ended up being something of a late bloomer.

Q : *Meaning?*

A : In the countryside the discovery of one's sexuality happens early. I was therefore as precocious in my discovery of sex as I was slow to practice it. Moreover I was a timid, embarrassed and fairly closed adolescent.

Q : *Didn't you ever fall in love when you were a child?*

A : No. Maybe I was too narcissistic to fall in love.

Q : *How old were you when you fell in love for the first time?*

A : Fifteen, at school. But I don't want to talk about sex, it doesn't interest me.

Q : *Why?*

A : I'd prefer to talk about slaughtering pigs.

Q : *Which pigs?*

A : Each year when I was a child I eagerly awaited the November mists because I knew they were coming to slaughter the pigs.

Q : *What did you like about this slaughter?*

A : The fact that it had been going on for years in exactly the same way and that it was a very elaborate ritual that took place in a festive atmosphere.

Q : *Can you tell me about it?*

A : In the courtyard of our farm, they hoisted the pig up on a kind of scaffold. Then the "masèn" arrived with a basket full of knives. He had about him an odor of blood you could smell ten meters away. When he came into the courtyard the pigs began squealing because they could smell the "masèn" too. He would seize one of the pigs, immobilize it and would thrust the "corador"—a kind of long needle with a ring on the end—into the heart of the animal. He didn't spill a single drop of blood. He was infallible. The animal died immediately without any pain. While he was at this, the other pigs squealed louder than ever. I was trembling and waited with bated breath for it to be over. This was the dramatic part. Then the festivities began. The peasants dragged the pig outside the stable and hung it upside down like Mussolini on a horizontal piece of wood which served as a scaffold. And there in the November mist of the open courtyard there was a huge vat heated by a fire where they boiled water. They took pails full of water and threw them at the carcass to soften the skin. The pigskin was raked with knife blades and then the "masèn" took his knife and in a single stroke cut the carcass from the guzzle to the zatch. The moment he made this cut there was an outburst of great joy. All the kids jumped up and down around this scaffold, and the peasants ran every which way to prepare the salamis, the hams and pig's feet, the lard. The pieces of fat which we called "ciccioli" were thrown right into the boiling water and were eaten piping hot. It was great!

Q: *How do you explain this attraction you had to cruelty.*
A: Maybe because my life was so devoid of cruelty. And then also because it was beautiful. It was like going to the theater. There was all the excitement of a popular show.

Q: *Did you suffer from any fears as a child?*
A: Yes. I was afraid of the dark. I was also afraid of cats and dogs. I've always had a very intense unconscious relationships with dogs. Dogs know I'm afraid of them and so they get all excited. The result is that they attack me. So I've never had a cat or a dog in my house. When I was a child and I scraped my knee I always really wanted a dog to lick my wound. It was a very strong desire but was never satisfied.

Q: *Were you afraid of ghosts, or spirits of the dead?*
A: No. For me the darkness was about loss of identity. In the darkness I touched my body to reassure myself I was still alive. I had the sensation of floating. I also suffered from vertigo. Fear of the void. I was also afraid of the tramway wheels. There was a yellow tram which circulated between Parma and the hill country. It had great iron wheels which scared me a lot. It was probably some form of castration anxiety.

Q: *So do you think you had a happy or an unhappy childhood?*
A: Very happy. So happy that I prolonged it as long as I could until it was no longer permissible to be infantile. I paid and suffered because of this.

Q : *Didn't you ever have periods of sadness as a child?*
A : Maybe I was sad at times, who knows? If I was, I wasn't aware of it. In any case the sadness of the day would disappear at night. Sleep was an immense thing that carried me off far from myself and my body. I became an angel when I was asleep.

Q : *Did you ever have problems relating to your family?*
A : No. I discovered the word aggressivity only after I was twenty. Up until then all the hard edges were softened by my father.

Q : *What about his anxiety?*
A : His anxiety was his only weak point, but I censored his anxiety. I tried not to be controlled by my father's anxiety and I succeeded.

Q : *How do you feel nowadays about your childhood?*
A : Since I'm neither religious nor a moralist, I feel any judgment would be out of order. In any case I live instinctively.

Q : *But do you think about it often, do you miss it?*
A : For a long time I exalted my childhood. Now, thanks to psychoanalysis, I have succeeded in establishing a more serene, more detached relationship with my past. I carry my childhood with me as naturally as hunters carry on their boots the leaves and mud that has stuck to them during their hike. When the hunter returns home in the evening and takes off his boots, he tries to scrape the dried mud off with a stick. Sometimes this mud comes off in a compact form which bears the imprint of the foot. I think I can see my childhood as if it were a mold of earth and leaves which has come unstuck from my feet and reveals the form of my past.

Every Sexual Relationship Is Condemned: An Interview with Bernardo Bertolucci Apropos *Last Tango in Paris*

GIDEON BACHMANN/1973

"THE ITALIAN COMMUNIST PARTY, I feel, ever more faithfully expresses the reality of the proletariat, and thus of Italian culture. I feel it allows space for the intellectual and serves as a link between him and those aspects of existence which he has often avoided.

"But I no longer feel the same need for the political element in my films; not in the same way. Not like we all used to need it: like an element of clear conscience, of programmed engagement..."

Bernardo Bertolucci, 32, director of *The Conformist* and *Last Tango in Paris,* is talking in his Rome apartment. Clearly divided on the shelves that surround him are his main interests: Mayakovsky, Gramsci, Goethe, and Tolstoy along one wall; Hitchcock, Bogdanovich, a complete set of *Les Cahiers du Cinéma* and things that have been written about him a few steps up on a steel shelf. In between, abandoned, perhaps, in midscript, magazines on interior decoration, mostly French. The objects in the room are all 1900–1925; a Goodwin painting from the last auction at Christie's, solid, satisfying colors, Jugendstil without Mucha's flabby pastels. Like his political views, Bertolucci's taste seems decisive; he appears to take from literature, art, and society that which he can employ.

Cosmopolitan origins, a rarity for Italy. His poet father, Attilio from Parma, lover of Proust, Conrad, and Svevo, wrote film criticism and dragged the schoolteacher Zavattini to the cinema until the latter, enflamed,

From *Film Quarterly,* Vol. 26/No. 3, Spring 1973. © 1973 by The Regents of the University of California. Reprinted by permission.

changed the texture of the art by authoring the classics of neorealism; his mother Ninetta, of Irish-Italian parents and born in Australia where her revolutionary father had sought refuge, wrote a thesis at the University of Bologna about Catullus. English, French, and ideas went flying about his head as far as he can think back; he received the Viareggio poetry prize for a slim volume at the age of 21. The same year he made his first feature film, *La Commare Secca*, scripted by a friend who lived in the same house in Via Giacinto Carini in Rome: Pier Paolo Pasolini, author of *The Ashes of Gramsci*, a book about the man who founded the Italian Communist Party. The circle closes.

Prima della Rivoluzione, his second feature, brought him his first acclaim: Talleyrand supplied the title, Italy's bourgeois revolutionaries, ten years after liberation, the subject. The sweetness of life in Emilia, where Bernardo was born; the poplars with their tops in the mist, the flow of enthusiasm and resignation, the useless parades and the incest of relationships and ideas; his pessimism even then founded in personal experience, mixture of intellect and earthiness, a deep sensuality of concept, sound, and vision. He seemed destined, even then, to become a cult hero.

His next film, *Partner*, form and failure à la Godard, and then psycho-analysis, some documentaries, and a protest film: in close-up, a typewriter, letter by letter, types a script they wouldn't let him shoot. After three years of stagnation and soulsearching, rescue by Jung and Italian TV, which commissioned two features: *The Spider's Stratagem* and *The Conformist*.

"Man is self-destructive, and destructive of his partner. In nature, it is usually the female that devours. Genetically, over the centuries, some males have understood her mechanisms, have understood the danger. Some spiders just approach the female, but stay within safe distance. Exciting themselves with her smell, they masturbate, collect their sperm in their mouth and wait to regain their strength after orgasm. Because that is how they get devoured, when they are weak after ejaculation. Later, they insemi-nate the female with a minimal approach, and thus she cannot attack them in the moment of their weakness."

The end sequence of *Last Tango in Paris* starts with a reversal of the roles from this Borges theme: Maria Schneider, the victorious snip, masturbates Marlon Brando under a table in the dark corner of a dance hall where his drunken prancing has convinced her of the end of their anonymous, sexual tango; weakened, he staggers after her as she escapes, through the streets of Paris with the wasted semen, breathless, up the stairs of her mother's home and into the study of her dead, military father; his strategy failed, he dies foetally from her bullet. The mantis, the while, recites what she will tell the police.

Ten years ago, when I first met Bernardo, his concerns were more directly cinematic, less literary. The camera itself as a subject of a film still seemed a possibility to him, the camera as an instrument of self-comprehension. And he didn't want to interfere with it too much; he was jokingly suggesting a law against montage. Films, he then thought, might well be divided into Pasolini's categories of poetic and prose works; he felt that because his work was primarily personal, it belonged in the first category.

The changes in the man are notable. The few years of inactivity and analysis seem to have left a mark: his eyes shift constantly and his tongue flicks from side to side in his mouth as he talks; his smile in secure moments is ironic, in others—more frequent—questioning. He continually speaks of his latest film as if he had discovered its meaning now, after it has been shown, in discussing it with friends. *"Mi sono accorto..."* "I realized...that the couple in my film are not isolated from the world as I had planned for them to be. You cannot escape to an island: even your attempt to do so is part of our social reality. It turns out that my characters are profoundly symptomatic. You can't hide in a room; reality will come in through the window."

The discovery of what he was really doing in making *Last Tango in Paris* came to him, Bertolucci says, after he had started shooting:

Originally, I wanted to make a film about a couple, about a relationship between two people. As I began to work and felt the film taking shape, *mi sono accorto...* I realized I was making a film about solitude, I think. I believe that this is its most profound content: solitude. It's the opposite of what I had set out to describe.

I let reality take over, most of the time. I set up a situation, and then make a sort of *cinéma-vérité* about the characters, the real characters I find in front of my camera. In the case of *Tango,* I felt as if I was interviewing Brando and Maria, seen within the narrative context of the film. Thus what results on the screen always represents the fruit of the relationship I develop with the characters, and of the relationship I develop with the things and the spaces I find myself filming. It is through the camera that I begin to understand the things and the people. That is why I am constantly open to learning and absorbing into the film that which the filming itself reveals, even if that should be in contradiction with what I have written into the script.

With Brando and Maria my subconscious relationship was extremely intense, but I think I managed not only to drop most of my defenses, but that I helped them drop theirs as well. I felt, finally, that this first film I was making about the present was being made without any sort of defenses, without excuses, of either a historical, narrative, or even a political nature. It seems to me now, that in this sense it's quite a liberated film.

In what way, then, do you consider the two characters as profoundly symptomatic?
The encounter of these two ends up being an encounter of forces pulling in different directions; the kind of encounter of forces which exists at the base of all political clashes. Brando, initially rather mysterious, manages to upset the girl's bourgeois life-style, at least at the beginning, by force of his mystery and obvious search for authenticity. His way of making love to her is practically didactic. Didactic in the sense that he seeks the roots of human behavior in that moment, the moment after his wife's suicide, when he has reached a peak and a dead end at the same time. He believes that he must seek absolute authenticity in a relationship, and this, I feel, gives the encounter its political sense.

A political sense, then, that you hadn't planned?
Absolutely not. In fact, I had been somewhat preoccupied by what seemed to me an absence of political terms in the script. I was beginning to get worried that I was being faithless with myself and was, perhaps, making a mistake. Because in me, too, there existed a certain conventional mental structure that demanded the use of a direct, political statement in every work. I was saying to myself, watch out! You'll end up making another *Love Story*! But I quickly realized, shooting, that when you show the depths, when you drown yourself, as it were, in that feeling of solitude and death that attaches to a relationship in our Western, bourgeois society, and when you begin to identify the reasons for this feeling of death, you inevitably make a political statement.

Do you consider the search for "didactic," anonymous sex an antidote for this
feeling of death in our society?
In the film, sex is simply a new kind of language that these two characters
try to invent in order to communicate. They use the sexual language
because the sexual language means liberation from the subconscious, means
an opening up. In no way, on the other hand, do I mean to identify sex
with the feeling of death, either. I am not setting up any eros-thanatos
theory. I am simply saying that when you describe a relationship thirsting
for authenticity, you discover all that surrounds it, all that hampers its
expression.

In any case, you link the concepts of sexual expression and personal liberation.
Do you feel that self-liberation must be a conscious process?
Self-liberation in the sense I employ the term is a first step towards living
better, towards the finding of an equilibrium with your subconscious,
towards the finding of a peaceful relationship with your subconscious.
These first steps can often be very dramatic, since we tend to suppress our
own attempts at making them. We suppress our aggressions and frustrate
our souls. Since that which is between Marlon and Maria is a sort of *amour*
fou that continually devours itself, I had been afraid it would seem isolated. Instead it became a centrally symptomatic affair for our times.

You don't feel, then, that the individual must necessarily be rationally aware of
his search in order to find that equilibrium?
No. One can also become conscious of the meaning of one's actions in a
completely irrational manner. In fact, "becoming conscious" seems to me
to be too limited a definition for what we are talking about. This does not
mean that I reject psychoanalysis or other systems of reaching consciousness, but I feel the system must be different for each one of us. I, for
example, walk this road towards self-liberation in a very unorthodox manner. I feel myself becoming conscious, but in an extremely emotional,
instinctive fashion.

Does your intuition lead you to an understanding of the feeling of solitude and
death in our society beyond our conventional answers found in Marx and Freud?
Both of these are still very important to me in my work. But I refuse to
limit my reading of their meanings to the conventional interpretations.

But certain references in this direction have been useful to me in under-standing the characters of my film. For example, how an encounter turns into a clash. Or, to quote Maria, how the casual becomes destiny.

I cannot deny a certain educational structure and background, of which Marx and Freud form part, but I try and see them in a political, existential way. In making *Last Tango,* I found that what I had considered points of arrival were in reality points of departure; I mean to say that understand-ing my characters with the help of conventional psychology or politics gave me only a beginning glimpse of their complicated, personal struc-tures, but it did help me in accepting them as living beings in front of the camera, and in accepting their contributions to the film.

I find that I must live through the relationships that a film creates in a direct way, without logical or rational references. You could say, of course, that the film is a form of dream, that the whole story is an oedipal projec-tion on the part of the girl; after all, she is 19 and Brando 48. And his story could be another oedipal projection—he feels, in a way, that he is as much the son of his wife as he is the father of the girl—but I prefer not to define things in this way. After all, the film is meant to mean different things to different people; the final, personal significance of a work always depends on the viewer.

The viewer, then, for you becomes an essential component of the work?
Absolutely; as essential as the lights, as the sets, as the man who pushes the camera dolly. Even when an audience is not overwhelmed by a work, in its distance from the work it remains an essential component. But I can-not think about it when I am shooting. After all, every conversation one undertakes—and a film is a conversation—presupposes the presence of a partner. In the case of poetry, my interlocutor is the reader, in the case of the cinema it is the public. I do not like to talk alone, and I do not talk alone. I do not talk for myself, I mean. This, by the way, is how the cinema becomes a way of weighing reality, that is, it becomes an instrument for understanding the world. And I think this is true for both creator and viewer.

In a way, then, you are exploiting the public?
I exploit it by giving myself, but I am also exploited. It's a two-way rela-tionship. By the way, I find more and more that there is no such thing in

human congress as innocence and guilt. There is only supply and demand, something offered and something requested, indistinguishably intermingling. And you can't even say that he who offers is innocent and he who demands is guilty, or vice versa. And this applies to personal, sentimental relationships as well: there are never faults. And as far as the public is concerned, the only sure thing I know is that I seem to be seeking an ever larger one.

Have you changed your demands, then, since you were writing poetry?
No, perhaps the offer has changed. I also feel, by the way, that my films, deep down, are quite generous, that I make no excessive demands. Perhaps part of my process of liberation was the acceptance of the fact that I had always wanted to create a *spettacolo*. It took me a long time to accept this idea, although even my first 16mm films, made with my cousins when we were children, told stories, rather than just documenting the death of a pig or the vain search for an abandoned cable in a forest. But I think that only with *The Conformist* I really accepted the role of author of story films. ["*Autore di film—spettacolo*" cannot really be translated; "*spettacolo*" essentially means a demonstration for a public, a notion situated somewhere between entertainment and spectacle. —GB]

Your difficulty is accepting this idea derived from the fact that you felt your political concerns could not be well expressed in the spectacular form, or because you found it difficult to give up the idea you expressed ten years ago, of the camera itself being the most important subject of your work?
I haven't really given it up. I had arrived at a point of rupture when I made *Partner,* the film in which I most violently went against my own nature of being a showman. Besides the fact that this film caused me a tremendous psychological trauma, because nobody, almost nobody, accepted it. Paradoxically I now find—now, after having finished and discussed it—that *Last Tango* is, of all my films, the one most closely related to *Partner.* Now that I have fully accepted my showman role I find I can return safely to a whole series of questions, obsessions, discussions over the meaning of the camera, of research and of experimentation which in the making of *The Spider's Stratagem* and *The Conformist* I had deftly avoided as if they were the devil. This means that now, with the security I derive from the show element, I can start afresh. That is why I find *Tango* very close to *Partner,*

because in *Tango* there is a continual enquiry in filmic terms, a research on the use of the camera, an attempt to question the structures of cinema.

You don't mean in the spoofing sequences, where Jean-Pierre Léaud satirizes Godard?
Certainly not. Jean-Pierre is not meant as a serious Godard character, rather as a character à la Jerry Lewis, perhaps. His part is superficial and strictly functional. He could also have been a carpenter. The reflections on the use of the camera are in all the rest. In that sense I don't think I have changed since we discussed all this ten years ago. I still feel I am looking for the very specific light that is typical and expressive of every feeling and of every epoch, and I still seek the very specific way of representing how time passes—that particular, psychological passage of time which gives a film its style. Perhaps it is a matter of *percorso*, of how a man moves through time, in the historical and in the practical, daily sense. That, in fact, is what holds *Tango* together, as I see it now: Brando's retreat from being a man of 48 back to being an adolescent and finally dying like a foetus. Jean-Pierre, filming his life with Maria, at one point, pushing the camera at her and forcing her to retreat, says: "*Avance en reculant!*" Advance by going backwards. That is exactly the *percorso* of the character of Brando in the film.

At the beginning of the film he is supervirile, desperate but determined in his despair. Look at how he fucks the girl the first time. But slowly he almost loses his virility. At a certain point he makes the girl sodomize him: going backwards, he has arrived at the anal stage. Let's say, the sadico-anal stage. Then he goes back even further and arrives in the womb of Paris, dying with mother Paris all around him, her rooftops, TV-aerials, her grey, grabbing anonymity. Much of this feeling was born during the shooting of the film, although I had planned for him to die like an embryo even when we wrote the script. But now I find that all this comes out very specifically; that there is a clear departure and a clear arrival in death. When we were planning the film, all this was only in my subconscious. My camera research clarified it for me. The irrational becomes lucid.

In your script, I found the words of the scene where he lectures to the girl on the restrictive structures of the bourgeois family, but he does not have anal intercourse with her while he is talking. Why did you add this in the filming?

It seemed clearer to me, if he accompanied the oral lecture with suffering caused to her in a direct way, performing for her, by using her, the double-faced violence he was describing. It is a violence that wants to teach, the violence of the teacher, and on the other hand there is the violence of the family, the destructiveness of the idea of the family. Her drive to be free, when she screams and repeats "Liberty, liberty!" is very real and also double-faced: she wants to be free of what he is talking about but also free of him. What he is doing to her, thus, is a sort of didactic savagery.

Do you mean to tell me that he uses perversion in the guise of anti-bourgeois teaching?
It's a moment of catharsis. He is conscious, but also divided, in that moment, between his consciousness and the pleasure of perversion. He immerses himself in perversion as personal catharsis, and also, partly, because perversion in that moment serves him as an escape.

Do you mean from impotence? Because he can never, obviously, live according to the principles he is talking about. Throughout the film you show him as a man who defends one principle and lives by another, or by none.
Partially yes, but also as an escape from the pain caused by his wife's suicide. There are many ways of getting over that kind of pain, perversion and sex are obvious ones. Sex is very close to death in feeling.

Certainly the metaphor you are suggesting seems to land the character of Brando in a duality of motivation. Your film, especially in America, where we tend to equate sexuality with liberation as you seem to do, has been hailed as an erotic masterpiece. To me it seems the opposite, and the sequence we are discussing, in its sadness and desperation, proves rather that you use sex as a symbol of the impossibility of relationships.
I didn't make an erotic film, only a film *about* eroticism. In any case, you can not separate "erotic" behavior from the rest of human action. It is almost always like this, that things are "erotic" only before relationships develop; the strongest erotic moments in a relationship are always at the beginning, since relationships are born from animal instincts. But every sexual relationship is condemned. It is condemned to lose its purity, its animal nature; sex becomes an instrument for saying other things. In the

film, Marlon and Maria try to maintain this purity by avoiding psychological and romantic entanglement, by not telling each other who they are,
etc., but it proves impossible, since dependencies of various types develop.
Brando tries in vain to defend himself from his innate sentimentality,
which is why he goes to such extremes in putting down both himself and
her precisely at the moment he discovers that the man she claims to love
is he. He already knows, deep down, that he will give up his strong-man
act, that he will put on his pointed shoes and his red tie and will, over
champagne, tell her who he is and accede to her bourgeois ideals, fearing
that they are in reality more his than hers. It is the last dance of his
chaotic solitude, his last defense. Asking her to cut her nails and insert her
fingers in his anus is like saying: Fuck me, break my virility, destroy it!

Why do you feel every relationship is condemned?
Every relationship is condemned to change, anyway. Perhaps it can im-
prove, but generally it deteriorates. It cannot remain just itself. Thus there
is always a sense of loss. It is this sense of loss that makes me use the word
"condemned" rather than saying "destined."

So you do not believe at all in the possibility of a romantic relationship?
Well, I am myself being a romantic when I say that first emotions cannot
be repeated. But I do not believe that relationships can develop on a
romantic level, because . . . well, because there isn't really a reason why
they should: history, reality, are all but romantic. And a relationship must
feed on reality in order to continue.

So what can develop between a man and a woman on a conscious level?
Not a very cinematographic question . . . What can develop is only posses-
siveness, which brings about the destruction of the loved object. That is
the sadomasochism at the center of the relationship, a constant presence
in all relationships. It is a component which in rare cases can be dominated and regulated and can find a channeling which instead of harming
the relationship itself finds victims outside, a sort of centripetal instead of
centrifugal sadomasochism. When we manage to channel and express our
aggression outside of the relationship, the relationship can be saved. But
most of the time it works against ourselves.

What about man's other, less personal relationships? You have changed your
emphasis away from social and political themes, at the same time becoming
more contemporary. And yet you defend a single political party.
In a way, I feel an even stronger political obligation now. But I think more
clearly. I feel that my political engagement is more mature, less linked to
personal neurosis. I feel my presence is a historical continuity, in a cultural
involvement. A modest presence, of course, but I perceive it in a more liberated way, probably because I am also less frustrated. At one time I could
not distinguish between that which was rational and profoundly necessary, and that which, on the other hand, was more of an alibi, that is,
linked to neurotic structures and the search for a clean conscience. In a
way, I think, all of us European intellectuals have lived in this distorted
political dimension for the past few years.

Do you feel there has been a lack of political clarity? We do not seem to have
been able to give the most recent generations any background by which to judge
their current political moment. They seem more rootless than we were.
This problem interests me greatly. The film I want to make next is, in fact,
concerned with the rediscovery of roots. The film will be called *1900*
(Novecento) and tells the story of two children born in that year at a distance of a few hundred yards from each other, one in the house of the
peasant and one in the house of the landowner, in Emilia. The film follows
their lives through the century, living moments of Italian history with
them. Friends at first, then enemies, with the rich one financing the first
fascist clashes and the poor one in the Communist Party, navigating
through the whole period of fascism in Italy. I want this to become a film
about the agony of the culture of the land, of peasant culture, of a civilization that lasted thousands of years and has practically died in only 50–70
years of industrial "progress." It is a film I want to dedicate to the young
generations; I want to carry them back to the rediscovery of their real roots
which are those of the peasant world. I want to carry the camera into the
cornfields, into the furrows of earth during irrigation, into the ground
itself; and in a less physical sense bring them to rediscover certain popular
values which we, for imperialistic reasons, have completely throttled. It's
for those who today are 25 or younger — that means for all those who
know this kind of world only from literature (and that, too, is a privilege,
after all), for all those of the great mass who know nothing at all about

these values, who are perfectly ignorant of their own roots, which must still be there somewhere—I just don't believe that a few decades can cancel out generations of genetic memory; in our nucleic acid there must be a memory of the values of the land. At least a sediment! Nobody has ever posed this problem.

Do you feel more clarity now, at least in being able to provide some guidance to this generation you are describing?
No, no. I have no clear lessons to impart. Personally, I do not see clearly, neither the problems nor the perspective. But I feel that within the party one is now given space to develop, perhaps, a clearer view.

1900 Has Taken Its Toll on Bernardo Bertolucci

SALLY QUINN/1977

"I THINK," SAYS BERNARDO Bertolucci in a sober Italian accent, "I think that I am a repressed person. I think I can express my energy, my libido, my aggression, only in my work. We are all Dr. Jekyll and Mr. Hyde. We know our ghosts. And we don't tell anybody, not even our partners, about our ghosts. We live with our ghosts. We keep the ghosts inside in our life. It's just in the moment that Jekyll becomes Mr. Hyde that I can put my ghosts on the screen. I think I have understood this through psychoanalysis."

Bernardo Bertolucci, once the *enfant terrible* filmmaker of Italy, the creator of *Last Tango in Paris,* the arrogant young artist who took sexuality to new limits of creativity, the passionate Italian who creates controversy with every new venture... Bernardo Bertolucci has done it again. This time he has done it with *1900.*

The controversy has taken its toll. The former wunderkind is now thirty-six years old, but he looks forty. The lines around his eyes, his forehead, weren't even visible when he first came to New York five years ago for the opening of *Last Tango.* He is quieter, calmer, easier, more comfortable with himself; somewhat fatigued, but certainly more mature. He is nicer, sexier. He is, well, grown up.

"The controversy is finished now," he says quietly. Then he shrugs and smiles, just a little mischievously. "I'm looking for the next one now."

From *The Washington Post,* Section G, 16 October 1977. © 1977 by The Washington Post. Reprinted by permission.

Bertolucci believes, though he doesn't want to, in destiny.

He sighs. "La forza del destino," he says. "If you're violent or provocative, you don't know it. You are what you are even if it's not your intention. You are what you are.

"This film, it's (explosive) in a way," he says with no little glee. "It's outrageous. I use any kind of material in an outrageous way. I use opera and drama, I use two boys born on the same day when Verdi is dying. It's outrageous."

He loves the idea. It pleases him. "I wasn't afraid," he says, "to go deeply. I enjoy it."

He laughs.

"But you know," he says, "I am not completely screwed up."

But sometimes, he says, when he is not working on a film, when he does not have an idea—as for the past year and half, during the political negotiations of *1900*, when he really did get sick—he is filled with anxiety, with despair.

"I was like a spinach," he says now that he can laugh about it. "Like a vegetable. My life passed by me like water from a stream passes over a rock. It was nothing. It was terrible. I was sick."

What he does, when he is in such despair, is simple. "Pills," he smiles. "I take pills." And he reaches in his pocket and pulls out a tiny plastic container of pills. "Here," he says, "read the label. Ansiolitici. That's what I take. My pills." And he says, "I have lots of symptoms when I have problems. I am a . . . how do you say . . . a hypochondriac.

"I deal with anxiety," he says, "by trying to analyze what's going on, by trying to understand why I am feeling this way.

"*1900*," says Bertolucci, "was really a great effort. It was very tiring.

"My partner, Clare, she was my assistant director. She helped me a lot during the fight. It's too bad she can't be here with me now. But she was very strong. She was, well, in Italy we say, 'If my grandmother had wheels she would be a wheelbarrow.' Clare was that for me. She was my support.

"Because you know," he says, "when I make a film, all of me goes into it. Otherwise there is no other reason to feel alive, to live. It is also communication, being in touch with a lot of people. Don't you think it is probably a great need of affection. See my movie. Look my movie. Touch my movie. It's always indirect but the movie is the extension of me, the extension of my dreams. To me, dreams are very important. I use my dreams. I interpret them. It's hard work. It's discipline. You learn to do it through Saint Sigmund."

He leans forward, very solemn, "Do you know that you die if you don't dream? It's true. . . .

"When you begin analysis," he says, "you think you will be cured. For me it has been eight years now. And the problem for me is not to be cured. It doesn't exist.

"The important thing is to find a harmony with yourself. Accept yourself as you are. I think I accept myself now. I couldn't before. I don't know how much I like myself but I accept myself. It's finished with these mixed feelings of a little bit of hate or love, the extremes. I live better now in the company of myself. It's strange. When I began in analysis I was afraid to lose something; I thought that to be analysed was to understand what used to be mysteries inside you. I thought it would make me give up my inspiration. But it was just a form to resist my neuroses that didn't want to be counseled by analysis."

He props his orange-stockinged feet up on the coffee table of his hotel suite and slowly lights a Winston as he reflects.

"But I don't," he says, "think I've lost anything. I think I've gained."

He still has a boyishness to him which is appealing, particularly when he is being serious. He is sincere, gentlemanly, polite, well-mannered. "Bien élevé" (well brought up), he offers with a grin. There is no question that he is intelligent though occasionally he will get carried away with his own philosophizing, his own political Marxist dialectic, his own attempts at profundity. And he has to be nudged into laughing at what otherwise could be considered pomposity.

At one point, after expounding on a philosophical point at length, he is questioned about a contradictory detail and his face falls, then he smiles. "What I tell you is paradoxical," he says.

"If you want to go into details then the whole theory, everything will fall apart."

What was, five years ago, an arrogance camouflaging insecurity, has been transformed into a humility based on self-assuredness.

He is dressed, this morning, in a maroon silk shirt open and hanging out, a black sleeveless undershirt, tan corduroy trousers and orange wool socks. No shoes. He is totally relaxed and comfortable, and sprawls in a comfortable chair alternating between smoking Winstons and chewing gum.

He has just finished reading what he considers a very good review in *Newsweek* and is quite pleased with the fact that his film is called an "epic."

Now he sends down to the desk for *Time*, and when the bellman brings it up, he grabs the magazine and begins to read it aloud as he paces back and forth in his room. "Listen," he says excitedly, "listen to this.

"... For years to come, those who love film will savor and analyze each exasperating moment.

"I like that," he says, plopping back down in his chair satisfied and pleased. "I like that. Exasperating," he repeats, savoring the word.

Bertolucci seems vaguely melancholy, his enthusiasm at the good reviews not as euphoric as one might suppose. He explains it as being a combination of things. He says he is enormously relieved that the film has been finally released, and that that has released him. And he says that at the New York premiere last Saturday night, "I felt I could finally get separated from the movie.

"The movie," he says, "was a sort of monument to contradiction. I'm not afraid to say it. But it was also a communication with the audiences. My earlier movies I didn't care about the audiences. I was much more arrogant before."

He says that though the movie was a celebration of contradictions, there was a change "from contradiction to dialectic..." And yet, he contradicts himself again by saying, "The audience doesn't care about dialectic, about those things. They care about emotion. And in the end it's the emotion that, God bless, cancels all this stuff."

And yet, he says, "I feel abandoned as if the movie has abandoned me. Not me the movie. I've been with it for four years. That's long enough to be a marriage. And all that time it was so up and down, up and down."

Part of what made him feel that abandon, that loss, was that, "In *1900* I faced my whole life in a way. I faced my adolescence, which is really very near me inside. To go straight ahead we must have a look back behind us. That's why, when I finished *1900* I got sick, I was sick for months, emotionally sick. Nobody knew. Because to me my adolescence used to be the lost paradise and I created again my adolescence, my childhood in *1900*. And I created a copy of the lost paradise. And I lost it for the second time. Now I have really lost it. To let go of the movie was letting go of my childhood."

Five years ago, when Bernardo Bertolucci came to America as the celebrated young director, he had just broken off a four-year relationship with
a young woman he then referred to as his "wife," though they were not
married.

Then he scorned marriage as bourgeois and had given no thought at all
to fatherhood. All that is changed, mainly, he says, because of his experience with this latest movie.

Now, he says, "I want children. I think to have children you must accept the idea that you are an adult. I think now I can manage it. It's not
a decision I made. It's something that happened. It happened because of
1900."

Now, he says, he has been living with the same woman for four years,
Clare Peploe, an attractive, but not movie-star beautiful, English woman of
thirty-six who has been his assistant director on *1900*.

Now, he says, he will probably marry her. "I have just considered it
recently," he says. "But only for practical things. She is English and it would
make it easier for her to live in Italy."

He is still, however, not totally sold on the joys of matrimony.

"We come from a world where marriage was destroyed by the generation before us. We are shocked by the examples of marriage that we have
before us. The idea of marriage was made empty, and our generation, I
think, is in the middle. But now the younger ones are getting married. For
our generation we took love seriously. We refused to make it a social pact.
The new generation is using marriage as a life raft. They are so lost."

Sex and marriage are themes that dominate most of Bertolucci's movies,
and they are subjects he thinks about a lot.

"I think it is a personal thing with me," he says, "but I think that sexuality is maybe the most important thing in a person's life. To me it is so
obvious because if you think about how you became a person, if you go
back with your memory, see your behavior is completely determined, not
so much by your sexual life, but by your sexual formation as a child. In
one way I think it is fundamentally important and in another way I think
it is completely natural. I think that is why you don't feel embarrassed at
the sex in my movies. And maybe why you do feel embarrassed in some
American movies."

For Bertolucci, sexuality is naturally wrapped up in his maleness and the
sex in his films is often personal.

"The male," he says softly, almost shyly, "we are very vulnerable with this object we have. If you think how fragile we are, we have to prove to everybody and ourselves our virility. And of course with all that has happened with the liberation of women, men feel much more vulnerable."

He was bitterly criticized by feminists for showing only female nude scenes in *Last Tango* and not male nude scenes. So in *1900* he has the two male leads totally nude in bed together with a prostitute. With close-ups.

He insists, however, that he feels differently than most men on this subject. "No," he demurs. "I feel better first of all because I agree completely with this movement politically. Oh," he says, stopping himself in disgust. "That is a stupid thing to even have to say. Of course I agree with it.

"I think because of the movement we can have better relationships.

"I don't feel especially Italian," he says, "not in the sense of macho. I'm not a macho." He pauses, looks slightly guilty and amends. "No more," he says with a grin.

Bertolucci is just now beginning to plan his first movie after almost two years of being, as he says, "a spinach, a vegetable." He says his next movie will be called *La Luna* (the moon) and "it is not a science-fiction film," he jokes. "It is too delicate a subject to tell about it because it might break it, but it explores a relationship. It is more like *Tango* than *1900*."

In a strange way he is both looking forward to making it and dreading making it.

"Because when I make a movie I am of the attitude that it is as if I was making my last movie. That's why my movies are always so full of things. Maybe as a director we are not immortal in this society of consumerism. We live as if we are immortal but our values are so false. You lose the idea that you could die tomorrow. When I shot *Tango* I couldn't even think of *1900*. I was totally consumed. I am that way with everything. I am that way with women, too. I am completely involved with things. I'm very romantic. When I make a shot I must think it is the only one possible, the only shot I will ever make. But when I say I think it is my last movie, I do not mean necessarily that I will die. I mean only that I may never be able to do one again."

He quickly reaches down and grabs his crotch and rolls his eyes heavenward.

"A superstitious Italian," he says laughing, "would touch his b———— against bad luck."

Bernardo Bertolucci

JEAN A. GILI/1978

J G : *In 1962 you became known simultaneously through your first film,* The
Grim Reaper, *and a collection of poems,* In Search of Mystery, *which won the*
Viareggio Prize for a first work of poetry. Was there a moment in your life when
you found it difficult to choose between cinema and literature?
B B : When I was a child, people would sometimes ask me, "What do you
want to be when you grow up?" I always answered, "I want to make movies."
Meanwhile, since at home there was this poet who happens to be my
father, Attilio Bertolucci, I set about writing poems. Better still, I began
writing poetry as soon as I could write, when I was about six. I guess one
could call this a strong desire to imitate my father. But, since my father
was also a film critic in Parma, I often went to the movies with him to see
the films he had to review. I even went so far as to identify Parma with
the cinema since we lived in the countryside and we really only went to
Parma to see movies. When I was about fourteen or fifteen, I had a 16mm
camera and made my first film, a fifteen minute short with a story. At sixteen I made another.[1] So at twenty, I had the feeling that it was a very
natural thing to make movies. When we think something is natural, it's
also natural that it happens naturally. So, in 1961 when I was twenty, I
became Pasolini's assistant for *Accattone.*

From *Le cinéma italien* (Paris), 10/18, 1978. Reprinted by permission. Translated by
T. Jefferson Kline.

J G : *How did you meet Pasolini?*

B B : My father had published Pasolini's first novel, *Ragazzi di vita*, in 1955 and after that some collections of his poems. When he first started out, Pasolini was helped a great deal by my father, who was working for Garzanti, one of the major publishers. So it was that I became Pasolini's friend who, by the way, lived downstairs on the ground floor of our building. When I was sixteen, I would write poems and then run downstairs to read them to Pasolini. It was he who encouraged me to publish them. Thus we developed a classic and very traditional teacher-disciple relationship, and so when he shot his first film, he naturally asked me to be his assistant. Pasolini came to film from literature, from the novel, from poetry, criticism and semantics; I, on the other hand, was more connected to film than he was. Yet neither of us had really had been actively involved in making a movie: the two 16mm films I mentioned were really an amateur's work. So I became his assistant for *Accattone*, and what did I assist in? I assisted in and witnessed the invention of cinema: Pasolini was inventing a language.

Accattone was very important for me because it rarely happens that you get to witness the invention of a language: what Pasolini did was truly an invention because he had no significant experience of the cinema he could draw on. At that time, the only film he really liked was Dreyer's *Joan of Arc*. It was only later that he began going to the movies more often. So, to repeat something I've said many times, the first day that Pasolini made a tracking shot, I had the feeling I was watching the first tracking shot in the history of film.

And then *Accattone* turned out to be a success, and Pasolini sold an idea to the producer, Antonio Cervi, who asked me to write the screenplay and direct what became *La Commare Secca (The Grim Reaper)*.

J G : *During these years, what were the films that made the biggest impression on you?*

B B : The same ones that still move me today: Renoir, Dovjenko, Godard, Mizoguchi, Rossellini, and a lot of American movies of the twenties, thirties, forties, and fifties. Back then I had already become a regular at the *Cinématheque Française* and was really interested in film.

J G : Accattone *is the film of a beginner and yet it already displays great stylistic maturity.*

B B :   Pasolini had decided to be a primitive, a very perverse, yet very authentic, choice. He didn't know much about the cinema, or rather he didn't know it very well. He went to the movies but never had much interest in them. The great maturity you find in *Accattone* is due to the fact that Pasolini had no avant-garde pretensions. When he was shooting the film, he was free to do what ever he wanted; his references were more pictorial than cinematic—pictorial and oneiric, Masaccio, Giotto and the dreams he had. In *Mamma Roma*, it was Mantegna; in *Accattone* the reference point for all those close-ups was really Masaccio.

J G :   *Was this reference to Masaccio conscious?*
B B :   Yes, absolutely. Plus there was the influence of his dreams. I remember that every morning we went together to the set, and on the way he would tell me what he had dreamed the night before. In a way his dreams influenced the work he did during the day.

J G :   *This way of working emphasizes the double nature of film as a dream language and as an objective language born of the reality in front of the camera.*
B B :   In dreams as in the cinema or in the cinema as in dreams, we have the enormous freedom to indulge in free associations. Film is really a language which uses signs from real life. Pasolini has said that the language of film is that of life itself. Cinema is made of a raw material that is woven on a dream loom. Moreover, I find cinema much closer to poetry than to prose, closer to music than to theater. Even films that seem the most theatrical are really using theater as a mask, as a travesty.

J G :   *When you wrote the scenario of* The Grim Reaper, *did you feel like you had a lot of freedom with Pasolini's treatment of the film?*
B B :   Well, I felt that I had to appropriate through my writing a story which at the outset belonged to someone else. So I tried to absorb Pasolini's subject. I co-authored the scenario of *Commare secca* with Sergio Citti, who was Pasolini's most faithful collaborator, in order to try to keep my feet on the ground and not falsify the reality Pasolini had described. On the other hand, I felt when I was shooting the film I was attracted and inspired by completely different things: I was beginning, however vaguely, to get a feeling for my own identity as a filmmaker. And so I was really upset—of course I was still very young, only twenty-one—when I would hear people say that

Commare secca was a very Pasoliniesque film. It is a film about very minor subjects when compared to themes as important as those in *Accattone*, which is a little like a Greek tragedy. My film is also a film about death—"commare secca" means death in Roman dialect—and yet death is portrayed in a more lyrical, more crepuscular way than in Pasolini's film. I didn't—and still don't—have Pasolini's sense of the sacred. The odor of death is communicated in *The Grim Reaper* more by the way I structured the film, a film entirely constructed on time passing which consumes everything without anyone seeing it. The idea is a bit like Cocteau's famous words: "To make a film is to capture death at work." It's strange but just today I was reading *Opium* in which Cocteau says that each of his books guillotines all previous books. What a beautiful vision of books being guillotined! A close-up is like the guillotine. So in *The Grim Reaper* all the characters are surprised by a storm at the same moment but in different places, with different friendships, in different situations. I really wanted to tell how time works: something like death at work, that is, time passing is death at work. The storm unified everything, recalled death, and the rain washed away this convention of death: at twenty, of course, I thought I was immortal.

J G : *What sort of reception did* The Grim Reaper *get in Italy?*

B B : The film did pretty well. What's more it's a film that didn't cost very much. *The Grim Reaper* was presented at the Venice Film Festival. A few days before the screening in Venice I learned I had won the Viareggio Prize for my book of poetry. I was too young; it didn't seem possible to win a prize for poetry *and* get a film presented at Venice. It was, in some ways, a scandal. The film was received with some reservations by the critics, so I had my first encounter with the conformism of film criticism. What's more, I discovered another kind of scandal, the scandal that is provoked when you try to play on people's emotions. That was a bit the same thing that happened with *1900*. Some of the Italian intellectuals rejected *1900* partly I think because, after the success of *Last Tango in Paris*, I had become physically unbearable for many people, and partly because *1900* is a film which requires the audience to give in to their feelings. Today there is a complete rejection of feeling; feelings are considered to be shameful. I, on the other hand, believe that in today's world, emotion is the only way to communicate. It's really through feelings that we can rediscover the source of reason.

J G : *Which is another way of saying that emotion is perhaps the only way to change anything in human relationships.*

B B : If film can change anything, it must be in concert with everything else. It's not because a film is seen by millions of people, whereas a poem is read by a few thousand, a few hundred, or a few dozen people, that it can change anything. It's a illusion to believe that even political film can change anything. If we don't come to grips with this, we are very naive and very guilty: the belief that after seeing a film the public runs to join the Communist Party is a kind of naiveté that we don't have the right to adopt. You have to realize that this isn't true. You have to realize that film is a complement to a great cultural movement, or rather of a great political movement. Film is only a piece of this more general movement. In 1968 everyone was spouting these grand statements that were as marvelous as they were stupid: "The camera is like a machine gun." There were a lot of people saying this. Even I was, for a moment, a bit swept away by this idea. But in reality, it was a romantic, childish notion that blinded us from the truth.

J G : *As for the political limits of a film, it seems to me that 1900 is less an opti-mistic film—or even a triumphant film as some have called it—than a profoundly despairing work.*

B B : I think *1900* is a desperately optimistic film, but surely not a tri-umphant one. It seems desperately optimistic to me in the sense that Gramsci gave to this idea. One could quote Gramsci's famous statement if it hadn't already been overused. I think that *1900* contains the kind of vol-untary optimism shared by someone who joins a leftist party and who can't help thinking that the common efforts of the masses will end up in victory. That is what we might call the optimistic side of the film, but at the same time, there is the despair of knowing that what we're talking about is, for the moment anyway, a dream, a utopia. And in the film that leads to a sense of despair.

J G : *Such despair seems to be shared by a lot of Italian filmmakers.*

B B : *1900* seeks to go beyond such despair with a prefiguration of a revolu-tionary moment which is still in the domain of the utopic. In fact, certain politicians have told me, "But at the liberation we never put the landown-ers on trial!" In my film this trial of the landowners seems to be taking place in 1945, but in reality it is situated in the future. It is a dream. This entire sequence is an anticipation; it is a dream of something yet to be. To understand this sequence, you have to read the film correctly. We have to teach people how to read films because when it comes to the cinema there is an unbelievable illiteracy... especially among intellectuals. The public at large has no problem; they abandon themselves to the emotions of the film. The intellectuals, however, leave the theater believing they've understood the films because they think they've understood the content of the films. There is still an emphasis on content exactly the way there was during the Jdanov and Stalinist eras. That's the awful thing and that's what creates the despair in *1900*. But, conversely, the film is optimistic because it's a film that believes in the possibility of communication with the masses and is conscious of the carnival of communication possible with the public and with the masses. In Italy it's the largest grossing film of the last several years. So from a purely quantitative standpoint, that means a maximum amount of communication of all films shown. As for quality?... In any case it's a hopeless film because of the small number of people who can read a film the way it's supposed to be read. More than anything else, it's upsetting to see how few cultured filmgoers succeed in understanding films: they don't see what the film is but instead they look for things in the film. When an intellectual reads a novel, he never proposes alternatives to what's written: the novel is what it is and it is judged as such. For *1900* people said to me, "Why doesn't the film portray the *leghe bianche*?" "Why don't you show the Americans and the Germans during the second world war? But why..." Why? Why? They're talking about other films. They're imagining other films. I have to add that the official critics, the militant ones, saw the film more or less correctly. Those who came after the first critics, on the other hand—since the film was a national phenomenon, it was discussed over quite a period of time—wrote unbelievable things about it. They were no longer discussing the film itself; it had become a kind of subcultural bull fight.

J G : *Did you expect this reaction?*
B B : No, in the same way that I didn't anticipate the success of *Last Tango in Paris*. For *1900* I had no idea the film would provoke such hysterical reactions from a certain group of Italian intellectuals. You can't predict reactions because in fact you never know what you're doing when you

make a film. Me, I never know what I'm doing. I'm the last to understand my films, the very last one—if I understand them at all.... I shoot films, I do a certain number of things, better yet, I react in a very contradictory way to what I've done. I don't know.... It doesn't interest me much to know.

J G : *And yet it must be said, to attempt to understand the climate that developed in Italy after the film's release, that 1900 sometimes poses some delicate problems. For example, the relationship between Alfredo (Robert De Niro) and Attila (Donald Sutherland) introduces the difficult subject of the relationship between the bourgeoisie and fascism.*

B B : If you analyze *1900*—the film is firmly grounded and is the result of much reflection and a very carefully worked out scenario—you see that it is not Alfredo who finances Attila; it's the previous generation who financed fascism and who, to some extent, invented it. Alfredo's generation inherited fascism, they didn't create it. What's more, Alfredo is a very passive and weak person. Attila and Regina (Laura Betti), the two fascists, are not Fascism personified, but rather two examples of fascism. They represent all the monstrosity and aggressivity that exists in other bourgeois characters but which these others don't have the courage to express. Attila and Regina are delegates, after the image of Elizabethan drama where certain characters are the delegates for the aggressivity of all the others. Alfredo cannot find the courage and strength necessary to free himself of Attila until his alter ego, Olmo (Gérard Depardieu), decides to leave. Alfredo is not the Old Berlinghieri (Burt Lancaster) who represents the nineteenth century, nor his father, Giovanni Berlinghieri (Romolo Valli), this prosaic man entirely deprived of the style of the Patriarchs. Alfredo is already a Dorothean,[2] a Christian democrat. He invents the opposite extremes and indirectly, even unconsciously, pits Attila against Olmo, and vice versa. This just occurs to me. I'd never thought about it before. When does Alfredo succeed in freeing himself from Attila? When Olmo leaves: with Olmo gone, he can split off from Attila and fire him. He no longer needs someone to mediate his relations with Olmo. Alfredo is profoundly and violently jealous of Olmo; moreover, there is a homosexual relationship between these two which is expressed through Alfredo's jealousy. For example, when, in the sequence in the inn, Alfredo tells Ada (Dominique Sanda) that he can smell Olmo's scent on her, we see a moment of delirious homosexual jealousy. What's more, as we move further and further into *1900*, we move from a nineteenth-century novelistic narrative to one more influenced by psychoanalysis.

J G : *You said that Attila is not Fascism personified, but rather a particular example of fascism. That seems to me a nuance that's difficult to understand since in the cinema everything becomes symbolic, every character takes on values which go way beyond his particular individual characteristics.*

B B : It's true that in film everything becomes symbolic, and yet, at the same time, cinematic language is one that has the least recourse to symbols: a tree is a tree, a house is a house — this very specific tree and this very specific house — and Attila is Attila. That's why I never used stock newsreel footage in *1900*. I never showed fascism in general but only the fascism that existed within a twenty kilometer radius of the farm, the village and the neighboring town. Also, from another point of view, I wanted to go beyond strictly Italian fascism and that's why I chose Donald Sutherland to play the part of Attila rather than an Italian actor. At first I thought of using an Italian like Ugo Tognazzi, who's from Cremone. Attila is also from Cremone, the birthplace of Farinacci,[3] the famous fascist blackjacker. Tognazzi is a very good actor, but I thought he would give too much naturalism to the character. I wanted Attila to be played in a naturalistic way, but beyond that, I wanted him to express something more than just Italian fascism, something like a universal fascism, with the violence and the sado-masochism of Elizabethan characters. That's why I went in search of an actor with a very particular physique. So it's no accident that subsequently an Italian, very well-known director chose him to create a kind of. . . . So, even if one interprets the character of Attila as a metaphor of fascism, I wanted it to be not just of the fascism which we witnessed between 1921 and 1945 but of all fascism — fascism as a spiritual dimension, fascism as a projection of the monster inside.

J G : *The film takes place in a very particular region, but at the same time it takes on a sense which goes beyond this locale.*

B B : For me *1900* is a microcosm, just as *The Spider's Stratagem* was before it. If you look at a piece of dust under a microscope, it's as if you were looking at the universe in a planetarium in a film by Nicholas Ray. A piece of dust can make us dream, and the microscope of *1900* should be just like

that: a tiny region of Italy magnified and thus rendered in a certain way—
what a horrible word—universal.

J G :   *But at the same time, Emilia is a region of Italy where there is a powerful
tradition of anti-fascism.*
B B :   Well, it's true that we couldn't have filmed this same story in, for
example, Sicily.

J G :   *So you told a story which takes on a universal value and yet at the same
time is situated in a very precise locale and a very defined social milieu.*
B B :   I became aware as I was making the film, and especially during its
editing, that *1900* is constructed on the principle of contradictions: the
contradiction between American dollars and the ideological and political discourse of the film, the contradiction between Olmo and Alfredo,
between peasants and landowners, between Hollywood actors and the
authentic peasants of Emilia, between fiction and documentary, between
the most detailed preparation and the wildest improvisation, between an
archaic peasant culture and a truly bourgeois culture.

J G :   *Ultimately your own contradictions are reflected in the film.*
B B :   I don't think I'm alone in this respect. Luckily I'm in the same boat
with a lot of other people. *1900* is even a film born of a feeling of guilt,
the guilt of being of country bourgeois origins. Maybe that's why I apparently paint the peasants much more lovingly than the bourgeois. I say
"apparently" because it seems to me that I love all my characters. In
France I was called a manichean, a ridiculous and false accusation—the
word is no longer even used in school except to label a very precise religion. In response to this accusation of manicheism, I answered three
things. First, that if it's an epic film, there are always good guys and bad
guys in the epic tradition. Secondly, and here I'm touching on another
contradiction, this is, on the one hand, an epic film, but on the other
hand, it's a very intimate film, quite opposite from the epic sense. Thirdly,
you shouldn't confuse manicheism with the fact that I subscribe to an
ideology of class struggle and of the struggle of the worker and the peasant. At the Cannes Festival the film was very badly received; later, when
it came out in Paris, some critics wrote that they had been mistaken. The
film was sent to Cannes by the producer for promotional reasons. From

Francesco Barilli, *Before the Revolution*, 1964

Pierre Clémenti, *Partner*, 1968

Giulio Brogi and Alida Valli, *The Spider's Stratagem*, 1970

Jean-Louis Trintignant and Dominique Sanda, *The Conformist*, 1970

Maria Schneider and Marlon Brando, *Last Tango in Paris*, 1972

Robert De Niro and Gérard Depardieu, *1900*, 1976

Ugo Tognazzi and Anouk Aimée, *Tragedy of a Ridiculous Man*, 1981

Wu Tao and Bertolucci on the set of *The Last Emperor,* 1987

Richard Vuu, *The Last Emperor*, 1987

Bertolucci and Debra Winger on the set of *The Sheltering Sky*, 1990

Donal McCann and Liv Tyler, *Stealing Beauty*, 1996

Thandie Newton, Bertolucci, and David Thewlis on the set of *Besieged*, 1998
(Photo credit: Alessia Bulgari)

my perspective, given the many years I'd worked on this film, I wanted to finish it in time for Cannes, be done with it, get rid of it, because I simply couldn't take it any longer. What's more, I thought that the film would excite the distributors, but distributors are made of wood and don't ever get excited. It's only now, four or five months after the release of the film in France, that the president of United Artists told me: "You were right, the two parts of the film should have been distributed simultaneously at two parallel theaters." This was evident to everyone except the distributors. The distributors told me in essence, "You're an artist so just do your artist bit. We're businessmen so let us to the commercial bit." The film would have done much better, as it did in Italy, if they had distributed the two parts together. In Italy they wanted to do the same thing, but luckily, since Part I was temporarily seized, they had to release Part II two weeks later. I thought that the film would be stimulating by offering distributors the possibility of doing things differently when showing a film which was much longer than the norm. All that is so discouraging because you work so hard to make a film — *1900* was very tiring to make, and not just for me — and then you end up with the film in the hands of these petty bureaucrats who are devoid of inventiveness, incapable of doing their job.

J G :   *Your films are often a meeting ground between outside elements and elements that are autobiographical. How is the balance achieved between these two sides?*
B B :   Well, this is true for anyone who expresses himself, not just in film but in any expressive form. The tricky thing is to find some harmony between what one has experienced and the imaginary. It's hard for me today to remember and to sort out what is autobiographical and what is invented in my films, even in a film as recent as *1900*.

J G :   *Does the work with the screenwriters help integrate these different influences one finds in your films?*
B B :   Well, it depends. There are films that I wrote alone and films I wrote together with screenwriters. For example, I wrote *Before the Revolution* alone, *Partner* with Gianni Amico, *The Spider's Stratagem* with Marilù Parolini and Edoardo De Gregorio, *The Conformist* was taken from a novel by Moravia but I wrote the screenplay alone, *Last Tango* was done with Kim

Arcalli, and I wrote the script of *1900* with my brother Giuseppe and with Kim Arcalli. Each time it's a different experience. The screen writers help wake you up if you're asleep and make you see things that you don't see, even though they're often right before your eyes. They also end up giving you parts of themselves believing, of course, that they're giving you other things. The more I work, the easier I find it to collaborate with others. When I began filming, when I made *The Grim Reaper*, I was coming from poetry, but from the first day behind a camera I stopped writing and never wrote another verse. But because I came from the very solitary and vicious experience of writing poetry, I believed that film would be the work of one person, of one person's feelings, of one person's eye. The more I do, the more I understand, especially since *1900*, which was a collective creation, that I have to open up more to others. The entire mythology of auteur cinema is connected to the fear of communicating with one's collaborators and especially with the viewer, the same viewer who is, ultimately, the one who really collaborates in making the film, by loving it, hating it, participating in it and then abandoning it. . . .

J G : *In your filmography, one might distinguish two periods of screenwriting, first a period of collaboration with Gianni Amico and then a period of collaboration with Kim Arcalli. Do these two periods really exist for you?*
B B : I knew Gianni Amico when I was doing *Before the Revolution*. With Gianni I shared a sense of complicity, a cinephilic delirium; we had the impression of taking great risks, while at the same time hiding behind pretexts of rigor and experimentation to justify our refusal to face the problems of communication. Kim Arcalli helped me a lot to free myself of all that and to accept a real dialogue. With Gianni we worked on elective affinities, whereas with Kim we confronted the brutalities of our differences. All the same, it would be too easy to think that certain people have such influence on you. I think, in fact, that we choose a certain kind of collaborator at a certain moment and that we choose a different kind at another moment when we feel ready to change. In my filmography, there was definitely an Amico moment and an Arcalli moment, and yet there was an intermediate moment, with *The Spider's Stratagem*, when there was neither one nor the other, but Marilù Parolini and Edoardo De Gregorio. That film was the first real opening after *Partner*. *Partner* was an experience that I lived through like a sickness; it's a neurotic film, a sick film, schizophrenic.

By contrast, *1900* seems to me from this point of view like a very healthy film. It would take a very long and probably boring explanation to clarify that. I would say that *Partner* is a sick film and that *1900* constituted a kind of cure for it by resolving certain problems. But as for those problems, I don't want to imply that I'm for or against sickness or for or against health — health that doesn't really exist anyway.

J G : Partner *was a sick film that reflected your own sickness. How did you get out of this state?*

B B : I began to get out of it gradually beginning with *The Spider's Stratagem*. That said, it's no accident that when I began this film, I also started psychoanalysis; or to put it better, I paralleled my cinematic career with a psychoanalytic career.

J G : *Did your analysis last a long time?*

B B : I'm still undergoing analysis full time. I've been in analysis for about eight years now. But it's a strange analysis that gets interrupted each time I make a film. When I'm shooting a film, the film replaces the analysis. I see the end of my analysis as something very far off.

J G : *You spoke of a psychoanalytic "career." What do you mean by this expression?*

B B : In general my films are constructed according to a stratification so mysterious to me that I could never separate the political from the psychoanalytic, linguistic, the means of production, etc. I feel that it's all mixed together. It seems to me that my films are all about finding the way out of this labyrinth, this chaos of politics and psychoanalysis. And yet, when I spoke of a psychoanalytic career, I was speaking of work I began in 1969. I call it work because at a certain time each day I have to go to work, I have to go to my psychoanalytic session. It's a strange relationship because I feel like a worker who's going to work and who, at the end of every month, has to pay his employer: that's the way it's constructed and this construction has its own meaning, its finality.

The Spider's Stratagem is the first film that I made while in analysis, a film that I even worked on a lot in analysis, almost without realizing it. I wrote the film during the first months of my analysis: the first months of an analysis are the discovery of a new universe, of a new methodology. I had to find a language for this new work, a language to express myself in this new "job." From this moment on, psychoanalysis became one of the most important elements of my films. In *Before the Revolution* and in *Partner* there was already an influence of psychoanalysis, the influence of my reading of Freud and of people who were in analysis. But it wasn't direct knowledge. The direct influence of psychoanalysis begins with *The Spider's Stratagem*. All my films have been elaborated in the framework of my analysis. My next film, if I don't change my mind, was conceived the day before yesterday during my analytic session. One day I told my analyst, "I should put your name in the credits of my films." I could tell that he was happy, sitting there behind me. It would take a long time to explain, but let's just say, to simplify, that for each film I go through an elaboration, a plumbing, a perverse simplification that is created through the working through of Freudian analysis.

J G : *Did you ever think of becoming an analyst yourself?*
B B : Well, all filmmakers are more or less indirectly analysts. Let's just say that analysis is to a great extent based on oneiric material, and aren't films constructed out of oneiric material? Aren't films made of the same material as dreams? This said, I've never considered becoming an analyst. I have too much respect for others. Psychoanalysis is a science and a scientist must possess the necessary faculties for his work. I don't personally have those talents, and I don't want to have them. The kind of liberties I take I'm able to take precisely because I don't have those faculties which otherwise would have made me an analyst and would have made me choose to be an analyst and not a filmmaker.

Besides the senses that are given to us as humans, anyone who practices psychoanalysis acquires a new faculty, an additional faculty, a sixth sense. Here as always we see the usual and age-old contradiction between reason, between the beauty of reason, and the impossibility of escaping one's own viscera, one's own unconscious: it's a conflict we can't ever escape. Here again, there is always the attempt to find some harmony between the unconscious and reason. Psychoanalysis is like having an additional lens on my camera, or an instrument that would be at once a lens, a dolly, a tracking shot, truly a tool of the trade that would combine all of these aspects together. Of course, I can indulge in this comparison because I have no scientific ambitions in this domain. And also, to the artist who seeks new forms of expression, all is permitted and all is forgiven. There are no limits; freedom must always be total and absolute, at least for me, even if it means total and apparent incoherence.

J G : *To return to the question of your collaborators, it's interesting to note that Kim Arcalli is both the writer and the editor of your latest films, two activities that are rarely combined.*

B B : Arcalli is the person most responsible for getting me to accept editing. Up until *Partner* and even up until *The Spider's Stratagem*, I had refused or even, in some way or other, put off the moment of editing. During those years, those marvelous sixties, I had theories about film. I considered that editing was a rather banal aspect of filmmaking, a moment when things have to be organized, when order is imposed on the marvelous chaos of the rushes that we've enjoyed without any order whatsoever. I really refused editing. Then, little by little with Kim, I was forced to confront the question, and he made me realize that the material already shot is much richer than one would think. It was already written into the strategy of auteur cinema; ultimately that author says: "I write, I shoot, I do the editing, but the editing is only a consequence of the way I've shot the film." Now, on the contrary, I edit *against* the way I've shot the film. This change of attitude vis a vis editing was very important. I'm not just talking about technique; I'm talking about a very profound evolution in my work. Also, Kim is a very stimulating person, full of very rich ideas. With him, collaboration goes beyond what we usually think of as making a film. There is always, at the moment of editing, a kind of reworking of the script based on the material that was shot. That happened the first time we worked together on the editing of *The Conformist*. From that moment on, I have asked him to serve as script writer as well, and we've made *The Last Tango in Paris* and *1900* together.

J G : *It also occurs to me that Arcalli has never written a scenario for anyone else but you.*

B B : He may have written the first film of Tinto Brass, *Chi lavora è perduto*. But that's really a film that they did together: Arcalli even had a role in the film. He played an old partisan who had gone mad and was interned in an asylum.

JG: *In his* Scritti corsari *Pasolini shows that the consumer society is a form of fascism which tends to destroy all cultures.*

BB: I made *1900* as a kind of dialogue with Pasolini on this subject. I wanted to show him that in Emilia, as if by some miracle, this phenomenon hadn't occurred. In this island—let's call it an island since all around it Italy has changed—the peasants succeeded in conserving their age-old culture of origin. When Pasolini was talking about the leveling and destruction of culture, he was thinking of southern Italy, of the expanding periphery around Rome and other large cities. By contrast, in Emilia, thanks to socialism and then communism, the peasants have really succeeded in becoming conscious of their culture as an important treasure, and the destruction Pasolini was describing hasn't happened there. That all happened thanks to communism: in southern Italy, by contrast, the left is very weak. It's paradoxical, but in Emilia, Marxism succeeded in conserving the original culture. With *1900* I wanted to answer Pasolini and open a dialogue on this specific topic. For his part, he had made a very apocalyptic statement, and I wanted to focus his attention on more everyday realities. I wanted to show him that I'd found hundreds of faces which weren't effaced, banalized by consumerism, but instead faces which had remained the same as those I remembered from when I was eight years old, the same faces as before the war. In short, I wanted to show him that the Emilian peasants—a bit like the Chinese—have become conscious of the great treasure that constitutes their culture.

JG: *Does living in Rome inspire a feeling of being uprooted?*

BB: In some ways no, because I've been living in Rome since I was eleven and so I've been settled here for quite a while. Still, I've always found that Rome was an unbearable city, a city which thrives on appearances, a city in which you can't work, where you can never get anything going, where you sleep all the time. It's a city that is good for editing which is a kind work of digestion. In fact, I've done very little shooting in Rome, *The Grim Reaper*, a little bit of *Partner* and some scenes from *The Conformist*. Rome is a city where you can't even go to the movies because everything is dubbed, even *1900*. You have the impression that if you filmed the city, nothing would end up on the film. Rome is going through a terrible time. Paris is worse. Certainly you can see more films there, but you have the terrible weight of the French bourgeoisie. Their bourgeoisie who made its revolution displays such arrogance, such insensitivity, such tyranny that you can even feel them physically. The Italian bourgeoisie is more vulnerable, less unified, less powerful, less historical in some way. In Italy, you feel more vitality, and yet at the same time I've felt it was more and more difficult to live here, and in Rome in particular. I think the problem isn't unique to Italy; it's the same throughout Europe. We're living through a moment of transition, a moment that is devoid of style.

J G : *The problem of identity recurs quite often in your films.*
B B : To come back to your previous question, I ought to begin by saying that in some ways I was uprooted, torn away from the region where I was born. My family was moved from the countryside to the city, a trip that took six hours by train: everything that existed before existed no longer; I had lost all my points of reference. During those first years, I rejected this city. So, as for my identity, I had, and maybe I continue to have pretty big problems. There is a theme that recurs all the time in my films, the theme of the double, the theme of schizophrenia. In *Partner*, I confronted the theme of schizophrenia head on. In *1900* it's the same thing. The two protagonists are born on the same day and represent two opposing social classes. In a certain way, they are a bit two aspects of the same person. In *The Spider's Stratagem*, the father and son are interpreted by the same actor: Giulio Brogi merely changes his jacket and shoes, but in everything else remains the same. The problem of the double is a double problem, so big that I really don't know how to talk about it. All I know is that it recurs frequently in my films; perhaps with *1900* it will be the last time.

J G : *Does psychoanalysis help you to confront this problem?*
B B : And how! Analysis helps me a lot to keep from avoiding problems, to keep from running away from them and to confront them in the interior of my films. What's more, as I told you, when I make a film, I feel good and I don't need analysis.

J G : *Could you explain precisely what it means for you to be a member of the Italian Communist Party?*
B B : Searching through my memory, I can first of all tell you more precisely why I first joined the communist party. In some ways I've always

been a communist. At first it was for sentimental reasons. It all began when I was a kid living in the country. Try to imagine the Berlinghieri and Dalco families, but on a reduced scale: a microscopic version of the dimensions these two families share in *1900*—on the other hand, a petty-bourgeois agrarian family and, on the other hand, a family of peasants numbering about ten people (rather than the forty you see in the film). Naturally I spent almost all of my childhood in the peasants' house: all sons of landowners love to live with the peasant families. I said "sentimental reasons" because the word communist is a word I was always hearing in the peasants' mouths. I learned one day that "communist" meant "hero" because the peasants were talking about a demonstration organized to protest the death of a young man who had been killed by the police and whose name was Alberti. That happened during the years 1949–1950, at a time when there were lots of general strikes. I recall that we were in a tomato field; the women were harvesting tomatoes, leaning over the low plants. I asked them who this Alberti was. And then Nella, one of the peasant women, gathered herself to her full height, towering over my eight years; I saw her stand up with her face shaded by her straw hat, look me right in the eye and say, after a pause only a great actress could stage: "Alberti was a communist." From that moment on, obviously, I became a communist. In that situation, with that dramatic pause, in that light, and also given the fact that Alberti had been killed by the *Celere*,[4] who wouldn't have converted? I have been a communist from that moment and I've never had any doubts. I must say that the doubts always come from the inside. I never have doubts based on exterior facts; I have great respect for exterior facts, for exterior reality. So I've never had any doubts about communism even if I didn't join the party right away.

J G :   *How did you end up joining the party?*
B B :   In a fictive sense I've been a communist ever since I was a boy. At the beginning of the sixties, I had some anxiety about the Communist Party, an anxiety expressed in *Before the Revolution.* When the film was released in Paris, at the beginning of 1968, it had a lot of success, opening in a theater in the Latin Quarter where it sold a huge number of tickets for a small art film.

Before the Revolution did well because in this film shot in 1963–64, there was all this anxiety about the Communist Party which had evolved into a new form in 1968. In Italy the film irritated a lot of people because it was ahead of its time. I think it expressed a number of concerns which only later became issues in Italy. In 1968, with the birth of the student movement which questioned all the parties on the left and in particular the communist party, I felt surrounded by such violent anti-communism that I immediately joined the party.

When I made *Before the Revolution,* I wanted to express the conflict that existed for a young bourgeois from the provinces who was full of intellectual ambition—the conflict between his cultural upbringing and the idealism he felt about the communist party. I was trying to get at the reality of the communist party of those years. The beginning of the sixties was a period of transition between the postwar mythical years of Stalinism and what was later to become the Berlinguer period. Those were the years that were later to make Togliatti die.[5] During this period, the Italian Communist Party lacked style, so to speak. I think that the Fabrizio of *Before the Revolution* reproached the party above all for its lack of style. In short, I would say that I'm not a political person and never have been, certainly not in the way that the majority of people are today. In any case, at that time I was not a member of the party. In May 1968, the year *Before the Revolution* enjoyed such great success in Paris, there was a great explosion of anti-communism among so many other very inspiring things. I think we all needed 1968, even if, despite the use of a highly politicized discourse, the events of May were one of the first signs of the way the bourgeoisie was trying to hide, to camouflage its anti-communism. And this anti-communism which originated among the bourgeois continued. I felt it all around me, especially among young people and even among the not-so-young people who had grown young again by embracing the movement of 1968. That was the reason that led me to join the party. In 1969 I could no longer stand this anti-communism. At that point, I told myself that for reasons of honesty, coherence and loyalty to the party and to my communist comrades, I had to join. So I've been a member of the party since that time.

J G : *I think* Before the Revolution *is a film that remains quite vital today.*
B B : In fact, when the events of May '68 occurred, it seemed to me that everything that was happening was all a sort of *déja-vu* or *déja-entendu*—in a general sense of course. It was sort of like a repetition of the discourse in

Before the Revolution, rehearsing old arguments I'd already filmed: the relationship between the communist party and the sentimental and cultural upbringing of a young bourgeois—exactly the position of the students of 1968. Last night I was listening to one of those maverick radio stations, one of those stations where they say, "that is to say" every five seconds. They were talking about the sit-ins in the universities and about Luciano Lama, the secretary of the CGIL who was supposed to talk at the University of Rome,[6] and they mentioned that the government counts on the abstention of the Communists. They were holding forth in such an infantile and politically stupid way on the communists who had left the opposition and who were supporting the government by their abstention. They had understood absolutely nothing in Berlinguer's remarkably brilliant speech about austerity. From time to time, Berlinguer has amazing intuitions: he had transformed the meaning of austerity and said that austerity was a great revolutionary weapon by which we could change society. The leftists keep talking about expropriating consumer goods. Thus, they refuse to understand or admit that from now on consumption is over and that it can never be brought back. They're going to have a hard time when they discover that better doesn't mean going backwards to a social model which we have experienced and still live with but which will soon disappear. Better means moving forward towards something maybe less comfortable but which will transform everything, especially the economic relationships between individuals.

J G :   *What connection do you find between your work as a filmmaker and that fact that you're a Communist?*
B B :   It is only with the greatest difficulty that I can describe the explicit connection I have with the communist party. It's a connection that reached its greatest intensity with *1900*, whether it be vis-a-vis what I had imagined would be the eventual reaction of the party to the film, or whether it be in relation to the reaction that eventually emerged. Ultimately I feel a lot of guilt vis-a-vis the party as an individual and as a militant: I find that I don't get to my section meetings often enough, that I'm not sufficiently involved in the life of the section because a party member should really work for his section. On the other hand, I feel very much like a militant for having made *1900* even if *1900* is an oneiric film, very nearly conceived and structured like a dream, made to the measure of the dreamer, that is

to say, the public. I find that the quarrel that was born partially—certainly in a minor way compared to the debate I had hoped for and had tried to provoke within the communist world, but which was, for the most part, ignored—that the quarrel provoked by the film was a fairly important one.

I find a huge gap between the intuitions of this poet and philosopher Berlinguer and the apparatus which functions as the exterior armature of the party, an apparatus which is very bureaucratic and is apparently very anti-Berlinguerian: but perhaps those are both sides of Berlinguer. Ultimately, it's an argument I've never made and so I don't have an answer for it. I thought *1900* was a communist film, and I still think of it as a communist film first because it's a film in synchrony with the postwar communist party line from Togliatti to Berlinguer. It's a film which accepts and fits into a capitalist mode of production in order precisely to emphasize the contradictions that govern the work of a filmmaker. That's already something very important for me, even if certain people simplistically accused me of having wanted to make of *1900* a model. It's quite the contrary, *1900* is an exception. Neither I nor anyone else will be able to repeat this type of experiment. It's an exception precisely because it's a film that self-destructs, a film that, given its mode of production, goes up in flames. *1900* is really a symptom of a particular moment, absolutely not a model. Everything that's been said so often about the seminar that was dedicated to *1900* at the Venice Biennale last year seems to me entirely off base: the Biennale was accused of creating a model out of *1900* by organizing such a seminar. It seems to me exactly the contrary: *1900* is unique, not an example of anything.

To turn to another problem, *1900* is a film in which I try to achieve a harmony, maybe an impossible thing to do, between Marx and Freud. It's a film not about "historical compromise" nor about a specific historical compromise, but rather a film which is itself cinematic historical compromise. By historical compromise—you must read these sentences with the kind of delirium that I feel when speaking them—I mean something very elevated because it's the most important thing that has appeared in political thought in Italy in the last several years, in fact the most important, along with Berlinguer's last speech in which he talked about austerity, a speech which caused a great deal of confusion and which wasn't really understood even within party ranks. Because of this that speech wasn't given the weight it should have. *1900* constitutes historical compromise even if some people are surprised that I should mix film with historical compromise. For me historical compromise signifies, as I already said, the possibility even for someone of bourgeois origins—as so many valorous men have been in the history of the communist party—of being able to find some way to put his own culture to work for the masses.

JG: *That's the problem of the organic intellectual.*
BB: Yes, that's the problem of the Gramsci's organic intellectual. I would like to add that in *1900* I consider to be communist the vital first principle of dialectics on which the entire film is based at every level. Likewise I consider to be communist the feeling of guilt that I experience as a bourgeois—a feeling which, according to some conformists, makes the film appear to be manichean. I read an article on *1900* in *Les Temps modernes* in which the author claims that the word manichean was invented by the ruling class, and that the true manicheans are the members of this class. As for me, the fact that I have a visceral feeling about my bourgeois origins, the fact that I accept the burden of a certain type of guilt which is not directly mine but belongs to my social class and those who support that class, is also a communist idea.

But to get to concrete facts, let's talk about how the Italian communist party reacted. The Federation of Communist Youth reacted with great enthusiasm because they recognized themselves in my film; but this same federation has some elements among its leaders who are great fans of Hitchcock. I don't think one can say the same of the Central Committee of the Communist Party. I don't know if Berlinguer saw *1900*: I tried to get him to see it, but there was always someone or something that got in the way. On the other hand, I heard some very disappointing reactions from important historical leaders. The first disillusion happens when you realize that they are all illiterate when it comes to being able to read a film. Of course, you immediately realize that that's normal: why should they be able to read a film when no other politicians know how? They only understand the content of the film, which greatly limits their capability of understanding the whole film. Take the example of Giancarlo Pajetta, who is not only an important communist, one who has struggled and made personal sacrifices for the cause, but is also a man linked to bourgeois culture. After seeing Part One of the film, Pajetta told me that he felt like embracing me with tears in his eyes; after Part Two, he was furious, furious over the last sequence which seems to produce a state of crisis among the communist comrades, especially those at the highest echelons of the Party. Why this reaction? First of all because they can't see the film without imposing a historical reading on it: the history that you read in books, history as written by historians. They just can't see any differently. Pajetta's first comment to me was, "We never conducted trials of the landowners." "Too bad," I replied, "and you don't even want us to conduct them in our dreams in a film?" Next he told me that he didn't like the feeling in the final sequence. He found it a little triumphalist. And here I could detect a kind of modesty and timidity in this communist leader: to see the joy, the happiness, the triumphalism—if that's what you want to call it—of these peasants who are going wild at this dance with the red flags and the music.... All that embarrassed him: "We were never like that, there was never any such outbreak of joy." Pajetta just couldn't make the leap between his memory, the truth of his memories, and the truth of the film. I tried to explain that the day in question wasn't really the 25th of April 1945 but some day in the future. *1900* is the history of a utopia. Maybe you can't ask politicians to look too far into the future because they might end up poets or artists!

J G : *Many of your films bring aspects of Italian history to the screen. Could you clarify your relationship to history?*

B B : Even though history is very important, I wouldn't define my films as historical films at least not in the sense that historians or even Marxist historians give to the word. Better yet, it is precisely the work of historians that has allowed me to adopt a particular view of history. I use history, to be sure, but I don't make historical films, I make falsely historical films, because in fact you can't write history through cinematic means: film knows only one tense, the present. That puts enormous limits on the possibility of writing history. *The Spider's Stratagem, The Conformist, 1900* are not historical films, they are films that try to historicize the present. All my films are films about the present even if they speak about the early years of this century, the twenties or of the beginnings of fascism.

J G : *The theme of fascism as a moment of Italian history recurs often in your films.*

B B : To speak of fascism is to speak of the present. In *1900*, if I had confronted the birth of fascism as a historian—and indeed the historians complained somewhat about my way of presenting things—I should have shown a whole series of stages in the relationships that were established between the ruling class and the nationalists and the interventionists who became powerless after the war. On the contrary, I tried to synthesize the birth of fascism in two sequences, one in which the landowners collect money in the church to support the fascists and the other in which a tailor fits a fascist shirt on Attila. They are, in my view—and this is curious— the two most Brechtian scenes in the film. I felt that, one way or another, I had to show the birth of fascism; I thus preferred to use a kind of Brechtian ellipsis rather than showing in the more naturalistic way you find in Italian historical films.

J G : *There is also in almost all of your films a connection to memory, notably in* The Spider's Stratagem *and in* Last Tango in Paris *where you have a confrontation between a girl almost without memory or a past and a man composed of memory.*

B B : Yes, in *Last Tango in Paris*, Marlon Brando is really the living matter of memory, made of memory. Maria Schneider on the other hand is without memory; in fact, she can calmly step over the dead body of this man, and she does this throughout the film with a kind of innocence and unconscious cruelty. In my view, the film is political because it's a film about the confrontation and power struggle between a character without a past—and then of course we discover that Maria has one after all because in fact the gun she uses to kill Brando belonged to her father who was a French officer in Algeria—and on the other hand a character made up of memory, of the past, of allusions to film and literature. Fundamentally, Brando resembles a bit the characters of Minnelli and Miller; he's part the Gene Kelly of *An American in Paris* and part the characters of *Tropics* who are living in Paris. In fact at first I wanted to call the film *An American in Paris, Part II.*

J G : *In your choice of actors, you draw on actors of many different origins, foreign actors, some beginners, others linked to the history of Italian cinema such as Francesa Bertini, Tino Scotti, Massimo Girotti, Alida Valli, Yvonne Sanson. What determines these choices?*

B B : The actors I don't know I always take based on my very first impressions, the first feelings I have when I meet them. I always decide to take an actor within the first two minutes of meeting him. That's the way it worked, for example, with Robert De Niro and Gérard Depardieu. In other cases, the actors with a long history behind them are like living quotations, quotations of nothing very precise perhaps, and yet if you look more closely there's doubtless a reason, some justification, for example, the choice of Yvonne Sanson to play the part of Stefania Sandrelli's mother in *The Conformist:* even if Yvonne Sanson's films, *Figli di nessuno*, (*Nobody's Sons*), *L'Angelo bianco* (*White Angel*), are posterior to fascism, they nevertheless express an entire petty-bourgeois mythology.

J G :   *When Massimo Girotti does his gymnastics in* Last Tango in Paris, *you can't help thinking about the very athletic actor who played in* La Corona di ferro (Crown of Iron) *in 1941.*

B B :   In the case of *Last Tango in Paris* I had thought about bringing Marlon Brando and Massimo Girotti face to face. They had both been so good looking when they were younger — one became an international monument and the other remained quite provincial, yet has his particular poetry as we see in *Ossessione (Obsession)* and perhaps in *La Coronna di ferro*, and also due to the fact that he never became a big star. The idea of playing them opposite each other was maybe a bit sadistic, and yet both of them are professionals. And then I got a kick out of the fact that Girotti has a trimmer waistline and more hair than Brando, so Girotti got a little revenge on Brando even so. Meanwhile, what Girotti did was a bit of self-irony, I think. There again, I was working with the theme of the double, Girotti being the double of Brando, with their identical bathrobes. Francesca Bertini in *1900* really connected the film to the beginning of the century. There was a scene in which she was holding onto a curtain, just like she did in her silent films. Unfortunately, given the length of the film, that scene had to be cut: the homage was too obvious. Tino Scotti, Alida Valli are also living quotations.

J G :   *The use of foreign actors, for example, a French woman and an American man opposite one another in* Last Tango, *emphasizes your search for a culture that isn't specifically Italian, your attraction for a kind of cultural cosmopolitanism.*

B B :   Here as elsewhere, I always act according to the principle of contradiction or, if you like, of dialectics. I think that in fact I'm very Italian and even, if such a thing exists, very Emilian. I was raised in a family for whom culture was really the road to freedom. At home we had a library full of books. But it was really film that gave me the international part of my personality and my culture. I loved going to the movies, a love I can no longer feel to the same extent given how difficult it is, especially in Rome, to see good films. To love someone or something you have to spend time with them, meet them from time to time.

JG: *Your cultural cosmopolitanism is maybe an attempt to move Italian culture out of a kind of provincialism which characterizes so many of its expressions.*
BB: That may be the result of my work, but it certainly wasn't anything that motivated my early work. It may be just the result of the way I work or of the nature of my films. At home, as I said, there were always so many books that I lived literature, and especially poetry, not as a particular, national or local phenomenon, but just as a general experience, a little bit as though all the poems of all the poets make up one unique poem. Fundamentally, I now believe that all films make up one single great film that is cinema. It's from this perspective that we must understand the contradiction between the way I place my films in very specific locales and my desire to be as open as possible. To be open to what you call cultural cosmopolitanism means to love many diverse things, for example, many different filmmakers and many different countries. Ultimately there is nothing that makes us want to make a film as much as seeing great films. Seeing beautiful films is the most stimulating thing there is. In fact, I think that film schools are useless; classes on style, on mise-en-scene, on diction don't serve any useful purpose. What's important for a director in a film school is to see films, lots of films. That's why Langlois is the greatest professor of the cinema, because he showed six or eight films a day.

Notes

1. BB is referring to two short subjects, *Morte di un maiale* and *La Teleferica*.

2. One of the important tendencies of the Christian Democratic party. The group owes its name to the convent of Saint Dorothy, where its members met.

3. Roberto Farinacci, founder of the shock troops of Cremone, later mayor of Cremone, one of the most violent protagonists of the fascist rise

to power. In 1925 he became secretary general of the National Fascist Party (PNF). He was executed by the partisans in 1945.

4. La *Celere*—the rapid ones is the equivalent of the Republican Security Forces.

5. Palmiro Togliatti died in 1964.

6. Bertolucci is referring to a meeting that was supposed to take place at the University of Rome the morning after our interview, a meeting which provoked, after the talk by the syndicalist leader Lama, serious riots and the shut down of the University.

Bertolucci on *Luna*

RICHARD ROUD/1979

LUNA, BERNARDO BERTOLUCCI'S FIRST film since *1900*, was one of the major Italian entries at the Venice Festival held at the end of August—the first Venice Festival since 1972. *Luna*, which was produced by 20th Century-Fox, is likely to be seen in London early in 1980. This interview took place in the summer, when Bertolucci was still working on the film.

BERNARDO BERTOLUCCI: The idea of *Luna* came two years ago during a session with my psychoanalyst. I suddenly realised that I had been talking about my father for seven or eight years—and now I wanted to talk about my mother. And my first memory of her—I was maybe two—was of me sitting in a little basket on her bicycle, facing her. We were in the country near Parma, and suddenly I saw the moon in the evening sky. And there was a confusion in my mind between the image of the moon and that of my mother's face. This image stopped me dead in my tracks. I couldn't get behind it and I couldn't let it go. So I thought that it was a point of departure for a film. And the film began from that image.

What surprised and excited me was the change in style from your previous films. It's more direct because it's less 'psychological' and much more existential. It's as if you had made The Conformist *but put the 'explanatory' sequence with the chauffeur at the end of the movie, not at the beginning.*

From *Sight & Sound*, Vol. XLVIII/No. 4, Fall 1979. Reprinted by permission.

Yes, I always used to give the 'key' from the start; here it's the reverse. I guess that's what we'll have to call the 'New Dramaturgy.' I think that *Luna* resembles *Breathless* more than any other film. *Breathless* was made twenty years ago (my God—twenty years ago!) but they are similar in their freedom.

Breathless *had a very close relationship with a certain American cinema and* Luna *is also much more American than your other films. It reminds me of the great period of the American cinema when everything was there in the film, but it was never explained. Like those American novels the French discovered just before and after World War II in which there was no psychological commentary— just a presentation of facts, events or things.*
That's true. For a long time I used to present a situation and at the same time make a commentary on the situation and analyse it.

Is that why there are very few set-pieces in the film?
One can't go on doing the same thing all the time; it gets boring. But when you see the film a second time, I think you'll notice that there *are* some bravura sequences, but they are more subtle, more discreet. There are some sequence shots, for example, but I cut in the middle of them. Then I take them up a little later, but in such a way that you don't realise that it is the continuation of the same shot. I think that generally I tried to substitute feeling for the usual narcissism of the camerawork. The camera movements are not so long, not so showy. Because I was too involved with the sentiments of the film—the mother-child story, the father, the father-mother-child trinity—there was less room for my usual exhibitionism. Of course the opera scenes are spectacular.

The first prologue takes place in a house by a very Mediterranean sea. There are four characters in this sequence: a mother (Jill Clayburgh) and her child, a man, and an older woman (Alida Valli).
The film begins with the child who takes a biscuit and some honey: he spills the honey on his leg. That's why I like to call the film mielodrama! [*Miele* is Italian for honey.] The mother licks it off. Then she takes her own finger with the honey still sticking to it and offers it to the child: he sucks it off her finger. What's important to me in the prologue is that we witness the moment of passage from the mother-child symbiosis which lasts dur-

ing the whole breast-feeding period up until the moment of individuation which, according to Freudian theory, occurs when the child sees—or imagines he sees—what Freud called the primal scene: the mother and father making love. In *Luna,* the primal scene is the Twist danced by the mother and a man we cannot clearly see. I didn't want to identify the man for two reasons: first of all, I didn't want the audience to know who the boy's father was, and secondly because the first image the child has of his father is often that of a stranger, one who is necessary to break up the closed circle of the mother-child symbiosis. This 'twist-as-primal-scene' is important because from this moment on the Oedipal process begins. And it's the only way the child can realise he is not a *part* of his mother.

One thing seems strange to me in this scene: why is there a large looking-glass leaning against the wall of the verandah? It reminded me of the title of Auden's long poem The Sea and the Mirror.
A house by the sea is usually furnished in a provisional manner, and I thought it would be beautiful to see the sea and the mother [*la mer et la mère*] reflected in the mirror. But it was also a little homage to Lacan and his views on the importance of the child's first recognition of himself in a mirror. I don't want people to think the film is a psychoanalytical dictionary. It's just that psychoanalysis *is* a possible key to *an* interpretation of the film.

Then it's not too fanciful to see the unrolling of the ball of wool as standing in some way for the umbilical cord?
No, that was intentional.

The prologue ends with an evocation of your childhood memory: the mother pedalling along on her bike in the early evening. The next sequence—the second prologue, as it were—occurs many years later, in New York. The Jill Clayburgh character is an opera singer: born Catherine Silvers, her stage name is Caterina Silveri, and she is packing for a European trip. Her fourteen-year-old son Joe (Mathew Barry) wants to help her and he also wants to go to Europe with his parents. 'I can do everything,' he says, 'the contracts, the hotel reservations.' But she answers, 'Your father does that.' 'But I could do it better,' he retorts. To no avail. 'No, no, you must go on with your schooling.' And then Joe skips out to

*find his father and proposes to him that he stay in New York with him. Of course
he succeeds no better with his father than he had with his mother.*

*And then comes the E. M. Forster-like sudden death of the father: he has gone
out to get the car, but he has a heart attack and he doesn't come back. At the
funeral, Caterina suddenly suggests to Joe that he come with her to Europe...*
As long as Douglas, her husband, is alive, she insists on Joe's need to go on
at school. The minute he's dead, she suddenly discovers that there are
plenty of schools in Italy! Joe naturally feels like an object that his mother
does what she wants with. She is a singer who is at the beginning of her
career, and I think that Douglas is a paternal figure for her, too. He's both
her impresario and her agent. He's the one who takes care of Caterina, and
in fact he's more of a father for her than for Joe.

*The film proper begins in Rome—but again it's a different Rome from the one
we usually see.*
Yes. Joe is completely uprooted, and I tried to underline that by showing
Rome as a city of the Middle East—an exotic, colonial city. That's why the
usher in the movie theatre in the Piazza Cavour is an Arab, and that's why
the bits of Rome we see are not the usual ones.

*The first we see of Rome is the Piazza Cavour with kids skate-boarding, and Joe
arriving with his girl friend Arianna (the name is not accidental: she does provide in some degree the thread to guide Joe through the Roman labyrinth) and
another boy friend of hers. Joe and Arianna go in to see the movie,* Niagara.
Why did you choose that film?
First because there's all that water, which reminded me of the sea at the
beginning of the film, but mostly because of Marilyn Monroe, who for me
is an image of Woman, like the Madonna, the mother.

Who never had any children herself.
Right. And I think she's one of the most poetic things in all cinema.
Furthermore, she's a mother in the film.

*It's a very puzzling sequence. Before going into the auditorium, they both go into
the men's room. But why? At first I thought it was to have sex, but later inside the
auditorium she says she is a virgin, and he replies, me too. So what did they do?*

Perhaps a fix, but it's not clear. I want the audience to think it's a love scene, but afterwards I want to disquiet them with the scene in which they both admit they're virgins.

Joe then goes to find his mother at the opera where she is singing Leonora in II Trovatore. *The scene is the one in which Leonora mistakes the Count di Luna (!) for her lover Manrico. Why did you choose this scene?*
I don't know why Verdi and his librettist Cammarano wrote that scene. It's like the equivocal comedies of Shakespeare where one character turns out to be another, but here I think we have two father figures. Furthermore, as we eventually discover, Manrico and the Count are in fact brothers, so they're in a sense the same man, but split in two. Perhaps I chose this scene to prefigure the discovery that Caterina has had two husbands, two lovers.

After the performance, Joe goes backstage and hears Caterina's friend Marina (Veronica Lazar) say: 'She sings better since her husband died.' This is the eve of Joe's fifteenth birthday and he also hears his mother say, 'If Joe stopped growing, I wouldn't be so old.' Then comes the birthday party the next day. During it Joe disappears into another room to shoot up. Initially it comes as a shock to realise that Joe is a junkie, although looking back one sees the signs that had been planted.
I particularly liked the cut from him 'shooting up' to the arrival of the birthday cake. She thinks of him as a kid who still gets turned on by cakes, but we know he needs stronger stuff!
That is a little joke. There are the Nouveaux Philosophes and the Nouvelle Cuisine, and in this film I wanted, as I said, to create a New Dramaturgy. It's what I've always done in my films—the contrary of what is called consistency in English. I really like to play on contrasts: there are a lot of them in *1900*. There are a lot in Shakespeare too. The English talk about consistency, but thank God they don't keep to it in their literature. Life isn't consistent. You can (and should) have consistency in the *structure* of a film, a play, or a novel. But one must avoid consistency if one is to portray the sudden contradictions which we find in life.

I very much liked the sequence that follows: Joe running away from the party with Caterina in pursuit. It ends up in the Piazza Farnese—the drug centre of Rome. Was it done with a handheld camera?

No, it's the first time I used this American thing called Steadicam; it was first used in *Rocky*, but now everyone uses it. I like it because it's not a dolly-track, and it's not hand-held. It's something between the two, and there's no jiggling.

They return to their flat, and the scene that follows is arguably the centre of the film: the first real confrontation between Joe and his mother. She turns on him: 'When I look at you and your friends, I think I'm on Mars.' They even start hitting each other. Joe escapes to his room to turn on. Then he sneaks out and the next sequence shows him wandering round Rome. With a piece of chalk, he marks out his itinerary by tracing a line on the walls.

The whole film is a kind of labyrinth. There is probably a connection between the umbilical cord (the unravelling ball of wool in the prologue), the chalk and the Ariadne thread.

In the Zanzibar cafe Franco Citti tries to pick him up. He buys him an ice-cream cone which Joe sensuously licks: they dance together, but then Joe falls asleep. When he finally comes home, his first words to Caterina are: 'I really miss dad, and you don't.' Then he passes out. After the doctor has left, Caterina decides to go out.

She puts on his clothes. The clothes stand for his skin. And where does she go? Well, she wants to understand Joe. So she goes back to the Piazza Farnese because she remembers that he knows someone there. She doesn't know what she'll find, but she goes anyhow. And there's nobody there. Suddenly, like an elf, there appears Mustafa, Joe's friend and dealer.

And at that moment, the film takes off on to a new level. There's something quite literally fantastic in that sequence with Mustafa.

A lot of people have told me that the sequence is too long, etc. Others think Mustafa is extraneous to the main subject, and that he should be cut. But he is the first person who enables her to begin to understand Joe. Above all, that's because he's *not her son*. After Mustafa she is no longer a Martian. She starts to enter into her son's world. Already she has decided to give up her career. Before, she was a kind of middle-class mother who was trying to understand 'modern youth'; from the moment she decides to stop singing, we realise it is because she feels that her son's loneliness has been caused by her career. Until she meets Mustafa it was a drama of noninteraction; after Mustafa the interaction begins. And it's only then that there is the first erotic incident between her and her son. So when she leaves Mustafa (who has forced a gift upon her—some heroin) she comes home with the feeling that she now understands Joe better. She has decided to take off her maternal mask. When she gets home, she finds Joe preparing a fancy dinner for her. What's paradoxical is that he indicates his need for being nourished by her by preparing a meal for her. I think heroin has become a substitute for the nourishment he hasn't had from his mother.

The sequence which begins as comedy ends in drama. 'Do you know why I take dope?' he asks. 'Because I don't give a shit.' 'About me?' she asks. 'About *anything*,' he answers. Like a lot of mothers, mistresses or wives, the minute she hears the other say I'm unhappy, her immediate and egotistical response is that it must be because of her. By this time he needs another fix, badly. And she does the only possible thing. She goes to her room and takes the package Mustafa has given her, saying, 'Take it, Joe will need it.' She never thought she would give it to him; she just took it because it was placed in her hand. But she begins to nourish Joe by giving him the heroin. She hasn't got a needle, and neither has he. So Joe takes a fork and sticks it into his arm. A desperate gesture. Once Caterina has accepted his need for dope, this leads naturally to her trying to compensate for his inability to take the heroin by 'suckling' him at her breast. [Both of them are fully dressed.]

But after he 'suckles' on her breast, he guides her hand towards his genitals.
Yes, he does take her hand, but she accepts: she begins to massage him through his clothes. It's the ultimate, the extreme maternal gesture.

After he comes, he falls asleep completely clothed, but the one part of his body that is exposed is his navel.
Well, that's no accident. Then she covers him up, blows out the candles on the dining room table, and goes out. At this point I see her as a kind of Mizoguchian heroine.

Then we cut to the next morning, and we see the maid cleaning the floor. Joe wakes up, goes towards the window, and sees someone. But it's not his mother, it's her friend Marina.

There are two or three brief shots of another town. An American could think we were still in Rome. But we see this Romanesque architecture, and the Palazzo della Pilotta (where we saw Adriana Asti on her way to the rail-way station in *Before the Revolution*). Then we cut back to Rome and Marina tells Joe his mother has gone to Parma to see her old singing teacher.

I wasn't sure the old man even recognised Caterina. Why does he put on 'Soave sia il vento' (from Cosi Fan Tutte*) on the gramophone?*
Because it was something she used to sing, and it's a heavenly melody. It's not Verdian, it's neither passionate nor romantic. It's elegiac, sublime. It's about everything that's been going on in her life.

What is the building that Joe (who has followed his mother to Parma) and Caterina walk past together, talking, but separated by the colonnade?
That's the Teatro Regio, the opera house. That was where she sang her first *Traviata:* 'It was snowing outside and I was throwing up on my costume because I was so nervous, so I had to wear it inside out on stage.' But I'm thinking of cutting all that in the final print.

Then she says, 'When I found out I was pregnant, your father fainted.' And Joe asks her if she will ever remarry. She doesn't answer, and they try to get into the theatre, but it's closed. Then they go off to the country to show Joe their old house. They get to a level crossing and have to wait until the train comes through. And the sequence that follows is the one I find the most uncomfortable. Caterina kisses Joe for no apparent reason.

She has just said that his father first kissed her here at this level crossing.
Yes, but that's no reason for her to kiss him. And she kisses him as one kisses a lover. Earlier it was the mother who was helping the son. But here, I don't quite understand it myself. I guess it's the New Dramaturgy!

Then there follows the scene of them looking for—and finally finding—Verdi's home at Sant' Agata. And the strange and, to me, not wholly relevant sequence when she is picked up by Renato Salvatori and flirts with him. Then she gets rid of Salvatori, and says to Joe: I didn't want to touch him, I wanted to be touching you. Does she really mean that?
I think that scene has to be improved a little. But she does, I think, want Joe in some way, although when they go into the bedroom behind the cafe and he tells her he's scared, she admits to being scared too. The real point of this sequence is that she doesn't know how to tell Joe who his real

father was: 'If only we could have found the house, it would have been easier... I could have told you... the house where I lived with your *real* father, not Douglas.'

So finally the truth is out, and we realise that the man in the prologue must not have been Douglas, but someone else. Who? And why has she not told Joe sooner?
That happens quite often in middle-class families. But there's another reason, too, that we only discover at the end of the film. Something very traumatic, obviously, happened between Caterina and Giuseppe (Tomas Milian), her first lover. Joe's father was not an adult. He was a man who lived with his mother (Alida Valli).

In Rome, we and Joe find Giuseppe teaching in a school. It's paradoxical that someone who has abandoned his own son has surrounded himself with children. And Joe is even a little jealous. But he does not reveal himself yet. He hangs around, and even manages to exchange clothes with Giuseppe: he takes his father's shoes and leaves his own. They both have white jackets. It's like Brando and Massimo Girotti in *Tango* wearing the same bathrobe.

Joe follows Giuseppe [Giuseppe and Joseph are of course the same name] surreptitiously and this leads him to the sea near Rome. And one realises that this is where the prologue took place. Then Joe asks Giuseppe if he ever wondered what happened to his son. 'Where is he?' asks Giuseppe. 'Dead,' says Joe. 'He died in front of my house of an overdose.' Alida Valli is cryptically strumming Debussy on the piano, but stops to ask Joe where Caterina is. 'At the rehearsal at Caracalla.' Then Giuseppe asks Joe to leave. Does Joe remember his father?
No, he was only a year old, but he does know that there was something missing from his life. He says that he, Joe, is dead, because....

Because in order for there to be a resurrection there has to be a death?
Exactly.

The final sequence takes place in the ruins of the Baths of Caracalla where outdoor opera is given every summer in Rome. It is afternoon, and they are rehearsing Act 4 of A Masked Ball. *Why this particular opera and scene?*
Because we have a woman between two men, and one of the two is killed. She (Amelia) is veiled; and she is trying to hide herself.

Caterina, we discover, is so upset she cannot sing her role at the rehearsal. When she sees Joe, she asks for a five minute break.
Yes, and then she dries his tears, and he dries hers. And then he takes the veil from her. She says, 'Now you're in love with your father!'

That was very funny because she says it with a particularly New York accent. First you were in love with me, and now you're in love with him. Where will it all end?
When Joe asks why she left his father, she tells him that Giuseppe was selfish; he hated her voice; he wanted something different. *He* was in love with his mother, too. Then Arianna arrives.

It's like the end of an opera when all the characters are on stage. You don't know any more whether the action is taking place on the stage or in the audience. I like the scene where Caterina, in effect, gives Joe back to his father. And then — smack! — the father slaps Joe's face. And then a few minutes later, he turns around, sees Joe sitting with Arianna, and gives him a little smile, as if to say, why did you make me suffer, why did you make me feel guilty? I am guilty, of course, but not of your death.
Joe has finally found his identity. There's no question of him going to live with Giuseppe, and the parents don't come together again, because Giuseppe is still in love with his own mother.

What are the last words she sings?
Ei muore: he's dying.

Who's dying?
Joe . . . I wanted to say the obvious: that every man is in love with his mother. And then, that Joe has now become an adult. The boy is dead. The adult has killed him. He had to die to live. You know, 'Except a grain of wheat fall to the ground and die, it abideth alone: but if it dies, it bringeth forth much fruit.'

Every Film Is a Nick's Movie: A Conversation Between Bernardo Bertolucci and Wim Wenders

ENRICO GHEZZI/1981

E G : *What are the connections between* Nick's Movie *and the American cinema?*

W W : Go ahead!

B B : No, you go ahead. I'm older so I get to go second.

W W : OK. This is a pretty vague question. *Nick's Movie* doesn't have much in common with American film. I'd even say it's the opposite of American film. There are two directors, but most of all two friends, and we never asked ourselves whether we were European or American film directors. The question was never raised; it was just a starting point. We did the film as friends and not thinking about this antithesis of American vs. European film.

B B : It's been a long time since I've seen *Nick's Movie*, when the film had another title, *Lightning over Water*. It was at the Cannes Festival, and I was very moved because Nicholas Ray had always been a myth for me—I'd met him in the States in the early seventies—and even if I didn't make a film about him or with him, I consider myself a friend of Nick's, who was always willing to help a friend. I think he resembled his films a lot, just as all directors resemble the films they've done. He looked like a tough guy

From RAI (National Italian Television), 7 October 1981. Reprinted by permission.
Translated by Fabien Gerard and T. Jefferson Kline.

who made tough films, but in reality he was very vulnerable and you feel this vulnerability in each of his works. I think the secret goal of his films was a kind of defiance to failure: I mean a kind of poetic game that is unique to his films and to his personality. But I find that for the first time in Wim's film we don't see Nick in the grips of some perverse logic of failure. Maybe because when faced with death, which goes way beyond the idea of failure, he finds himself faced with a huge surprise. It's a film about a man of great vitality. I don't know what people will think when they see this film. I remember the first press conference after the premiere of the film at Cannes, the audience was a bit sad. That is, either people were sad or they were upset that such a young filmmaker had chosen to make a film about the death of an older director whom he considered a great master. And so in the theater they kept asking Wim questions like "How many feet of film do you shoot?" or "How many weeks did his final illness last?" i.e., ill-at-ease or very prosaic questions. For me, on the other hand, I found it a very exciting film, a film about vitality, and at a certain point I got up to say something in public—a thing I never do in public since it's already difficult to talk about my own films so to have talk about others' films is really hard—and so I said several things like, "Why is everyone talking about extraneous things and no one is saying, 'This is a terrific film!'" In fact I was making a declaration of love about this film.

w w : Yes, that was very courageous of you. It really helped me a lot at that moment. As for me, it was a very dramatic experience. In fact, that showing you were at in Cannes was the first time I'd seen the film. In fact, I hadn't been very present during the editing, since after the shooting I felt that I simply wouldn't be capable of editing this film, and so it was better to give it to a third person who would be able to tell this story in the third person. And that's precisely what my friend Peter [Przygodda] did. This work took him an entire year and was very heavy. It nearly drove him crazy. And sometimes I'd go find him in the editing room, but I was about to shoot another film, so I didn't insist. So I discovered the film in Cannes, and despite the fact that I knew every shot, it was there that I realized that it was really necessary to tell this story in the first person. And that was the version that Bernardo saw. Then I went back to the U.S. with the reels under my arm, and I started from scratch. It was the same story but told from a first person point of view. That's why I re-edited it, and it completely changed the perspective of the film. Everyone who has seen the two versions agrees that there's a huge difference between them. So this work took another six months, but for me it was like a kind of exorcism. It was only at that point that the film was really completed. Though I'll never forget everything that happened during the shooting because it was such a difficult and important experience for me. Now, of course, we're talking about it as if it were merely a film, before it was really something else, and it bothers me to talk about it as if it were only a film. But that seems false to me because the film wasn't just something you see on a screen but was the whole human experience that it represented and what remains of him in me. So each time it's always the same; you talk about a film and I don't want to talk about it that way.

B B :   I find you a bit formalist when you talk this way because it's my impression that Nick's death in the film is a pact to say the least, but every time you make a film you have people who are aging in front of the camera, especially if it's a long film, and you can see the changes in their faces. My feeling is that what you experience in such a dramatic way happens in fact every time you have people aging in front of the camera—even within a single take. For example, in a long take. Because in some sense they are getting closer to death. So I have the impression that you've experienced in a more overwhelming way something that happens every time that we shoot a film. That's why you could almost say in this regard that all films are Nick's movies without going as far as quoting Cocteau, and indeed why not, that to make a film is to watch death at work. Evidently in the case of your film this quote is practically written in capital letters on the very celluloid that you were using. In America they have what are called "sneak previews," which are the first chance to show a film to the public before its commercial release so you get to see what works or doesn't work in a film based on the reactions of this audience. And in fact I have the impression that in Europe where sneak previews don't exist, the Cannes Film Festival plays this role for the director. As Wim said just now, I finished editing *Tragedy of a Ridiculous Man* just a few days before showing it at Cannes, so it was at Cannes that I discovered my film, just as he discovered *Nick's Movie*. Moreover it's always the audience who completes the film and gives it its finishing touches. In the case of *Ridiculous Man*, I understood that the mystery of the film was a bit too arrogant and irritated the audience. I was in a sense violating the audience. That's why I worked on the film and brought it back to what it had been at the level of the screenplay and which I'd changed during the shooting, i.e., a film told in the first person. And I added a voice-over of Ugo Tognazzi which had been eliminated during the filming. I don't think that this element really helps to clarify the mystery, which is the mystery of today's Italy. In fact it's not up to me to clarify this mystery, but rather up to the judges and magistrates, but the addition of the voice-over gives a less arrogant feeling to the mystery and allows the spectator to identify more with the character and allows the public to get inside this mystery.

Now I'd like to come back to something we were talking about before we started recording this interview. You were talking about Coppola, Scorsese, Brian De Palma and Steven Spielberg, of this whole group of directors who at the end of the '60s and in the early '70s "woke up" American cinema, an industry that had gone to sleep at this time as if suddenly blocked by an inferiority complex they'd gotten about the European New Wave. In other words, the old guard in Hollywood had lost their way, and thanks to this young group of directors, Coppola, Scorsese, etc., the American cinema began to live again. But then I was disconcerted when they talked about shifting their work from Los Angeles to San Francisco which seemed terrific at the time — a bit like storming the Winter Palace during the Russian Revolution! In a sense the younger generation was beginning to wrest some of the power from the hands of the major companies. OK, very exciting! But what was going to happen next? How were they going to manage this beautiful movement of renewal? What films will these young independent guys make once they've seized power? What bothers me, you see, is that the films they've made so far are films that could also have been made by the big studios, films that don't seem to have a new identity, no real "difference," and so it's a bit as if the new independent filmmakers had reestablished the studio system within their own movement. . . . I mean that this movement which all of us in Europe found so interesting to follow because it meant a very hopeful change at the heart of the "empire," didn't really lead to such different films from what Hollywood would have done anyway.

w w : No, my feeling is that the independents discovered that they already believed in the way the Major Companies worked. So maybe it's more a question of the American taste for films that was developed over fifty years by Hollywood; the entire system of production and distribution is at risk here, and I think it's illusory to believe that from one day to the next they're going to start making films that are completely different in the States and that they could do completely without the major companies and make films that really bring something new and different to the screen. American taste is what's really at stake, not just in the major companies, but throughout the American system of distribution, television, newspapers. . . . No, it's pretty unthinkable, in my view, to produce something radically new in such a short time.

B B :   I should add that you had the experience of *Hammett* with Francis. . . .

w w :   Yes, when we began three years ago, Coppola had his own company in San Francisco and he wanted to do a little independent film there. Then during *Hammett*'s preproduction period, the company he'd started up moved from San Francisco to Los Angeles. Coppola bought some new studios, and suddenly my film was the first to be shot in his new Hollywood studios, and Coppola found himself in a situation where he couldn't make films that were really different from the usual Hollywood films. Once he found himself in Hollywood he really had no choice: he had to work in the same way they've always worked in the major studios. So there was the film and there was all this machinery behind the film which was just like you'd find in any major studio. That's why I doubt the possibility of a new independent circuit ever being born in the U.S.

B B :   Which means that American film will always be dependent on the logic of the studios? Which doesn't prevent the studios from representing what people like you and me have always loved in the great American cinema.

w w :   Of course, but I'm not at all against studios since it's these same studios that made the films that I literally adored as a kid.

B B :   Yes, we always have to made distinctions. I realized that I maybe have a tendency to generalize in what I just said, and it's always a mistake to generalize. Coppola is obviously someone who's extremely sensitive to everything that's happening in Europe and the rest of the world and the proof is precisely that he asked you to do a film on *Hammett*. Moreover we know that all of his films, whether it's *Apocalypse Now* or something he's just made like *One from the Heart,* are always films that problematize the language of film while the other films we were just talking about scare me because they exemplify a kind of regression that American film is going through with the approval of the American public and indeed the whole world. It's clear that the best of today's American film have been films aimed at kids, which seems a bit unfortunate. That's the case of *Raiders of the Lost Ark,* for example, which is entirely based on a philological obses- sion with the best comic books of the '40s, and this lack of ambition seems too bad. Of course it's this philological obsession which creates the interest of such films, but it also constitutes their limitations, for there's not a trace of the innocence that characterized their models. But you could say the same thing of *Superman* and lots of other films that have been released recently. The problem is that you have to be careful not to take refuge in regression.

To come back to *Hammett*; when you spoke of the impossibility of doing the film as you'd originally intended it, I recalled a similar experience I'd had. Do you remember that when I was making *1900*, I wanted really badly to do an adaptation of *Red Harvest,* also a Hammett book. The idea was to develop the dialectic between two opposing world views: that of the "Con- tinental Op," the detective inspired by the real Dashiell Hammett, vs. that of the union leader, Bill Quint, who had the vision of an American ideal- ist—not to say Socialist—which no longer exists in today's America. Ultimately I didn't do this film because I realized that American audiences are deprived of a sense, in the same way one might lack sight, hearing or touch—the sense of Marxism, which for us Europeans, even if you're not a Marxist, is an integral part of our culture, even if we get it only from a sense of conflict or dialectics. That's the main reason I abandoned the idea of doing that film. So, in this respect, you could say Hammett unites us and separates us!

w w :   I remember meeting you in New York one day when you were writ- ing the screenplay for *Red Harvest.*

b b :   I remember it too, but I think at that point, even if I didn't say it, I'd already decided not to do the film.

ww: Quite by chance, two weeks ago, I came across *Luna*, which was being shown on TV. I watched the whole thing even though I never watch movies on television, especially my own. It's something awful that I completely refuse to do. And of course someone always comes up to me the next day and says, "I saw your film on TV, it was great!" That's something that makes me furious. Well, anyway, watching *Luna*, I said to myself, that for once here was a film that really worked on TV. Now I have to tell you that my attitude is slightly contradictory on this point, because I've always considered television as the enemy, ideologically speaking. And yet, quite obviously, for certain films in any case, it works really well. Indeed, I think it doesn't depend so much on television as it does on the particular film. It's particularly true for films that are capable of remaining films because they've got lots of form, and it's that that allows them to survive this terrible experience! Who knows, maybe I should try watching my films on TV too.

BB: I don't ever look at my films again either, and especially not on TV. I'd be even more ashamed to watch them in a movie theater! As a matter of fact the only film I have a video cassette of is *The Conformist,* but I never dare watch more than a few minutes of it. Cassettes are very useful, but a bit masturbatory: but what's great is to be able to choose the parts that I prefer in the films I like, fast forwarding over the other parts. That's how I made my own personal *cinémathèque.* Most of all it's the possibility of intervention I like even though the ritual and liturgy of watching a film are completely different. The spectator who watches a film on a TV screen is completely different from the spectator in front of a big screen. And then the most important thing is that it makes a huge difference for the director, or at least that's how it should happen. Several years ago, for example, I was convinced to make a film for television, *The Spider's Stratagem,* originally made for RAI, the national Italian TV station. At that time my idea was to use television as a producer, but in fact to make a real film for the cinema, with wide angle shots, etc., without caring whether it would be distributed to the theaters. Today, on the other hand, I believe that everyone who continues to think as I obstinately did, makes the same mistake I did at the time. When you make a film for television, you have to have the courage to explore in depth all the possibilities of this medium, which is different from the cinema; you really have to have the courage to get inside it.

As for me, the essence of television is first and foremost seeing live coverage of President Sadat being massacred in a crowd in front of the cameras from the entire planet. That's why I'd like to shoot live for television, because anything that isn't live is not really TV; it's just cinema you can watch comfortably at home—your little private *cinématheque* which I was mentioning just a moment ago. In fact I think I could make any film I wanted for TV as long as it was shot live.

w w : As for me, I must confess that the idea of seeing *Nick's Movie* on television is really a problem, because the film is so personal, so private, that I feel like TV screen is going to make it even more vulnerable than it already is. I wonder if it's even going to survive this medium which I consider so cold and distant. If you look closely at the film, Nick and I were always trying to make a story. We shot with a 35mm camera using studio lighting, exactly as if it were a real film. And Nick's real effort, I believe, can be seen precisely in this choice of format, in his desire to go on making movies in spite of everything. It's also true that there was a kind of consciousness of television in the film, since there are scenes shot with a video cam parallel to the 35mm camera. We were often unaware that this video camera was on the set; they are maybe the cruelest images of all. As someone said, the presence of the video cam in *Nick's Movie* already represents in some way the cancer of the film. So I'm really scared to look at it on a VCR, and I know that I wouldn't be able to sleep at night if I knew that it was on TV the next day.

b b : If at some point I had to envision shooting a film for television television television (as they say when a traitor goes over to the enemy camp)— I'm repeating it three times to emphasize that I'm really talking about a film made for TV with no attempt to inject cinema qualities into it, not just a film you'd see on TV—I'd really like to make it live, because I feel that live is without doubt the most specific characteristic to which this medium owes its charm. What I'd really like, for example, would be to direct something which doesn't exist in Italy. In France they call it "Feuilletons,"— magazine novels, in Brazil "Telenovelas" and in the U.S. "serials" or soap-operas. So my temptation would be to make a kind of live soap opera, with, I don't know, let's say a family and all the things that happen to them during the day. I'd like to shoot each evening and have it broadcast live. I think it would be fascinating to imagine this kind of drama entirely influenced by what happened each day, over the past few hours, and, why not?, *while* I was filming. In this case the medium of television could become really interesting.

Not long ago, I met Francis—your friend Coppola—and we talked a bit about electronic media. He's a real maniac on the subject. I, on the other hand, am a little too conservative, still attached to good old film, which I've always had a kind of physical relationship with. I like working with my hands, in the same way an artisan measures a piece of cloth, and I'm beginning to understand what it will be like with a whole new generation of editors who can bring all the shots into alignment without ever touching anything but a bunch of buttons. In that respect I didn't feel like I was on the same wave length with Coppola, who is a great entrepreneur, a real manager, a sort of Citizen Kane desperately seeking Orson Welles inside of himself. I also understood that he needs to enlarge his space as much as possible, and that electronics offer him at least the theoretical possibility, he tells me, of projecting the same film throughout the world at the same moment. I entirely understand that this is an interesting element, and one which could bring enormous satisfaction to a creative artist, but the problem remains for the electronic artist of what to film, and when I ask Francis, he doesn't answer. So we're faced with the same question, once you wrest the power away from the major studios, how to use electronic media to change the direction of film, to make something different? What I'd like to see is for electronics to bring something poetically new beyond simply the technical questions of the medium. When it does, electronics will really interest me. Of course, you have to realize that in Europe we're living a little on the margins of the empire, so we see all of this from a distance and we may have a tendency to mystify things a bit. And what would you like to do?

w w :   Me too. If I had to make something for television, I think it's the idea of doing it live that would interest me the most. The ideal would be to be able to use this type of technology to work without having to move the usual film crew around. I'd really like to film certain travels live, just recording my voyages on video. Every time I go to a rock concert, for example, I think it's really too bad that there's no technology that would allow me to record it just as I've seen it, and not just to record it for myself but to be able to show it live to others who aren't there at that moment, without having a huge crew, shooting with a single camera, exactly as if it were the eyes of a single person who happens to be in the audience. Or again, to come back to the idea of the film-voyage, I'd love to be able to travel with a camera which could be connected to an electronic system which would allow me to share this trip live with other people who might be on the other side of the world. That's an idea that fascinates me enormously, but I don't think that technology has reached a level of perfection which would allow such a personalized way of doing it. And such a trip would have no meaning at all if you had to travel around with a crew of even two or three people. It would have to be something completely personal, and it's only then that it might turn into something really interesting. And it's only if it were completely personal that something like that would be worth showing to the public. For example my favorite TV show this year was presented by the apartment building where I live in New York. While waiting for the elevator, you can watch this little monitor they've installed over the door, which shows what's happening inside the elevator car. This way you can watch the people going up to the first floor and the people getting out on the second floor, or a guy who gets on at the tenth floor, and you watch him all the way down and then find yourself face to face with him as the door opens and he gets off, while you get on knowing that other people waiting on other floors are watching you. That something that interests me.

BB: That's a lot like Zavattini's old dream! He called that "the poetics of the neighbors on your landing." He imagined following his next door neighbor in the street a bit like a voyeur.

WW: Obviously we're not talking about a kind of television for a huge audience. In fact, I'm for a television system that would offer thousands and thousands of different channels.

Interview with Bernardo Bertolucci on *Tragedy of a Ridiculous Man*

MICHEL CIMENT/1981

M C : *When Primo (Ugo Tognazzi) asks Barbara (Anouk Aimée) why she married him, she answers, "Because you made me laugh and because you were working so hard."*

B B : They represent the confrontation of two different social classes. Barbara, as Anouk's allure implies, comes from the French *haute bourgeoisie*. At twenty, she studied art restoration in Parma which would explain her connection with painting, her fake Pisarro, etc. And she met this ex-peasant who got rich. Given her leisure class origins, she's fascinated by his materialism. Throughout the entire film we see the confrontation of admiration and rage because of her social class (as Selznick said, "There are two kinds of class, first class and no class.") And she envies his energy and vitality. Anouk Aimée is thus in a dialectic relationship with Tognazzi. This is connected a bit with *1900*, because what's at work here is the fascination that each class holds for the others. She represents someone who has never been able to work and who is seduced by the positive side of her husband, and also by a certain kind of poetry that emanates from his vulgarity.

M C : *The film ends in the dance hall like* Luna *ends in a theater. Here the father finds his son. There the son finds his father. In both situations we have theater and music.*

From *Positif* (Paris), November 1981. Reprinted by permission. Translated by Fabien Gerard and T. Jefferson Kline.

B B : Just like at the end of *Last Tango* and *The Conformist*. I suppose I have always needed to end with a musical moment. In a dance, in the theater, maybe I feel I can allow myself to take some liberties with my characters. Then anything can happen. In this case there is the resurrection of Giovanni, the son.

M C : *Where did you come up with the idea of this film after other such cosmopolitan films like* Last Tango, 1900 *and* Luna.
B B : I wanted to get back to the Italian language. It was a sort of wager. The hardest thing to do and the least successful part of Italian films in general is the dialogues. Screen writers, and I include myself here, tend to write dialogues that are too literary. I wanted to see if it were possible to strip the language of its finery, to strip it naked and even invent a new cinematic language. I'm fairly happy with the results, which are mostly thanks to Tognazzi, who is from the Po valley where the film is shot. He's a guy with a lot of common sense who for years played the music hall circuit, the real epic theater according to Brecht. Ugo's experience was a great help to me: his spoken language wiped out all traces of literariness from the script. As soon as I'd finished writing the screenplay—which took about forty days—I cut a lot from the dialogues, keeping only the essential.

M C : *To what degree was Tognazzi's work different from what he did in certain comedies which were also inspired by popular culture?*
B B : He got invested in this film to a degree that almost scared me! First of all he identified with the character, and then he totally understood the idea that is contained in this story, this utopia that Primo is living. I didn't want him to act as if he were doing Italian comedy. Ultimately, my relationship with him was a bit like the one I had with Brando in *Last Tango in Paris*. What interested me was his personality and what he could bring to the role from his own private experience. Tognazzi occasionally changed his lines during the filming. Originally I had written the film in the first person and there was a voice over narration that was completely eliminated from the film. [After the presentation at Cannes, Bertolucci reintroduced the voice-over narration.] This is a film seen from Tognazzi's point of view—this voyeur who watches everything with his field glasses. He's a sort of guru-mogul-monolith in the middle of this story, and all the other characters revolve around him. Tognazzi is a sort of Jean Gabin-like mon-

ster, capable of running off between takes and cooking a "risotto à l'éjac-ulation" as he likes to call it, which consists of putting a bottle of champagne in the middle of a plate of rice and dropping some sugar in the champagne which then bubbles over into the rice. With him there was never any continuity between the take, the recipe and the following take. In some ways, though, we never had to work things out or even talk much in order to achieve a true meeting of minds.

M C : *It's interesting that the film was written in the first person whereas you are, by age, more in between the generations portrayed. Primo could be your father and Giovanni your son. In other words, how did you come up with the idea for this film?*

B B : About a year ago I was in Los Angeles and pretty depressed because I'd wanted to produce a musical comedy in Brazil with Gianni Amico as director, and music by Gaetano Veloso and Chico Guarte. We had everything signed with Fox and then, because of a change in their corporate leadership, the film was dropped. I was really upset because I really believed in this project. Once again I was face to face with the narrow-mindedness of these producers. I got several offers to do films in Los Angeles, but none of them really caught my interest. On the other hand I'd been feeling the need to make a film in Italy. So I returned home and my wife, Clare Peploe, discovered in a paper this news item which had taken place in the *Puglie,* in Southern Italy. The son of a local political boss had been kidnapped and killed. And the father had been looking for money to save him. I changed the locale and the personality of the character. I saw him as personifying a refusal of the very negative logic of violence in Italy where sons, mothers and fathers are used as merchandise. In Primo there is a kind of utopic force that makes me think of *1900. Tragedy of a Ridiculous Man,* though not directly political, is in some ways the third act of *1900.* Primo is an answer to the current cynicism in contemporary Italy. Out of an event as tragic as the kidnapping of his son he manages to extract something quite positive; he tries to save his cheese works from bankruptcy and help his workers at the same time. On the other side there is the utopia of the younger generation, Laura and Adelfo.

This said, I stupidly set about writing the scenario in the first person because it bored me to write it in the third person. I didn't quite know where I was going, but what kept me going was the idea of doing another Italian film, near my home in Parma, in Emilia—which is maybe the reason for identifying with the character and using the first person. I wrote the script in a bit if a trance working between eleven at night and five the next morning, completing it in less than forty days. I had run into Tognazzi briefly at Cannes in 1980, had told him the story in a few words and asked if he'd be interested. Since he was delighted, I set to work immediately always with him in mind for the major role. I didn't know him well, but I'd met him several times at the home of the producer, my cousin, Giovanni Bertolucci, who is one of his buddies and who produced, among other things, *La Camera del Vescovo (The Bishop's Chamber)*. During these high society evenings where we saw each other, I saw in Ugo a deep capacity for false appearances as well as a certain heaviness. And it's always interesting to go looking for the real self of the tortoise under the shell . . . Tognazzi's ego. From the start of the shooting, he displayed an exquisite spirit of generosity and finesse. He surprised me for I really didn't expect this. In fact, I don't go to many Italian films, and I knew Ugo only from a few roles like the one he had in *Venga a prendere il caffè da noi* where he was extraordinary. I found myself face to face with an actor who had degrees of depth and stature which I hadn't anticipated. I wanted to make a "dirty" film from a stylistic or structural point of view. I didn't want beautiful calligraphy. I began writing at the end of May, and I said we'd begin shooting on September 29 which left everyone incredulous. And yet everything happened exactly as I'd predicted. We spent fourteen weeks shooting, including interruptions. The editing went very quickly. It's a film that was made at the speed of life rather than the speed of cinema.

M C : *This is your most "provincial" film with* Before the Revolution *and* The Spider's Stratagem.

B B : It's closer to the second, I think. This is in part due to the space off-screen that you don't see, to the perfume of the place. Primo's villa is located in Langhirano, which produces the best ham in the world. That gives it a connection with *Before the Revolution*, the good meals and the ham. But there's also something which reminds us of *The Conformist:* it's not an autobiographical film. I created one character older than I and others younger. There's no immediate identification.

M C : *What did your director of photography, Carlo Di Palma, add to the film?*
B B : For the first time in eleven years I changed cameramen. With Vittorio
Storaro I'd carried on the longest love story of my life (it's never lasted so
long with any woman!). When Coppola came to Rome last year, the three
of us had dinner to try to work out the dates we'd be filming. But I didn't
yet know what film I'd be doing or when. When I'd made up my mind, it
was too late; Storaro had already signed with Coppola to do *One from the
Heart*. There was this cameraman who'd been telling my producer that he
wanted to work with me and that was Carlo Di Palma who, after *Blow Up*,
The Red Desert, etc. had gone into directing. The idea of signing on someone who was starting from scratch and yet already had a wealth of experience fascinated me. I met him and I discovered in him an artist like
Vittorio whom I was going to ask to do the opposite of what I would ask
of Vittorio. I wanted a lot of focus, aggressive shots where lighting wasn't
used in a dramatic way, a more hard-edged photography closer to hyper-
realism. I was also looking for an interior-exterior relationship. This is
difficult with Storaro because he's always putting projectors in windows:
he wants the lighting to come from natural sources (doors, windows,
shades, etc.). With Carlo I was able to use the large window looking over
the valley and which I find quite magical. There was also the problem of
nights: Vittorio cries when he has to shoot at night, especially in the country where there aren't streetlights, because, once again, he needs to build
from the real. I could ask Carlo to light the night scenes—like the scene
after the kidnapping—according to cinematic convention where you don't
know the source of the lighting and where it isn't realistic but rather hyper-
realistic since you see everything.

M C : *There's a very strong contrast with* Luna *which was so lyrical, close to
melodrama and opera with long camera movements, whereas here they are so
fragmented and broken through editing.*
B B : Yes, *Tragedy* is closer to *film noir*. I wanted to rediscover the dialectical
force that montage can give. Sometimes you get it. Sometimes you get so
attached to a scene you have shot that you can't bear to cut it. For example, Jean-Marie Straub never touches a shot either to cut it or integrate it
into another scene. Even though he's so Brechtian and Marxist he refuses
dialectic. In *Tragedy* I saw montage as in a dialectical relationship with
shooting. By breaking up the camera's movement you emphasize it maybe

more than if you keep the scene untouched. While I admire Rosi's *Three Brothers* or the films of Angelopoulos, I nevertheless sometimes want to jump on their sequences and tear them apart because they display too great a respect—and especially Angelopoulos—for the way they shot the scenes.

M C : *From* Luna *to* Tragedy of a Ridiculous Man *we move from harmony to dissonance.*

B B : But it isn't a planned dissonance. The structure of the scenario was simple and linear. But we shot the film in such a delirious atmosphere, with such a mix of anxiety and happiness that I almost never looked at the script. And I was working in such a way that I could radically alter the structure during the editing, and that's what happened. For example, the search of Primo's house carried out by the police was originally set near the end of the film whereas now it takes place in the first part. The succession of episodes was thus greatly modified. That's inevitably how you get this sense of dissonance. The choice of such structural liberty lets the film float free like a work in progress.

M C : *And yet in the midst of this free floating narrative, the major characters have a sense of real solidity.*

B B : Ugo, this cheese producer, this "casaro" turns milk into a solid. He's a strange man, sitting on a throne at the center of his fiefdom. I think it was Apollinaire who said, "Our image is noble and tragic like the mask of a tyrant." He has the nobility of his peasant origins the way Barbara has the nobility of her education. Primo is a bridge between a culture that's being destroyed and the present. His wife, for her part, has from the very beginning a kind of absolute faith in the bourgeois merchant economy. We pay, she thinks, and we get our son back.

M C : *You've often filmed in this region, but for this film you chose new landscapes.*

B B : Usually I shoot in the Po valley where the only reference points will be a church tower or a poplar tree. This time I went right into the hills for the first time. They're not far—about twenty kilometers away. I even went as far as the mountains. The forest where we were filming is a place I spent summers as a kid. It was there I made my first film, at fifteen. It was called *The Cable*, shot in 16mm. It was a ten minute film. My brother, who was eight at the time, went looking for the telepherique he remembered seeing there "as a child." The cables can be seen from time to time in the foliage, but he lost the trail in a stand of chestnut trees. It was a summer's afternoon's dream. So twenty-five years later I went back, and, being superstitious, I was a little afraid that this would be my last film because I was shooting it where I'd made my first one. Parma and its environs are a kind of microcosm for me. Going into the hills was a real adventure, a kind of exploration.

MC: *Tognazzi is from Cremone. Is there a big difference between his region and Parma?*

BB: No, the difference is mostly cultural; the landscape is pretty much the same, as is the appearance of the people. But Parma had the distinction of being occupied by the French and they pronounce their *r*'s like the French. There were French architects, pastry chefs, cabinet makers, whereas Cremone never experienced such an influence. And also in Parma we eat better than they do in Cremone. But the cheese factory which dates from the beginning of the industrial age is located in Cremone. Ugo was really the lord of this realm. Everyone from Cremone came to pay homage to him. Ferreri really understood Tognazzi's taste for good eating, his hedonistic side. He never forbids himself anything. That's what he's expressing when he kisses Laura and she tells him, "You've got guts," and he answers, "I'm never afraid *beforehand.*"

MC: *He also says to her another key phrase: "What's important isn't morality, it's sincerity." That's a very romantic conception of life.*

BB: But Primo is a romantic. He was a partisan during the war and a member of the Communist Party; he talks about "the cause." A lot of small industrialists in Emilia vote communist and they display a great deal of creative imagination in their work. They are real inventors with a huge amount of energy, and if the Italian economy is still functioning, it's undoubtedly thanks to them. Primo is the type of industrialist who can't accept the rules of the game dictated by the consumer society. Although he's on the inside of the economic logic of our system, he says — in a scene that was a cut — that, unlike the makers of TV's or cars or refrigerators who work with dead materials, he works with a living material, milk. The fermenting cheeses are all alive until you eat them: it was a source of pride for him as an industrialist. He also has guilt feelings associated with his social origins. And yet, when he speaks of collectives, he evidences a certain irony. He's a little what Olmo in *1900* would have become if he'd followed the route set out for him by our society. He has identified with what was the enemy for him when he was younger. In this sense, the film really speaks to the Italian present, to the constant cowardice of today. In the looks exchanged by the characters, we see the search for sincerity and at the same time the inevitable character of treason.

M C : *But you avoid directly focusing on the politics of the situation, the problem of terrorism.*
B B : We don't talk about it at all. I was more interested in showing the vertigo that takes hold of each generation when they find themselves face to face with the other one.

M C : *Which is summed up by Adelfo at the end of the film when he says to Primo, "Did I lead you here or did you follow me?"*
B B : When they go to the dance hall together, you get the impression that they're going to mass, right? In fact, Primo doesn't understand a thing about this generation, which doesn't even understand itself. For his part, as he says, "The sons who surround us are monsters. They sneer but they don't know how to laugh. Either they have too much scorn for their fathers or too much complacency. We don't know how to interpret their silence: are they crying for help or do they want to shoot us?" This last sentence is a variation on an article Pasolini published at the end of his life in the *Corriere della sera*. It was at the time he made *Salò*, a film I didn't like the first time I saw it because it was right after the death of Pier Paolo, but which I now find quite extraordinary, because he's really talking about his relationship with the younger generation. The truth of this work has nothing to do, really, with Sade or profligacy. It's much more an act of vengeance against young people who betrayed him by losing their innocence.

M C : *The title of your film brings to mind the irony of Gogol and the ambiguity of Dostoyevsky, suggesting the tonality of a Russian novel with its opaque characters.*
B B : There's something a little bit Russian for me in the Po Valley, with its snowy winters and its poplar trees which resemble the silvery birch trees of

Tchekhov. Dostoyevsky also wrote a short story called "The Dream of a Ridiculous Man." You have to interpret the title quite liberally. I think in today's Italy anyone who becomes ridiculous is tragic. And when you see that you've become ridiculous, you become tragic all over again. There's a strict connection between these two feelings, and I myself feel ridiculous when I look in a mirror. That's why this film is ultimately neither a satire nor a tragedy, but moves back and forth between these two terms.

M C : *It's not just the characters that are veiled in obscurity but the plot itself. Is he dead or alive? We keep asking that question.*

B B : In my view the film's spectators and Primo should be asking whether his son is dead. Barbara is the only one who believes he's alive. Adelfo learns he's dead in a confessional booth. But this confusion is meant to reflect the state of politics in Italy. In Moro's case as in Mattei's we know in fact *nothing* about their deaths. When I made *Before the Revolution*, I started out from a position of ambiguity, but it was more esthetic than cultural, more an adolescent's malaise about his relationship with reality. Today ambiguity is our daily bread; we no longer have any certainties, including facts themselves. When at the end of the film, Primo watches Giovanni, Barbara, Adelfo and Laura dancing, we can see that he's afraid, and he goes out to look for some champagne to get away from this spectacle. He no longer understands anything; he sees everything he has built crumbling and sees himself as powerless after having believed he was omnipotent.

M C : *We can even imagine that the son "organizes" his own kidnapping.*

B B : That's a possibility. There have been such cases in Italy. The son of an industrialist had himself kidnapped but died during the kidnapping: in order to make his family believe it was real, they gave him too much ether and he died. It was one of the most complex psychodramas of the Italian terrorist dramaturgy. I based my film on events I'd read about in the papers without being too liberal because I never wanted to get into all the little details of terrorism.

M C : *Morricone's music is put into a popular register.*

B B : Yes, it was inspired by popular waltzes and catchy tunes. He composed the music before the film based on certain melodies from Northern Italy using instruments like the accordion and bandoleer. For Barbara's character, and in particular for the night scene in which she meets Laura for the first time, we wanted to use a more cultured "French" score with references to Satie and Revel. I directed the film with this music running through my head since it had already been composed and that helped me shoot, as usual. I listen to a lot of music when I'm filming, morning and evening, whether it's Verdi, Prokofiev or Bernard Herrmann; it gives me ideas. This time it was the two themes of the film which directly guided me: the theme of the ridiculous man and Barbara's theme.

M C : *What's the opera aria he's humming at the end?*
B B : That's "Di Provenza il mar, il suol," the theme of Germont, Alfredo's father in *La Traviata*. It's a quotation from Visconti's *Obsession* where the husband sings at a talent show.

M C : *The film has a somber tonality which is almost oneiric.*
B B : This film had another ending. Primo was to wake up after the scene in the dance hall. That would have closed the loop with the sequence in his office at the beginning where he's having a nightmare. The story was a dream, like a premonition of something that was going to happen. The tone corresponded to the heaviness in his stomach after a birthday party where he's drunk too much. The film maybe kept this dreamlike quality — with the opening nightmare — through the use of the first-person narrative.

M C : *The more the character of Primo "comes down from on high" and returns to earth, the more Barbara's rises and seems to take flight.*
B B : In my view a psychodrama like a kidnapping pushes everyone involved toward their most extreme truth. Barbara seems to take flight but also seems to be a snow bride. When she is on the terrace waiting, wearing her pelisse, looking through the same field glasses he used at the beginning, she is viewed against a background of snow and sun. I like this change of climate which accompanies the sense of the film. You move progressively from the end of summer with the corn to autumn in the woods and then finally to winter.

M C : *All of your films speak about the family, even* Last Tango in Paris *where the relationship between father and daughter is essential.*
B B : I don't know if I'm condemned to speak about the family or if it's a deliberate choice. Obviously I haven't settled all my personal accounts.

I've been in analysis for the past twelve years and it's enough to look at my films to see where my analysis is going.

M C : *In your previous films (*Tango *and* Luna*), psychoanalysis was more explicit in a sense, as was politics in 1900. Here we don't see a trace of any theory. The Freudian symbols are never offered as such but instead are subsumed in the general opacity of the film.*

B B : There comes a moment in analysis where you stop dreaming, where you stop interpreting dreams, and seem to talk about something else. That's a little bit what's happening in this film. It's for this reason that I said a while ago that it's not as autobiographical as the others. It's as if I had gotten rid of certain ideological, psychoanalytical and political millstones, as if I needed to see things outside of these schemas, as if I was looking for the unexpected. If there's less of a position taken at the outset then everything gets more mysterious.

M C : *Where did you find the young actors Laura Morante and Vittorio Cavallo?*

B B : Vittorio is an actor well-known to a small circle of people. He works in the "off-" theater circles of Rome. He's of the generation of Benigni, who plays for students and intellectuals. This is a very different tradition than the major theaters of thirty and forty years ago where Tognazzi and Sordi were trained, but you find the same freedom and the same possibilities of advancement for new talent. Laura began doing theater two or three years ago. In the script their characters were very hazy because they were figures of Primo's dreams. They only got definition during the filming; since I don't know young people very well, they were very helpful to me in defining their roles. I mostly wanted them to represent the mystery of today's youth. I don't think all young people are mysterious. My generation's youth wasn't. Maybe because we were born after the war, my generation seemed very sunny. The youth in this film are more obscure—they both have black hair and a dark look. Laura and Vittorio were very nervous because they didn't know what was expected of them. And I could only help them on a day-to-day, shot-by-shot basis. I told them I knew what they were supposed to be when they were on camera, but that I would maybe never understand them in their totality. My relationship with them was like the one I have with the story: never knowing, never judging, never giving clear signals to the spectator.

M C : *Were there many non-professionals among the actors?*

B B : Yes, as in the majority of my films: the maid who dances the rock, for example, is a woman from that town. The creditors also come from that region. One of them already had a part in *1900*. The people dancing at the end are not professionals either. That's what's great about the cinema: to take documentary and make fiction of it. You get things from amateurs that you can't get from actors.

M C : *In your shots there are often several levels. In the city or on the road we see horizontal planes where different characters are in movement.*

B B : I try to make the interior life of my characters visible. The richness of the visual field is meant to render the contradictions of these people. These contradictions fascinate me in life. As a director, what interests me is a taste for contradiction, and therefore of risk. That's what I want to tell colleagues my age whom I like a lot but who don't have the courage to take risks. They defend themselves by claiming that they want to remain faithful to themselves. I, on the contrary, believe that you have to betray yourself.

M C : *What contradictions do you find in yourself?*

B B : If you look at my first films, *Before the Revolution, Partner,* and the cinema I'm making now, it seems pretty evident. I used to be for a cinema that talked about the cinema. It was, let's say, a cinema in the spirit of Godard. It was also very romantic, but I was enjoying myself and getting established. Now I'm still trying to get my footing, but in a way that is, I believe, more generous. In the sixties we felt panic at having to confront our public and invented theories to avoid having to confront the spectator. We voluntarily frustrated our need for love. From this point of view, I think I've changed a lot.

Bertolucci: The Present Doesn't Interest Me

GIAN LUIGI RONDI/1983

"IT'S BETTER TO TALK about the past rather than falsify reality to try to communicate with a public more and more degraded by the films they see." A return to the '30s with the adaptation of Moravia's novel *1934* will be filmed next spring and probably right after that an adaptation of Dashiel Hammet's *Red Harvest* (1929). A career in teaching about change has gradually evolved from a first phase, dominated by stylistic arrogance and a sado-masochistic relationship with his audience into a second phase in which monologue has given way to a search for dialogue.

Nineteen Questions for Bernard Bertolucci

Bernardo Bertolucci, forty years old, twenty years in his career, ex-child prodigy of the Italian cinema and today one of its most prestigious directors.

Q: *How do you happen to be in Rome? I thought you were supposed to be in Montana to begin shooting* Red Harvest, *adapted from Hammett's novel?*
A: We are in a temporary rest period. It often happens with big productions. The film is in a parking lot which will allow the producers, and especially the Italian producer who is in the U.S., Alberto Grimaldi, to review the situation and to study new production possibilities. I could sit around and wait for him to finish his review, but I've never liked sitting around

---

From *Il Tempo*, 2 January 1983. Reprinted by permission. Translated by Fabien Gerard and T. Jefferson Kline.

doing nothing, and so I'm already looking ahead to the production I'll
undertake after *Red Harvest.*

Q : *And that is?*

A : An adaptation of Moravia's last novel, *1934.* I've already requested a
screenplay from a young English writer Ian McEwan, whose novel *The
Cement Garden* and a short story *First Love, Last Rites,* are quite popular in
Italy. It's a new experience for me to have a scenario of one of my films
written by someone else who will work entirely independently from me.
The reason initially was because I was working with my wife, Clare Peploe,
Jonathan Demme and Marilyn Goldin on the scenario for *Red Harvest,* and
then when that was done, I realized that I could also try this experiment
of directing a film written by someone else. Now, in any case, given that
we're about to start filming next spring, I have begun working on the scenario myself. In any case I'd be making changes on the set of the film.

Q : *Have you already chosen the actors?*

A : The decision to shoot *1934* before *Red Harvest* was only made a few
days ago, so no agreements with any actors have been signed yet. Two
weeks ago, though, I met with William Hurt, in Hollywood, who struck me
as a possible lead, and, given that the main female character is a German, I
thought of Hanna Schygulla. But I haven't yet made any final decisions.

Q : *Why an American actor for the leading role?*

A : I see the film a bit differently from the way Moravia saw his novel. The
real protagonist in my view is Capri, during the thirties, which witnessed
the rise to power of fascism and Nazism in Italy and Germany. All around,
the world is going up in flames yet Capri, at the center of the action, is
doubly an island: on the one hand because as a popular tourist site for foreigners it is completely isolated, but on the other hand it is assaulted by
the changing world around it which will upset everything that went before.
The character has both faces of a German (the old romantic face and the
new Nazi face full of cynicism and aggression), and this suggests, I'd even
say *reveals* quite effectively the changes that are happening at this time
throughout Europe. The character of the young Italian, on the other hand,
who has a difficult relationship with the German woman (in the beginning, he believes her to be two different women and there is a lot of sus-

pense around this double identity) doesn't seem to me, as an Italian, to have enough distance vis a vis what's happening to bear witness to these social changes. That's why I thought it would be better to make him an American. Not being implicated in the rise of fascism and nazism, it will be easier for him to observe and understand these two directions that Eupope was beginning to take in these years.

Q :   *Again, "these years." In* 1934 *and in* Red Harvest, *the end of the '20s. The* Conformist *has left its mark on your films.*
A :   In America a strange thing happened to me. I met a young, widely reputed architect who told me: "*The Conformist* was a fundamental film for young American architecture. We have heard a lot about Fascist architecture; we read books about it and saw documentaries on it, but it was only in your film that its real face was revealed." He was referring specifically to the sequence of the EUR, and those great walls of white stone, to the backgrounds like theater sets. Mostly he was amazed by the whole visual idea of the film and found it hard to understand how a director of my age could have conceived of it. I explained to him that even though I wasn't old enough to have a direct memory of these years, I was greatly aided by the collective memory that was filtered through the films of that period. The true face of the '30s was often presented in detail by Italian, German and French films. I found this image in one film after another almost as if it were in my unconscious. And suddenly it came back up to the surface.

Q :   *But why the '30s especially? They're not positive years for any of us, especially in Italy.*
A :   I don't know. Through an identification, perhaps, since it was a period when our parents were young. And then, who knows? because I feel in me the beginnings of a kind of refusal of the present, a refusal which preoccupies me—of course I'm only speaking for myself—which in any case has nothing to do with a lack of interest. It's an awareness that the times we live in are becoming more and more depressing, and we're beginning to feel the repercussions of what Pasolini called "cultural homologisation." Local and national cultures are fading in importance and in many cases are completely losing their identity, being swept aside by a kind of "international style" in which it's no longer possible to recognize them. I spontaneously get the idea of looking at a period when culture still had a face, an individ-

uality. Without nostalgia, of course, because these years were not positive ones for us or for our country. Nevertheless, when we turn toward the past, we still have the present as a mirror and as a point of reference. I remember quite well that during the shooting of *The Conformist*, I felt that the film had a direct relationship with the times we were living through.

Q : *And 1934, what connection might it have with today's Italy?*
A : An extremely indirect, even subterranean connection. I'd say that the more time passes, the more I am convinced that the true message of the film — if we can still talk about "messages" which has become something of a joke — is the pleasure it affords the people who make it and the people who see it, the emotional pleasure. This is an idea I've only had for a short time, but even in the past I felt that a very important part of the cinema lay in the pleasure of seeing, the pleasure of feelings. For a long time, the left thought that the idea of pleasure was a right-wing idea. A huge stupidity. Also because when I talk about pleasure I'm not talking about frivolity and estheticism. And speaking of estheticism, think about how many times Visconti was accused of this! Empty accusations without any weight, now entirely forgotten, all the more so since the more you see Visconti's films the more beautiful and important they seem.

Q : *In 1934 will you give us "the pleasure of looking"?*
A : Visually, scenographically, they were the years of art deco, but aside from the fact that I don't know to what extent art deco may have reached Capri, I wouldn't like to use art deco in the decor (if you will permit this pun), but I'd like the viewer to feel it in the story, in the way it's told. From a cinematic point of view, I want to make a film in which shadows will have a special importance, great weight. The idea is still a bit vague and difficult to explain, but I feel that the more important the shadows are, the more value and meaning the film will have.

Q : *You and your... Diaspora. You travel a lot, you work abroad, sometimes like Antonioni, it's hard to know if you're still an Italian filmmaker.*
A : I've never felt entirely defined or even accepted by Italian cinema. I began making films in 1962. It was a time when Italian comedy was flourishing and I still loved neorealism, but it seemed to me that the most interesting cinema was French cinema. I felt much closer to Godard, to

Truffaut and to Resnais than to the film that was being done here in Italy at that time. So much so that today I think how ridiculous it was at the time that when journalists came to interview me I asked if we could speak in French because that was the language of the cinema I loved and, in a certain sense, felt I belonged to. I felt all the more comfortable in French given that in Italy my first films had no success either with the critics or at the box-office, whereas in France no sooner had my films arrived (I'm thinking especially of *Before the Revolution*) than they were hailed as "classics." In any case, I know that my films are also very Italian. *Novecento*, for example. Despite its multinational aspect and all those American and French actors, it could only have been an Italian film, especially with its melodramatic view of things which grew directly out of my practically atavistic love of Verdi. Even my last film, *Tragedy of a Ridiculous Man*, is an "Italian" film. Above all, this film was born of the malaise I felt living here for the last several years given the state of total indecision, nebulousness, doubt and uncertainty that has been weighing on this country. Now I feel that things have cleared up a bit. Perhaps now in our country people are beginning to live a little better than a few years back.

Q: *And this is why you're going to Hollywood?*
A: The idea of going there to shoot *Red Harvest* originated during the preparation of *Tragedy of a Ridiculous Man*. I also wanted to do it because I like change. My whole career, if you think about it, has been conducted under the sign of change. After *Spider's Stratagem*, for example, there was *The Conformist*, two very different films. Then after *The Conformist, Last Tango:* how could there be two any more different films than these? Then I did *1900*, which resembles neither *Last Tango* nor any of my other films. This need for change leads me to search not only for new themes, but for new subjects, to explore new worlds, new modes of production and other ways of life. In this sense, Hollywood was really a new world for me, but at the same time, *Red Harvest* put me in contact with a milieu entirely different from anything I'd experienced before, i.e., an American mining town in a period of major transition.

Q: *But I seem to recall that the idea of a film adaptation of* Red Harvest *was already on your mind when you were working on* Last Tango.
A: Yes, but it wasn't the film I'm writing now. At that time I saw Hammett's novel almost entirely as a political film from which emerged a story in-

spired by socialist syndicalism of the late '20s in America. For all intents and purposes, there were two protagonists with two very distinct ideologies: on the one hand a liberal, Continental Op, the detective whose mission was to destroy gangsterism in this western mining town where the action takes place, and opposite him, the syndicalist, Bill Quint, a Marxist. But the psychological perspectives are reversed, because the liberal turns out to be a revolutionary (like Hammett himself) and the Marxist ends up a traditionalist, a conservative. So as I said, everything was seen from a political perspective.

Q : *And now, have those perspectives changed?*
A : Yes, because I realized that, to be faithful to Hammett, the film's politics should be dissolved into the story and get filtered through the confrontations and reactions of the protagonists. In my first draft of the scenario, as a post-'68 Italian director, I had put politics not just in the foreground but also completely exposed. This was a mistake from both an aesthetic and a logical point of view. It was enough to get to know Hollywood and American audiences a bit better to understand this.

Q : *So this new* Red Harvest, *what will it be like?*
A : It will focus primarily on the detective, Continental Op, who arrives in Poisonville to clean up all the evil inflicted by the gangsters who have driven everyone crazy by their oppressive control of things: gambling, prostitution, alcohol, money lending. He acts a bit like the protagonist of Sergio Leone's *For a Fistful of Dollars*, or, if you prefer, like the hero of Kurosawa's *Yojimbo:* he rubs everyone out and ends up winning big. When he goes to leave, however, his mission completed, the city is like dead, which raises the question of whether all this evil he has eradicated wasn't in fact the sign of its life. Certain situations aren't always easy to understand at first glance.

Q : *Will Warren Beatty play the lead role?*
A : In June when Warren Beatty was in Rome, we talked a lot and did some more talking two weeks ago during my trip to L.A. At first I had thought of Robert Redford or Clint Eastwood or Jack Nicholson. I simply had to make up my mind, but with this postponement of the project until after *1934*, I'll need to see where things are. I can't ask anyone to wait for me.

Q: *How did you get to this "immersion in Hollywood" after your love affair with French cinema?*

A: It was precisely my love of French cinema that brought me to Hollywood. I came to the realization that what I liked in Truffaut's films, and even in Godard's, was the intelligent way they had proposed a new vision of American film. I loved Truffaut's films before getting a taste for Hitchcock, but one day I came to the realization that Truffaut's films were modeled on Hitchcock's. It's like with love, you realize that everything is the result of an original source of love. Moreover, when I talked with my friends in the New Wave, I realized that their deepest aspiration was to someday make films like they were made in Hollywood. This perspective is supported by Parisian criticism of the type read in *Positif* or in *Cahiers du cinéma*, which has begun to spill oceans of ink praising American techniques and citing certain Hollywood films as exemplary.

Q: *Especially at the level of dialogue.*

A: That's right. Dialogues were of my happiest surprises when I was working in Hollywood. In Italy we have perhaps the best directors in the world, but if you look closely, where their films are weakest is at the level of dialogue. In Italian film the dialogues (and often the scenarios) are written to be published; it's rare, on the other hand, that people write them to be spoken. In Hollywood, it's the opposite. Screenplays and dialogues are only a stage of the film as it's being created and everything is written as a function of the shooting. That's why, when you listen to an American film, you always feel it's real, without a hint of literariness. Because everything comes out of events and the recording of these events.

Q: *I see your "Hollywood immersion" was really total.*

A: But that's not all, and it isn't just a matter of that. I'm living a very unusual moment of my life when I'm open to all kinds of different suggestions. Japanese culture, for example. They invited me to a showing of *1900* in Tokyo. We stayed in Japan for two weeks, and I confess that I came away very impressed and full of nostalgia. It's another dimension, another rhythm, and naturally, another civilization. What do you make of all that? Should you give it all up, uproot yourself and go there? Paulo Rocha did, but I don't think I could manage to do it, but I feel the temptation is there. Even if it's only in my dreams. Imagine, with our friend Shibata, the daughter of Kawakita, I wanted to go kneel on the tomb of Ozu. "There is nothing on the tomb," Mrs. Shibata told me while we were looking for the grave in a little park where they also had a little Zen school, and I looked everywhere to find a stone on which nothing was written. Mrs. Shibata, however, stopped in front of a gray gravestone on which there was an ideogram. This is the one, she informed me. The meaning of this ideogram was "nothing." No name for Ozu, just the inscription meaning "Nothing."

Q : *Bernardo you've been on the cinematic barricades for twenty years now.*
A : As a man I still feel young, but as a director I could already be counted among the older generation. Twenty years is a long time, and maybe that's why I feel so transformed. When I started out, it was at the beginning of the '60s, and the fundamental cinematic problem we addressed then was "Qu'est-ce que le cinema" (Bazin's famous title, "What Is Cinema?"). You see I even say it in French. What mattered was technique and the study of the language of film and its exaltation, let's say, even a kind of stylistic arrogance. I needed to make *Partner* to understand this and to understand that the masochistic relationship I maintained with my audience wasn't the right way. It wasn't just with *Partner* I understood this, but I also had a profound intuition that my detachment from the audience was nothing but a terrible fear of the audience and therefore also a great desire, a need for an audience. Thus from the long monologue that constituted my early films, I moved on to films which were decidedly dialoged as you can see with *Spider's Stratagem* or *The Conformist*, until I allowed myself to be entirely invaded by the success of the big commercial films. Which, at a certain moment, was accompanied by a megalomaniacal trip, which coincided with the production of *1900*. Megalomania purely in the sense of production, and it's not coincidental that some directors of my generation then abandoned it, like Coppola or Cimino. Maybe it was inevitable, or maybe it was the necessary consequence of a period when we paid no attention to our audience. First there was nothing, then came the hunger for a colossal embrace by the public attempted by colossal productions. Now on the other hand, I'm again making less overtly ambitious films like *Luna* or *Tragedy of a Ridiculous Man*. With this new, contradictory and somewhat painful desire to privilege the past, hence the '30s setting of *Red Harvest* and of *1934*.

Q: *But we already noted that nostalgia didn't enter into this.*

A: No, but what is important is the painfulness of the present and the difficulty of representing it accurately. For me the experience of *Tragedy of a Ridiculous Man* was very frustrating. One of the qualities of this film is that it reproduced quite accurately the malaise we were living in Italy, but this aspect provoked a certain hostility from the public; to which was added the fact that the audiences that go to the movies today didn't identify with the film's protagonist, played by Ugo Tognazzi, i.e., with an older man. On the other hand I need now to make films that communicate, and if, to represent the present we can manage to communicate with audiences degraded by the average films that are out there, I must bow to the need for certain compromises that include falsifying the present, then I'd prefer to speak about the past. Yes, that's the way it is: I just have no desire for the present. But I don't want to make a theory out of this or make this refusal into some kind of final statement. But also, I would insist that when you make films you're always talking about the present. Even a historical costume drama can be related to the present.

I Was Born in a Trunk

ANDREA GARIBALDI,
ROBERTO GIANNARELLI AND
GUIDO GIUSTI/1984

I COULD SAY LIKE Judy Garland in *A Star Is Born:* "I was born in
a trunk in a Paris theater." I mean that somehow I am a "son of art." I
always knew that my father, besides being a teacher of art history in a high
school in Parma, was a poet. At home one could often hear a word used in
the most bizarre, funny and unexpected occasions: the word was "poetic."
My encounter with poetry was extremely natural; I wanted to imitate my
father and up to a certain point in my life, with the spirit of conformity
typical of children, I thought that as an adult I would become a poet, as
the son of a farmer would become a farmer, the son of a carpenter would
become a carpenter, and the son of a firefighter would become a firefighter.

My poetry school was my father and his environment, which was then
called "the farm." We lived about three miles from Parma at Baccanelli, a
cluster of houses on the road that goes to Pisa and then descends toward
La Spezia. There was our house, the "patronal," and near it were the houses
of the farmers called the "rustics." Surrounding these was our little farm,
not like the farm of *1900* in which these memories become gigantic. Baccanelli is more or less halfway between the city and the hills and from the
upper windows of the house, on very clear days, you could see the towers
of Parma on one side and the hills on the other. Beyond the hills there are
the Apennines with Casarola, the original village of the Bertolucci family,

From *Qui commincia l'avventura del signor…Dall'anonimato al successo, 23 protagonisti del
cinema italiano raccontano,* 1984. Reprinted by permission. Translated by Claretta Tonetti.

another place of my father's poems. We used to go there every summer on vacation after a month or a month and a half spent at Forte dei Marmi. Sometimes we stayed for two months in this mountain village without a road and inaccessible even to occasional tourists; the postwoman delivered newspapers some days and some days she did not.

As soon as I learned how to read, I found this apparently rather constricted universe in the first things I read, my father's poems. Thus he was for me sentry, cantor and king of his microcosm. There is a poem dedicated to my mother which says (I am quoting by heart): "You are like the white rose at the end of the garden, visited by the last bees. . . ." If I went to the end of our very small garden I would find this white rose. It is an example of how, for me, poetry was never something tied to school as it happens to almost everybody. It had to do with my home and my daily landscape.

I have a very vague memory, but I know that in my first years of life I was confusing the paternal and the maternal figures; I had fun calling my father "maddy" and my mother "dom." My mother was born in Sydney, Australia from an Irish mother and an Italian father; her family returned to Italy when she was two years old. I was proud of my grandmother whose name was Mulligan, and I liked the idea of being one fourth Irish. My mother, also a literature teacher, always accepted living partly in my father's shadow as a necessary image of extreme reassurance. I am not revealing any secret if I say that my father is a great hypochondriac, a very anxious man, as one can well understand from his poems since he says so constantly.

I gave my poems to my father to read, fortifying the game of imitation-competition that often exists between parents and children and is at the base of the entire dialectic of sons and fathers. I know of the existence of a notebook kept by my old nanny with my first verses written with an unsteady handwriting. Between the age of six and twelve I imitated the poems that we read in school, and I wrote verses in rhyme. I think I have a remarkable mimetic spirit: for this reason I later hid myself behind a camera since this is the most mimetic object in existence, a mirror in front of which one cannot lie (even if it is often used to spread lies).

Until I was twenty-five or twenty-six years old I always remembered my childhood and my adolescence as moments of great serenity, happiness and magic. I lived with a strange awareness of the passing of time because one of the fundamental elements of my father's poetry is the passing of time, the passing of hours, of seasons, of years, of minutes, of seconds. It was a childhood in the countryside, full of great imagination, of great games which are not permitted in the city and not permitted by the size of urban apartments; since then, even when we moved to Rome, I always needed a lot of space. It was a childhood inundated by the smells of the countryside, by games that trespassed into adventure and sexuality much earlier than would happen in the city. In the countryside, through examples given by animals and people, the discovery of sexuality is precocious. . . .

I went to elementary schools in Baccanelli and my companions were generally the children of farmers and of commuting factory workers, children of very poor families in the humble provincial post-war period. Sometimes I led them to steal grapes or tomatoes in the fields, but after having provoked this "theft," I was overcome by some kind of violent sense of property and like a repentant owner, I would send them away and we would argue. Again, the day after, I would lead them to repeat the same game out of sight of the farmers. I went to the city only to go to the movies. For a few years my father was also a film critic for the *Gazzetta di Parma* and he would take me along. Very early I started to see westerns and war films with Americans and yellow faces. As I returned to the countryside, I would repeat in games with the group of boys that came to our house the films that I saw; this way I was doing my first little productions in which I would of course save for myself the principle role . . . or the role of the person who was going to die. I remember this long period of my life up to the age of twelve as some kind of a long dream. Or so I thought until the age of twenty-five or twenty-six when I began psychoanalytic therapy.

Several of my films have to do with the countryside and therefore with the warehouse of memories of those years. One of my last films *Luna* derives completely from a memory, one of the first of my life: I must have been three years old, we were coming back from the house of my maternal grandparents, I was sitting in the basket hanging from the handlebar of the bicycle, my mother pedaled, I was looking at her, it was dark and I could see the very old face of the moon in the sky behind my mother's very young face. This image, buried for years, came back in a dream, and I thought that I could not understand . . . that I was confusing my mother's face with the face of the moon. Many people remember with anger, or they prefer not to remember, the childhood years and the years of adolescence. This is not my case even if now I know that those years contain the pains of later on, of adulthood. I am very tied to that period; one could not otherwise explain this slightly obsessive return to those places, searching for roots, like a private eye of memory, searching for those lights, for those faces....

When I was twelve, my family moved to Rome. I believed that my father wanted to do more than teach school in Parma and that he wanted to have contacts and relations with the Roman cultural life.... But what I just said seems to me an excuse. In reality I think that he also needed some kind of freedom from his father; he had to get away, to search perhaps, to demonstrate his own identity.

My father and my mother got themselves assigned to Roman schools. Then he began to work for a program on the radio; he was also an art critic and wrote about cinema for a paper called *Giovedì*. It was very traumatic for me to move from the countryside to Monteverde Vecchio; it was like being parachuted in enemy territory. There I stopped writing poetry. It was a kind of refusal. My father was saying: "Your vein has dried up." Monteverde Vecchio is a very pretty neighborhood with nice homes on a hill and little traffic and many gardens, but something was wrong ... for example, the change from the school companions of the countryside of Parma to the Roman companions: the former were mostly children of farmers, the latter belonged to the small Roman petty bourgeoisie and were mostly children of government employees. (The Ministry Of Public Instruction was near by.) I experienced what was supposed to be a social promotion as a demotion in lifestyle, because after all, farmers have something more ancient and are therefore more aristocratic than the petty bourgeoisie; it seemed to me that this demotion could be sensed from the type of values that these children, my new companions, had in comparison to the values that I left behind.

I did not write poems for three or four years, I went often to the movies instead. I used to go continuously to the three cinema houses of Monteverde Vecchio: one belonged to the priests and it was situated right under our apartment in the Piazza Rosalino Pilo, the second was the Del Vascello, and the third one was San Pancrazio, also run by the priests. The Del Vascello still exists; I filmed a scene of *Luna* in it, the scene in which Joe and Arianna, instead of watching the movie, see the ceiling opening and the moon appearing. The exterior and the corridors of this shot belong to the Adriano in the Piazza Cavour; but the interior was filmed at the Del Vascello for purely sentimental and, let's say, exorcistic reasons.

I tried to go the movies every day; I often went alone because my friends went only once a week. The problem was that they would show the same movie only two, three or four days, and this was very irritating. I did not yet go, as they say at Monteverde Vecchio, "inside Rome."

Whereas the films I saw in the countryside represented an escape from the countryside, now that I lived in the city going to the movies meant a return to the countryside, a two hour refusal of my surroundings, the horrible and charming piazza Rosolino Pilo and the city around it, a city that lived unaware of its "graffiti." It was the '50s; every school vacation we returned to my grandfather's house in the countryside. At the age of fifteen, during one of the great summers of Casarola, I filmed my first short movie, *La teleferica (The Cable)* and a few months after, during the winter, the second one *La morte del maiale (The Death of the Pig)*. Now I ask myself why I filmed them . . . maybe because I wasn't writing poetry anymore and I was telling myself: "Instead of writing poetry I will do something else, I will make movies."

I found out that a cousin of my father had at Casarola, in the mountains, a 16 mm Paillard-Bolex and I was able to get hold of it. The actors of *The Cable* were my brother, who was nine years old, and two cousins. After lunch, while the grown ups rested, Giuseppe left with the two girls looking for a cable that he had seen when he was a small child (who knows how small, since he was only nine.) They walked and walked far away in the fields. They arrived in the woods, and, without realizing it, they bumped into an abandoned cable with the cables collapsed and covered with grass a little as it was to be in *Strategia del ragno (Spider's Stratagem)* when the final scene shows grass growing on the tracks. Then my brother and the two girls got lost: after a moment of fear they found the right road again. That's all. It lasted ten minutes and I also added two or three captions.

After seeing something really materialized in that film, I no longer doubted that I would be a movie director. The film left me the impression that I could do cinema. From the moment I held the camera in my hands I felt like a professional movie director, I don't know why. It's as if objective reality coincided with a dream of childish omnipotence. Perhaps it was this kind of furious determination that led me to film my first movie at the age of twenty-one, the second at twenty three and so on.

Even the subject of *The Death of the Pig,* filmed a short time after *The Cable,* is something that returns in my films: it exists in *1900* and in *Tragedy of a Ridiculous Man.* Our farmer had only one pig and I filmed at dawn, when it was not yet day, the two pork-butchers who arrived on bicycles to kill the pig and then work on it as they still do nowadays. However I thought that their arrival on bicycles was not "epic" enough and so, I remember, I did two things. I asked the two pork-butchers to wear cloaks instead of coats, and I had them arrive in the middle of the fields, on foot on the snow in order to begin the movie in a way that seemed to me more exciting. Most of all I did some *mise en scéne.* They didn't understand and kept saying, "He is taking a picture of us. . . ." *The Death of the Pig* was completely seen through the eyes of a seven- or eight-year-old farmer boy: his mother gives him his backpack because he has to go to school, but he turns around and hiding, observes everything. The pork-butchers enter the pigsty with a sharp "corrador" with which they kill the animal. One turns the pig on its back holding it by the front legs, and the other stabs its heart. Maybe because of the presence of the camera, the pork-butcher was nervous and missed. The furious pig came out of the pigsty and ran into the courtyard bleeding all over the snow. And so for the first time I got a demonstration of how in the movies chance can be fundamental; in fact that pig running through the snow soiling it with blood, though filmed in black and white, seemed to me like something that I could never have foreseen; this somehow marked me: since then I always tried to leave as much space as possible to chance in my films.

At this point I miraculously started to write poems again. When I saw that another way lay open to me, I heaved a sigh of relief that I was not condemned to be a poet. The poems written in those years were then published in the collection entitled *In cerca del mistero (In Search of Mystery)* which won the Viareggio Prize for first work in 1962, the same year as *The Grim Reaper,* my first film.

After *The Death of the Pig,* when I was seventeen, I thought about a more ambitious film, the story of a mountain priest who during the war helped the partisans and was then killed by the Germans. I filmed only a few shots; the project was too ambitious, and I needed more money to buy more film. But with this material, with these sequences of a never made film, I went to visit Cesare Zavattini, a great friend of my father. Zavattini in the '20s was a young substitute teacher at the boarding school Maria Luigia of Parma, and my father was one of his pupils. Trembling, I organized a showing for Za, who fascinated me. There was also a boy my age, maybe a little older, blond with blue eyes, who when the film was over, while Cesare was saying, "Hurrah! We have a director!" said with a little grimace: "Too many low angle shots." I hated him a lot, but when years later we met at the Venice film festival, and I was no longer seventeen, we became great friends and discovered that we had the same passion for film. It was Adriano Aprà who started his career as a film critic on my film. Some years later he wrote encouraging and very intelligent things about *Before the Revolution,* which almost every Italian critic detested.

After passing my baccalaureate exams I asked to go to Paris as a reward. I really loved French cinema, and I felt closer to the French directors than to the Italians. It was a time when Italian style comedy was the vogue and neorealism was on its way out. I took this trip to go to the Cinémathèque Française. It was my initiation; I saw many films and when, later on, I filmed *The Grim Reaper,* I said, with a little arrogance but also a bit naively, to the journalists who were interviewing me, that I would have preferred to speak French since French was the language of cinema. I was convinced that everything, everything that was new, was happening in France.

I remained in Paris a month, and going around the city, I felt as if I were moving inside *A bout de souffle (Breathless)* by Godard, a movie that was completely filmed outside, night and day, in Paris. The great screen of the Cinémathèque at the Palais de Chaillot remains imprinted in my memory. The hall was big, long and narrow, and the screen occupied the entire end wall. I asked Henri Langlois, the founder and the leader of The Cinémathèque and indirectly of the New Wave, the reason for it. He answered: "It's for Rossellini's films. Because," he continued, "his frames could expand from one moment to the other, upward, downward, on the right and on the left and therefore we must be ready."

I came back to Italy and a year or two later served as Pasolini's assistant director for *Accattone. Breathless* had just been released in Rome, and I was trying in every possible way to convince Pier Paolo (Pasolini) to see it. He was not a *cinéphile*; he knew very few films, he liked Dreyer's *Joan of Arc* (one can see this in *Accattone,* which is a series of close-ups like *Joan of Arc*), and he liked Chaplin. I felt he should go to see *Breathless* in order to understand what was happening in the world of cinema outside Italy. I was completely in love with this film, and I wanted Pasolini to share this love. He greatly disappointed me because finally one day, it was a Monday and I had stopped insisting, he told me: "By the way, yesterday I went to see your *Breathless.*" It was then playing somewhere in Torpignattara, and he told me that his friends, the local boys, laughed a lot and jeered at the film. They were right, Pasolini said, because the film was pretentious. I was almost personally offended. A few years later Pier Paolo wrote a long poem in which the refrain is "As in a film by Godard...." Pier Paolo converted completely to Godard and that was for me a great victory.

I had known Pasolini since I was a boy because he often met with my father; they were very good friends. I saw him for the first time not long after our arrival in Rome; when I was twelve or thirteen years old, he dedicated a poem to me entitled *A un ragazzo (To a Boy)* in which he tells the story of his brother who joined the partisans leaving home with a pistol hidden in a book by Montale, and who died tragically in a battle between catholic partisans and Yugoslavian partisans. My father helped him a lot; when Pasolini wrote his first novel *Ragazzi di vita* my father took him to Garzanti. Pier Paolo lived at Ponte Mammolo; then he moved several times coming always closer to the center of the city, first in via Fonteiana then in via Carini where my parents still live. He had an apartment on the first floor and we on the fifth. Pier Paolo somehow was a father figure. Something similar happened later with Godard. Later on in the mid-sixties, when I felt a certain distance between me and Pasolini, I thought that he had pushed me away a little. Instead, as always happens with two people, the responsibility was on both sides. I was very infatuated with Godard and since I was born to cinema with Pier Paolo, maybe he experienced my new passion as a kind of treason; the disciple betraying the teacher.

I used to ask Pasolini to read the poems that I wrote in those years, and I greatly felt his influence. At that time he did not work in the movies with the exception of some screenplays *La notte brava, Una giornata balorda* and a sequence which he wrote for *La dolce vita*. Then one day, suddenly, we met in the stairs as we often did, and he said: "You know, maybe I will make a movie...."

The memory of *Accattone* is for me the memory in which the dream of cinema becomes reality. Since we lived in the same building, my first duty in *Accattone* was to accompany Pier Paolo from home to the set. We always met downstairs early in the morning, and while driving his Giulietta (he always drove Alfa Romeos), he would tell me the dreams he'd had the night before; he attached great importance to them during shooting. Then, when we arrived on the set, I had to take care of the pimps. There was a group of six or seven real pimps, Accattone's friends; I had to make sure that they memorized their lines and I had to keep an eye on them. They may have given their profession as jewelry salesmen or similar things, but they were pimps, and I must say that they were generally nice. Pier Paolo always surrounded himself with people who had some special quality; he never had uninteresting people around. That was, after all, a lesson. Because I was twenty years old, and one is a great moralist at twenty, I believed exploiters were totally evil. But on closer inspection, things were slightly different. In general, these young men were absolutely dominated by their women, and they did not have any real authority. They were worried about rushing home in their convertibles to boil water for spaghetti so that dinner would be ready at two in the morning when their women came back from work. They really loved Pier Paolo who knew how to make himself loved because he always knew how to establish an equal relationship with others. Pasolini had a great mimetic spirit; one can understand this even by reading his works: the absorption of the Roman dialect in his novels is extraordinary. He could mime not only the speech of his characters but also their way of thinking and their way of dressing. The first time I saw him it was a Sunday afternoon. He was wearing a blue Sunday suit, a white shirt, and he had combed his hair in a wave . . . he was very strange, he looked like a kid from the slums.

After a few days of shooting he did his first dolly shot, and it was rather extraordinary. I said to myself: something just happened here; Pier Paolo just invented the dolly shot. It was very important for me to watch a director discovering a new medium, a new language, with the talent that Pier Paolo had in inventing cinema, especially given that he'd come to film from literature. It was more exciting than working on the set of a director with a lot of experience. It was like a loss of innocence.

I don't believe that a technical school is important; all you need is three days on the set to understand how things are. I didn't go to a film school. The only real initiation is to see as many films as possible. The *Cinémathèque Française* was a great cinema school precisely for this.

After *Accattone* things moved very quickly. Producer Tonino Cervi had a short treatment written by Pier Paolo entitled *The Grim Reaper,* but Pasolini was already thinking about *Mamma Roma* and suggested to Cervi: "Why don't you have Sergio Citti and Bertolucci write the screenplay?" Cervi said: "All right, if you can keep an eye on them..." and he started looking for a director for the film. Citti and I wrote the screenplay. Cervi was enthusiastic and said to me, "Do you think that you would be able to direct the film?" So, with total irresponsibility on both parts we embarked in this adventure. Cervi risked a lot and I am very grateful to him. *Accattone* was a success; therefore *The Grim Reaper* had to follow the "Pasolini genre."

I was really very young, twenty-one years old; I had to fight to get credibility with the crew, one of those cynical Roman crews, and I think that it happened during the first days. We were filming in black and white. We didn't have much film or much time, only six weeks. The chief cameraman told me that he had rarely used the dolly so much: the camera was extremely mobile. I don't know what inspired me, certainly something that cannot be defined rationally...expressive necessity maybe. Most of all I just enjoyed being on the set, being the director; there was a *jouissance,* an enjoyment that, it seems to me, is present in all my films and that I discovered as one of the goals of my cinema. I don't mean that the pleasure of the film maker is necessarily communicated to the audience, but for me the pleasure you feel seeing a film is very important.

At the Venice Film Festival, *The Grim Reaper* was presented in the session on new films; a lot of critics didn't like it, a minority loved it. The fact that I had also won the Viareggio prize with my poems provoked envy and dislike. Many people found me obnoxious. Some critics wrote, "It is a Pasoliniesque film." But in my opinion it's not that at all; it doesn't have the religiosity of Pasolini's films and visually it was also very different. It seems to me that *The Grim Reaper* already contained many themes that were to be found in my later films.

Pasolini came to see the film and said: "So many dolly shots, so much panning! This camera is never still!" He liked my second film, *Before the Revolution,* more. He also wrote an essay entitled *Cinema of Prose and Cinema of Poetry* in which the example of cinema of prose was Ermanno Olmi's *Il tempo si è fermato (Time Stopped)* and the example of cinema of poetry was *Before the Revolution.*

During those years I was not part of the world of Italian cinema. I had French and Brazilian friends, and I was trying to go abroad as much as possible. As I already said, I did not feel I was an Italian director. In Italy, very few of my contemporaries were making films. The only one who comes to my mind is Marco Bellocchio, whom I held in high esteem; even if we rarely saw each other, we shared an unspoken rapport expressed primarily in the way I was watching his films and he was watching mine. A few times I met the director whom I adored from a distance: Roberto Rossellini. He had been completely refused in Italy and rediscovered by the French. Ultimately I saw him through the lens of *Cahiers du cinéma*. The naturalness with which he spoke of his work impressed me greatly. I asked him about his films; I thought that the birth of modern cinema occurred with *Viaggio in Italia* (*Voyage in Italy*) and that Antonioni's *L'avventura* (*The Adventure*), another fundamental film, would never have been made without *Voyage in Italy*. I believed that the road that all those who spoke of contemporary characters and stories had to take was in that absolutely unpicturesque, un-folklorist South seen through the Anglo-Saxon eyes of George Sanders and Ingrid Bergman. The extraordinary thing about Rossellini was his ability to move through the forest, through the jungle of production. He was genial and very cynical at the same time, but his cynicism served the purpose of focusing on very precise things and then allowing his geniality to express itself. He created conditions in which he could do what he wanted.

After *The Grim Reaper* I went through a difficult period until I met Mario Bernocchi; he was a young Milanese industrialist who loved cinema. I asked him to read *Before the Revolution*. He liked it and decided to produce it. The following story may be instructive, on a practical level, for those who are now starting to make films. We needed a distributor and so I went to Milan to speak directly to old man Rizzoli. I had to evercome a series of barriers, of secretaries, but finally I was able to meet him: "I am sorry, but I have to return to Rome in the afternoon, I must see you now." He said: "O.K. Come with me, young man."

I entered his office as a terrorist commando enters an Embassy; I had never seen Rizzoli before. He received me and he liked me. He kept me for several hours and took me for a tour of the new departments at Rizzoli's. Then he started talking about himself. In the meantime I had told him in a few words the plot of the film, and he told me that he would do it. We were talking about a very small amount of money—I believe I asked for thirty million lire.

Two weeks before beginning to shoot, I called Mario Bernocchi, the producer, and spoke with his secretary who told me, "Too bad! Mister Mario was drafted." He was twenty-six or twenty-seven years old; I was twenty-three. "He was drafted? But we have to start shooting in two weeks." "The police came. He had to go." "Where is he?" "In Palermo at the training camp."

I left immediately for the training camp and looked for Mario Bernocchi. He was under arrest because he had argued with his sergeant. I was able to talk with him and said, "What are we going to do? The film is about to start." He answered: "I'm very sorry, but I'm in here and I can't do anything." Then we started thinking, and he remembered the name of a person who knew an important member of the Sicilian Mafia. I left the barracks and made a few calls. . . . After a while I was able to find this important person. He took me to one of the best restaurants in Palermo, and I used the only reasoning that could work with this head mafioso of the old Mafia. I told him: "Bernocchi is an important person in Milan, his is a family of well established industrialists. . . ." My point was: you help him and one day he could help you. This gentleman had heard about them; there was also a bicycle race called the Bernocchi Cup. So in three days, through the Mafia, I pulled Mario out of military service. Production of the film started on time.

Before the Revolution was my first autobiographical film, a film in which I pour myself out completely; it also marked my return to Parma. In Italy it had no success; just a brief showing and, in general, very negative reviews. One important critic practically wrote, "Bertolucci, change your profession." When the film was shown in Cannes, the French critics talked about a "discovery," the American and English critics of a "revelation"; the film won the "Jeune Critique" prize and the "Max Ophüls" Prize. I'd never seen anything by Max Ophüls and so I looked for his films; now he is one of my favorite directors. After *Before the Revolution* I went to Paris and met Henri Langlois, Jean-Luc Godard, Agnès Varda. I met these people knowing that they were responsible form my extremism of those years. In a way I had been adopted by *Cahiers du cinéma*. On the one hand there was film making which was considered to be *praxis,* and on the other side *Cahiers* represented theory and reflection; but I felt that the two things ought to be combined. Therefore, for four or five years, until 1968, I did no work because I refused to accept things that were not what I immediately wanted to do; I wouldn't even consider the possibility of compromise. I believe that the knot of those years of inactivity was only untied much later. In other words I was telling myself: you can't think about the audience; the best way to think about the audience is never to think about them at all. The cinema I made and appreciated in those years was after all a cinema of cinematic analysis, a cinema about cinema. There was such fear of emotionally investing in the audience, of offering oneself to the audience and then being rejected, that the result was a kind of complete block hidden behind current theories. This is, I believe, a mechanism that blocked many others of my generation who were paralyzed by the idea of a cinema that was after all the refusal of the audience, almost a cinema against the audience, a somewhat masochistic cinema. This does not happen to young directors today; they don't have these problems, maybe because we overcame them. Luckily for them, they are more cynical and very pragmatic.

Bernardo Bertolucci: Back from China

ULRIKE KOCH/1987

U K : *Bernardo Bertolucci as a symbol of Western "Leftists" and a European doing a movie about China; what could be the expectations of today's young people (the public), the so-called '68 generation and the Italian Communist Party?*

B B : I am not a symbol. Period. I have feet, legs, a bottom, and I do movies. And especially, if you talk about young people, they know very little about the past that goes more than three, four years back. So young people aren't expecting anything. Also, I don't like to think about the public, the audience in terms of "young people" and the "old generation" because it's the beginning of giving up. The audience should remain in the darkness of the movie theatre, a mass of human beings without a face, with an interclassist identity. The moment you start to read the faces of the audience, you start to do acrobatic movements in order to please this audience. And that is the moment when you betray them, and yourself.

U K : *'68 generation?*

B B : I would like to say, like a travel agent: "come with me, I'll bring you to China." In fact, there's a bit of that because it is the first Western movie done in China about modern China, China of this century. However, the movie doesn't want to be a brochure for tourism. It is much more a story—that could only happen in China—of one man. It's a private story. To make a long story short: it is the story of a man who wants to walk out of his house and they never allow him. This is the minimum resumée of the

Reprinted by permission.

Last Emperor. I didn't go to China with all the prejudices that I could have had towards China in '68, which were full of aestheticism and illusions. I am going to China at a time when one can no longer have any illusions, for example, about the nightmare of the Cultural Revolution, and about the fact that many things that have occurred in China since "Liberation" have been criticized by the Chinese themselves. It doesn't make sense to use the term "Western Left" today in the same way that it was used ten years ago.

UK: *The Italian Communist Party?*

BB: My relationship with the Italian Communist Party is a kind of senti-mental, strong, affectionate, and again aesthetic relationship. The Italian Communist Party, I think, is the only party one can eventually vote for in Italy, and that's all. And I think, with *Novecento,* I try to analyse and to rep-resent my relationship with what could be for me in some paradoxical way my church, my religion.

Also, China is in such fast movement. When I came back from China, the thing that shocked me here was the kind of still image of my country. My country, like maybe Germany, is in a moment of quite good economic results, but there is this sensation of immobility. Italy seems still to me, even if the economy is dynamic. I was shocked because I was coming from a country which is moving very fast—China. And I was very, very im-pressed by the great energy which runs in China from every direction and how fast the people there move.

UK: *Would it have been possible to have done the movie before, during or after the Cultural Revolution?*

BB: I don't think so. It was even impossible to go to China during the Cultural Revolution. I don't see a Western crew, a Western director with all his people shooting the story of the *Last Emperor,* and being free to say what I wanted to say about this character.

UK: *Did you encounter any objections or restrictions while doing the movie?*

BB: The Chinese had to approve the screenplay, of course. But, in fact, we had two meetings on two different versions of the screenplay, and then we had the meeting on the final approval; and there were no discussions, apart from historical inaccuracy which we were pleased to correct. Maybe sometimes, with Mark Peploe, my writer, we've been a bit rude with the figure of the emperor, and the Chinese were trying to make us more smooth, less rude. There was a scene, which we then cut, where the emperor at ten years is trying to escape from the Forbidden City. He was in a tunnel under the level of the street, and he was seeing the life outside the tunnel which had this grill at the end. While he was looking at what was going on in the street, a camel came and sat right there, closing the view—and shit on the young emperor, who was covered with camel shit. And the Chinese told us that it was a bit of bad taste to cover the emperor with shit. That amazed me a lot. In fact, I was using a kind of transgression which is typically Western. Apart from that, there were a few historical mistakes, and they told us and we changed them, and there were some mistakes in the Chinese formalities. They never said anything against our reading of the story of Pu Yi.

Maybe during shooting there were some practical problems. We were doing the movie with the Beijing Film Studio, and they are not used to our methods of work. They are very slow in doing movies, and we are very, very fast. Sometimes, they were spaced out by our system of work. Sometimes, the old Chinese bureaucracy was appearing in the figure of an employee of the Forbidden City. For example, there are hundreds and hundreds of gates and doors in the Forbidden City, and every doorman has keys, and at 5 o'clock all the doors were closed. So we couldn't get the equipment which was just behind the door because all the keys were going to the office, to be seen at the office. And that was slowing down the work. But those are little things. In fact, we shot every day for sixteen weeks; there were never big, big problems. The opposite, we found a smiling collaboration in there—smiling because the Chinese, as everybody knows, smile a lot.

U K : *Would China accept "cheap" productions, for example, China only as an exotic background?*
B B : I think they are ready for cultural and economic exchange; more than that, they are *looking for* cultural and economic exchange. They are waiting with open arms for any kind of enterprise.

U K : *Why didn't China invest in the movie?*
B B : I think they are right. Why should they invest in something which they don't know, which is the market of the world? China had been cut

off from the movie world since Liberation because they were, they wanted to be, isolated. I think, first of all, they don't have a lot of Western money. They could have invested with local things; but between the choices of putting things like work, people, extras, etc. in a formal investment in the production and seeing some interest and profits later or earning money immediately, they chose the second thing. I think they are right; they are not taking any risk. Also, they don't have any way of knowing what this movie is and what it represents in the production of the world outside China. Because they don't know it, it would have been a blind investment.

U K : *You started working on this project three years ago and had been to China several times during pre-production. Did you have to alter your conception, your vision of the movie when you had to face the reality of shooting in China?*
B B : In the beginning, it was of course a very utopic project, which was through the figure of Pu Yi to tell the history of China of this century. But I realized, as it happened to me all the time, that I am much more interested in the destiny of a man than in history itself. So I became more and more close to the story of the character than to the history of China. And shooting the movie focused a lot on the character. This is a movie with one character at the center more than a dialectic between many characters, even if it's full of characters. But it comes from an autobiography; it is more or less seen through the filter of his eyes. That means somebody who is condemned to prison, all his life, since the age of three. To show China outside the walls of the prison would have meant to abandon the character, to abandon Pu Yi, and that was impossible. When you shoot the reality, it makes you choose or, I would say, the reality chooses for you. This reality has been to stay with the character all the time.

U K : *This was not different from your vision?*
B B : My vision doesn't exist, not a fixed vision; the vision is in progress. So it was very different, every day things were different from my vision. I think cinema is the language of reality. Reality expresses itself through literature, poetry, music, painting, sculpture, but especially cinema. Literature uses symbolic elements in order to talk about reality, or let's say, reality talks about itself through words. Those words are symbolic. The word "woman" is symbolic; when you read "woman" in a book, everybody thinks of a different woman. In a movie, if you show a woman, it's that

woman, not any other woman, so it's less symbolic, it's more realistic. Cinema is the language that reality has chosen to represent itself, more than any other art, any other language. You have to accept that, and you have to accept all the eruptions, the intrusions of life into the movie. You must in fact try to open the maximum number of doors to allow life to enter the movie. And the Forbidden City is full of doors.

U K : *Did you find all the doors that you were looking for?*
B B : The doors are often closed, they must be opened.

U K : *Didn't you feel limited by the reality of China?*
B B : On the contrary, no.

U K : *What about everyday reality, people who don't immediately understand, who have different habits?*
B B : The moment you say that they don't immediately understand, you are also saying we also do not immediately understand. I tried to absorb the most that I could, and above all not to hide behind my Western cultural categories. I attempted to go to China forgetting as much as possible my neurosis, my European intellectual perversions. When there were problems, I tried to employ the art of dialectics; that is to say, to contrast the reality that assailed me with my own ideas and to see what emerged.

U K : *Did China surprise you in one way or another?*
B B : Yes. You see, the Chinese are four thousand years old, so it's easier to be surprised by them than to surprise them. They are a much more ancient people than we are. I hope that my film will have the curious, fascinated and eternally surprised vision of someone who is seeing China for the first time.

For example, I didn't know that China and the Chinese would give the sense of a nature sublime and passive, sophisticated and feminine, that is very different from the Japanese for instance, who are, on the contrary, rather virile, hard. China is soft, and Japan is hard. I didn't know this, it's what I discovered in China.

U K : *Have you become a Taoist?*
B B : You have to be a Taoist if you want to survive in China. In that sense, yes. And also a Confucian. You have to be three things, Confucian, Taoist,

and Marxist. This is the incredible thing. The Chinese cultural river never stopped, so China never dropped Taoism and Confucianism. Even after Liberation they were able to harmonize together the old philosophies, the old religions and *le vent d'est,* that is, the ideas of revolution. I'm less Taoist now that I'm back in Rome. In China, in order to understand the reality and the people in front of me, I had to . . .

U K : *You also have a lot of dialectics in Taoism; and the Chinese art has been very influenced by Taoism . . . ?*
B B : In reality, I know very little about it. But reading the gospel of Taoism which is the *Dao De Jing* has been very important to me.

U K : *Did you miss Freud in China?*
B B : I didn't miss Freud because I couldn't drop it. Freud has a big part in the root of my personality. But I love contaminations. I love purity in other people; I'm not. If you look at my movies, they're not pure. But it's my nature, and it's what I like.

One of the places I love most in China is Shanghai because it's an example of the greatest architectural *contaminazione.* Where you have Western architects feeling quite free because they are far from the West, free to be bizarre. So you have a mixture of New York, London, Paris architecture, even Italy in Tianjin. In Shanghai you have this Western volume with Chinese influence; it's very strange how the shape of buildings which could be in New York is emerging in the Chinese atmosphere. It's irresistible in some way, especially if you pan down from skyscrapers to the ground and you see twelve million Chinese, and you have the feeling the Chinese have invaded the West and you are the only Westerner remaining there. This is a dream I had once, that I was walking very early in the morning in Shanghai, I think I was on Nanjing Road, and I felt I was the only Westerner in all Shanghai and it was a kind of ecstasy.

U K : *Could Freudian concepts by incorporated into Chinese thought?*
B B : Now, there is a tendency to think that Freud was perfect for Vienna's middle-class society in the years between the turn of the century and Nazism when he had to leave for London; that that social environment was where Freudian therapy could be at it's best. I don't think that this is true; I think that Freud had a much more universal soul. Even so, I think that Freud is an instrument for comprehension.

U K : *Which doesn't exist, has no equivalent in China?*
B B : I don't know. It would evidently conflict with all that exists in the
Chinese culture. Freud is based on individualism whereas the oriental culture is rather collective. So, there would already be this big problem to
overcome. Art in China belongs in the collective domain. I worked for
months and months in the Forbidden City, and no one was ever able to
tell me which architect was responsible for which building, which sculptor
for which sculpture, who was responsible for the decor..., this just isn't
known. In any small Italian church, they know exactly which monastic
order constructed the church, who was the commissioner—who disbursed
the money, who were the architects and painters who made the frescos,
and they are very proud to know this. For example, in a madonna by
Raphael or Masaccio, there exists an artistic unity that is the poetic representation of an often conventional situation and the precise expression of
the identity of the creator. In China, this doesn't exist. In Western art, the
presence of the creator in the artistic work forms a part of the artistic object.
In China, to get back to the Forbidden City, instead of reflecting the creator of an artistic work, things are there only to reflect one thing, the
Emperor, who is the representative of the Chinese people. The Emperor is
a collective moment. Everything is done and organized in such a way that
there is always a throne in a room. Real or imaginary, but there are hundreds of thrones in the Forbidden City. And I don't think that the Emperor
sat on all these thrones; they are all there to remind you of the Emperor, and
they are the only reason for the existence of this place. Thus, to be three
years old and to find oneself in this place must have been very traumatic.

U K : *Except for Peter O'Toole, you were facing only Asiatic actors and people.*
What have been the problems in directing them? Has there been a difference
between actors from Mainland China and those from Hong Kong or the U.S.A.?
B B : I will never forget Victor Wong, who in the movie is the first tutor of
Pu Yi, who is a Chinese-American coming from San Francisco. The second
or third night, we had dinner together. I'll never forget the childish amaze-
ment in his eyes; he was saying: "that's incredible to be here, have you
seen how many Chinese there are in the streets...." He's a Chinese, and
he was looking at the Chinese with American eyes. It would have been
very nice to do some video work about all these Chinese-Americans coming to China for the first time, discovering their roots for real. They're used

to their Chinatowns. I tried as usual, as I told you before, to take the part of reality, to be also sometimes violated, raped by reality. I always try to turn into material for the movie what is in front of the camera. *Questo stupore,* this stupor of certain Chinese Americans, I tried to use it. Generally, however, I would have preferred Chinese of the People's Republic, but it was not possible.

U K : *Why?*

B B : Unfortunately the film is in English, so I was forced to use English-speaking actors. Since there were very few of those in China, we had to have them come from abroad. But John Lone, who plays the emperor, lived in Hong Kong until he was eighteen years old, so he knows China well; having been an actor in the Peking Opera of Hong Kong, he also is familiar with Chinese culture. The Empress and the secondary wife of Pu Yi are both actresses from Shanghai. The prison's governor is one of the most important actors of Chinese theatre. There are other actors who were not born in China, but generally speaking, I was able to use many native Chinese actors. There is also a great deal of Chinese reality in the movie, which gave me the confidence to use Chinese-American actors. Let me repeat: I love contaminations, and I love contradictions.

U K : *What is the story of the movie? A man under changing circumstances or a man in the process of changing?*

B B : It's a story of a process, of a voyage from the center of the night—of darkness—towards the light. It's also the story of a healing, of someone who was injected with the syndrome of omnipotence.

U K : *What happened during the process? What does he get out of it?*

B B : One has to see the movie. I'm not going to tell the story of the film. Otherwise, there is no longer any need to see it.

U K : *What happened, this process that we will see in the film, is its origin in politics or culture, Mao or Confucius?*

B B : I believe that it is the Confucian aspect of Chinese communism. Instead of chopping off the head of the Emperor, they want to re-educate him. This has many implications. It means that what is true for the communists was true for the Chinese of the past: man, and man's origin, is good. It's the circumstances that will change man. So, there is a confidence in man which is very Chinese. Perhaps this is also due to the fact that Mao, in 1949, found that there were important forces which were lost because they were either Guomindang or enemies of the revolution, and that it was necessary to gather them back for the good of China. These were intellectual, military and economic forces. Pu Yi was told "You are here to change. If you do not, you will never get out of here." In the beginning, I believe, he didn't think that he could change. How to change? Through the analysis of his errors. So they obliged him to reflect about himself, which was, I believe, extremely painful for him to do, because his life was full of suffering. He had always lived in prison, his entire life, in different types of prisons. That is to say, that prison for him was also a protection from life. He also might have liked to sabotage his possibility of leaving this protective environment. A great change was necessary for him to become an ordinary citizen. He was unhappy, but even so, extremely protected.

U K :   *Could one say that this movie is a fairytale?*
B B :   It is the story of a man who has problems growing up, who is rather regressive. His itinerary is to become an adult, that is to say, when he enters prison, at the age of forty-five. In that sense, he has a tendency to look at life as a fairytale.

U K :   *He himself sees life in this way?*
B B :   Yes. Even the Chinese, when they speak about China, look at it with curiosity, as if China were mysterious even to them.

U K :   *I have heard you speak about a "true fable," or a "seductive parable." What did you mean by this?*
B B :   Also in life, you can live your life—not necessarily like a fairytale, but like a novel. All this is connected to the desire that you have to represent. The moment you represent, you create novels. That is to say, the fever to tell a story, one tells a story with a kind of fever, I find. Perhaps for me, telling a story is a way to understand life. All my films help a little to understand bits of life.

U K :   *The movie gives a rather negative representation of the Japanese. Is this in contradiction with China's attitude towards Japan today?*

B B : Not at all. There is an immediate economic attitude that presents itself. Japan is obviously the closest capitalist country to China. And the Chinese want to do business with Japan, thus they are very open with the Japanese. On the other hand, there is the collective attitude that has evidently still not forgotten what happened in the past, first during the invasion of Manchuria, followed by Japan's invasion of all China. Chinese schoolbooks teach this history and what transpired. But at the same time, there are many Sino-Japanese joint ventures, many business transactions. It's like between England and Germany where there are also very solid commercial relations.

U K : *Germany didn't do much self-analysing, wasn't really able to work up, to master its fascist past. Could the movie, the way it represents re-education, offer an instrument, an analytical method of how to deal with the past on a personal/collective level?*

B B : I don't know. The re-education is based on the memory, on going back to the past, on reading the past with a new knowledge. Meantime, the interrogator tells the war criminals, including Pu Yi, many times: "We know very well your crimes. So we want you to tell your crimes not because we don't know it but because we want YOU to live through the experience of investigating and saying actually your crimes. You have to say it with your words and with your mouth." This is a big part of re-education. So I think that re-education is a very Chinese, let's say, ceremony. Because Chinese consider themselves eternal students; they always say they're learning, they are learning until the day they die. In fact, if you look at the Cultural Revolution, they didn't have machine guns in their hands, but books, red books, as a proof that they were learning. Of course, students need teachers; a teacher could have been the emperor in the past or Mao Tse Tung in the recent past. I noticed that there is a dialectic of teachers/students in China which more or less is there all the time.

Chinese after Liberation also have a great sense of their identity. Somebody was telling me that, if they ask the students who did the recent demonstrations, "why have you done that," they will say, "for that and that, for democracy, liberalization, freedom ... and for China." They have a great sense of their own country which is not fashionable in the Western world.

I think a movie can be a kind of very deep experience, but I never believe that political movies could change the reality in some way. There was a moment in '68 when everybody doing movies thought cinema was like a machine gun to do revolution. I didn't believe that.

U K : *So Pu Yi, also for China, cannot be considered as an example for the "New Chinese"?*
B B : An example to avoid.

U K : *I mean, the way he changed?*
B B : Yes, I think that's why the Chinese gave me the authorization to do the movie. Because they think that the image of China which will be represented in the movie all over the world—this movie shall be seen everywhere more or less—is an image that they allowed, an image they are pleased with. Because it's positive, the experience of Pu Yi in the end. Maybe an American simple viewer would say "what do you mean, he was an emperor, and then he became poor and a person like everybody else, this is not positive." But this is not the right way of reading the story of Pu Yi. It is the story of a liberation.

U K : *Do you think Chinese people believe in re-education?*
B B : I think they believe in something which is formal and deep. Who knows how Pu Yi had changed? Where are the proofs of his change? I think that Chinese believe in the ceremony of the change, in the ritual of re-education. Chinese are great formalists. And I think that it's rooted in the culture, the idea that we are all born—not equal—but all good. When you believe in that, you believe also that redemption is possible. And if your life is full of crimes, there can be redemption.

U K : *While doing the movie, did you try to avoid an Eurocentric point of view? What was your approach?*
B B : It's what I think I have said before, that I try not to bring with me all my static cultural and philosophical categories, but try to be invaded by Chinese culture. I know, it is a bit of an illusion to think to be able to wash away completely your *formazione*, your background. But there is this effort, and I think I tried to leave myself as open as possible for me to receive as much information as I could.

U K : *How did you see the Cultural Revolution while it occurred? How do you represent it in the movie? Were you emotionally involved doing the scene?*

B B :   There is a scene in the movie, towards the end of the life of Pu Yi, which is during the Cultural Revolution. Pu Yi is in a street which suddenly becomes full of young Red Guards going to the great Tiananmen Square. So I attempted to give the emotion that I had at the moment, in '68, '67, but at the same time not to ignore what I learned about the Cultural Revolution actually going to China in the last three years. I had never been pro-Chinese in the sixties as many of my friends used to be. But I was fascinated by the spectacle, by the show of the Cultural Revolution; the aesthetic of this kind of theatre in the street was very fascinating for me. So in the movie I tried to create that fascination and then to contradict it, giving a judgment about what had happened. All Chinese I spoke to, either from the side of the Red Guards or on the side of the victims of the Red Guards, agree that these ten years were a nightmare. It was a case of incredible collective fanaticism, almost religious. Moravia in his book about the Cultural Revolution talks about a "crusade of children," which is very interesting because there was this kind of quality. That is the way I tried to represent it, to show how innocent these young Chinese were, but how innocence can be atrocious and totally wrong and destructive.

U K :   *How shall the movie be promoted? As what shall it be accepted in the world?*
B B :   I can't answer. I don't know. I'm a moviemaker, not a movie salesman.

The Physiology of Feelings

FABIEN GERARD/1990

BERNARDO BERTOLUCCI: While I was in the final stages of editing *The Last Emperor,* and just as I was finishing with China, the inevitable question popped up again: "What should I do next?" After the film on Pu Yi, in which the man's private history became intertwined with HISTORY in capital letters, I was on the lookout for a subject that would allow me to put the soul under a microscope.

How did you get to know Bowles' novel?
BB: For a number of years, I had been hearing about *The Sheltering Sky* from at least three friends: Mark Peploe, Ferdinando Scarfiotti and Marilyn Goldin. They were members of a secret society, the sect of Paul Bowles' "worshippers." I had been holding out, resisting their pressure and their best efforts to ensnare me, perhaps because I was irritated by the fanaticism with which they spoke of the book.

Overcoming my natural suspicion, I finally read the book on one of my trips to China. At once I thought: "This is a movie!" I was fascinated by the idea of these "figures in a landscape," so like the paintings of Caspar David Friedrich. At the same time, I had the feeling that the story of Port and Kit would give me the possibility of exploring the *anatomy* of the char-

From *The Sheltering Sky: A Film by Bernardo Bertolucci from the Novel by Paul Bowles* (eds. Livio Negri and Fabien S. Gerard), London: Scribners, 1990. © Fabien S. Gerard. Reprinted by permission.

acters even more than their *psychology*. I suppose that my secret ambition was to shoot a kind of endoscopic film, using a fibre-optic lens!

Your first impression of the book?

B B : Suffering. At a certain point in the story, Port walks out onto a sloping plain from which you sense that there is simply no return. Only then do we realize that this "odour of death" began on the first page of the novel. I identified so strongly with Port during his agony that I suffered physical pains I had never felt before. It was an overwhelming emotion that I couldn't explain. Confronting that emotion by making the film was the only way of exorcising it.

So, three years later, as the Chinese chapter came to a close, I felt a strange kind of nostalgia for those pains. Before making any decisions, however, I travelled to Tangier with my co-writer Mark Peploe in order to meet the elusive writer Paul Bowles. He had not replied to the telegram sent to his legendary PO Box. We met at his flat, located in a shoddily built fifties apartment-block. The first impression was that of an extraordinarily elegant man, but consciously outmoded in his dress. He seemed physically fragile, but somehow also a man of iron. Invulnerable. Once his cover was blown, Paul seemed to me to be revealed as intimately delinquent, almost without restraints. That's his particular fascination. In the depths of the liquid blue gaze of this cautious eighty-year-old man lurks one of the wildest natures you could imagine.

A few hours later, in front of the entrance of the Hotel El Minzah, I was the victim of an assault that might have ended very badly. Faced with death flashing in the eyes of a Moroccan boy wielding a knife, my wallet taken, and gripped by an overwhelming anxiety "a la Genet," at that moment any remaining doubts vanished. I had to make *The Sheltering Sky*.

A lot has been said about the fact that the protagonists of the film are based directly on Paul and Jane Bowles.

B B : *The Sheltering Sky* is a profoundly literary novel, giving a lot of room for its characters' thoughts. By its very nature, cinema has to leave a lot of room for what happens. There are some beautiful literary films like Wenders' *Wings of Desire*, but I was headed in another direction. One of our concerns while writing the screenplay was that of filtering the literary values of the book. The goal was to arrive at some sort of "physiology of feel-ings," substituting the inner voices with the physical presence of Kit and Port. From the start, we wondered how much of Paul and Jane's story had found its way into the book. Then I had the idea of building our characters by "drawing from life" — from the original models.

But Bowles has always denied that the book is autobiographical.
B B :   Certainly, half of this writer's life has been spent defending his privacy — though recently he has begun to admit a few things. Paul now maintains that in creating Kit he was inspired by Jane in the same way a painter is inspired by a model. He liked the example I gave — that of Caravaggio witnessing the recovery of the body of a woman drowned in the Tiber and then remembering that livid corpse and painting *The Death of the Virgin*. Once you have got over the false problem of the "autobio-graphical" nature of the work, I think the most important point is that the mystery and secret of Port and Kit revealed in the film is not far removed from the mystery and secret of Paul and Jane.

Beyond the character of Port, Bowles is also physically present on the screen.
B B :   A few days before the shooting started, I suddenly had this feeling that something was missing. The "literature" was totally absent. Together with Mark, I decided to insert Paul into the film. Through the physical presence of the novel's writer, we would represent the literature itself. I don't think there are many examples of this, where the author of a book plays himself on the screen. But how do you direct Paul Bowles? I just told him one thing: I would like to see on your face the sorrow of memory, the pain of remembering.

And the actors? How do they match up to the characters in the book and in the screenplay?
B B :   I think it was one of the most difficult and tiring casting jobs I've faced. In my mind, I imagined Port and Kit as the elegant children of Scott and Zelda Fitzgerald — beautiful and damned. I needed two American actors whose chief attraction was the intelligence that shows on their faces. Thus I came to choose Debra Winger and John Malkovich, so differ-ent in their approach to their role, and yet so harmonious in creating a couple that is both symbiotic and unhappy.

Debra has to identify completely with her character. From day one of the shooting, there is no difference for her between the film and life itself. She turns her life upside down to enrich the film just as she might turn the film upside down to enrich her life. I've never seen an actor suffer so much or be so obsessively and unceasingly in contact with her character. This way of working, which creates a constant emotional tension, is not unfamiliar to me. I, too, when I'm shooting, often fail to distinguish between my life and the film that I'm making.

On the other hand, John Malkovich walks into the shot aided only by his own intuition. He succeeds in becoming the character by nimbly leaping over the whole process of rationalization. Or at least it seems that way. But who knows what goes on in John's head the night before he's acting? He's really something out of mythology. To me John appears like a centaur — these strong soccer-player thighs — whereas the upper part of his body seems softer, becoming at times almost effeminate. (In the same manner, Debra's incredible energy at times seems to have something almost boyish about it). John would slouch onto the set, and then as soon as the cameras rolled, he'd have all the lightness of a ballet dancer. In any case, right now I cannot imagine any other Kit and Port than Debra Winger and John Malkovich.

But for the part of Tunner you chose someone completely unknown.
B B : Campbell Scott fills me with pride. He's very young, almost a beginner in films, with a background in theatre. I believed in him and was rewarded with a consummate performance. He demonstrated all the experience of a seasoned actor. Of the three of them he's the one who came closest to expressing the "body language" so typical of the forties. I'm pleased to think that I discovered him.

On the other hand, Jill Bennett and Timothy Spall — who no doubt some people in England will think of as vaguely "hammy" — represent the great tradition of English theatre. To be honest, what I was looking for were two actors who recall the minor characters of John Huston — types like Peter Lorre, Elisha Cook Jr or Sidney Greenstreet or Robert Morley. You know, a bit sinister, a bit comic, almost caricatures of themselves, but always suggesting in some way that they are bearers of death.

If John Malkovich is a false ballet dancer, Eric Vu-An, who plays Belqassim, is the real thing.

BB: Yes, Eric is one of the most extraordinary dancers of the "post Nouvelle Vague" in international ballet. I have asked myself how I came to make such an eccentric choice. Perhaps the explanation is that Belqassim is a figure who, both in the book and in the film, stands outside all known psychological convention. Hiding beneath that turban is desire, the desirer and the desired—all at once. He is the man without a face and without a country. The true nomad. I also discovered that the Tuaregs are great narcissists; the sand is the mirror in which their shadows are reflected.

The Sheltering Sky *seems as much a road movie as a love story: an escape that leads them to the middle of nowhere.*
BB: The children of Scott and Zelda have discovered that all the glamour that fired the stories of Fitzgerald is gone, cancelled forever by the war. So Paul and Kit, Jane and Port, turn their back on the United States—on New York and Long Island and the mentality that's associated with all the values of the "American dream"—to head off to another continent, in search of something different. And this is how they wind up in North Africa, in exactly the same place where existentialism was even at that moment being born.

Port and Kit love each other, but they know that they are not going to succeed ever again in being happy together. To love without being happy. Love as a mutual blackmail that unites two people, each of whom is aware of the absence of happiness. Two persons who love one another, adore each other, but are unhappy. They fail to experience love for its own sake, but rather as something horribly conflictive and endlessly sad, and their journey across the desert is an effort to patch up a relationship that's shattered into a thousand pieces. It is paralleled by the "journey" they are making into themselves in search of their own identity—for they have lost a sense of identity in the conjugal osmosis, in the ceaseless intermirroring of their personalities one against the other. If I look around me today, I see lots of people in this same state.

After we shot the scene in which Port and Kit try to make love among the rocks on top of the ridge, I was speaking on the phone with my wife, Clare, and I told her how painful a day it had been for me and for the actors. It's very sad speaking about a couple divided, as it were, by an invisible wall. The next day, Clare sent me a fax in which she wrote: "*While you were filming about a couple divided by an invisible wall, the Berlin Wall came down.*" It was a shock for me, because I was completely unaware of what was happening in Europe. The selfishness of unhappiness. By becoming so absorbed in the pain of this unhappy couple of 1947, I'd lost touch with the outside world. The news brought me back.

Bowles' book is universal, yet strangely topical.
B B :   The book, which was a success when it came out, soon became the bible of this "secret society" I was talking about. Then, in the past two or three years it has burst again onto the literary scene. In effect, I think the novel was ahead of its time, since the isolated melancholy experienced by Port and Kit forty years ago has now assumed epidemic proportions. All that we said about the paradox of love condemned to continue even in the absence of happiness is a notion very typical of the late eighties. We could also speak of the renewed search for alternative values developing as a reaction to the overdose of consumerism, and it isn't surprising that existentialism should once again take hold of the popular imagination. Due to the media bombardment, the encroaching desert, so pervasive in the book, also pervades our thoughts now. A desert world about to become tomorrow's reality. A symptom of the greenhouse effect.

So as you were saying, love equals unhappiness. But whenever separation takes place, it's always a terrible thing.
B B :   One day, just before Christmas, Port Moresby slipped from the final stage of agony into death. I remember feeling sick as a dog. More precisely, I was totally identifying with John Malkovich's suffering, and I couldn't bear the separation from Port. Or was it that I feared being abandoned by John? This is a perfect example of how, all too often, I end up by confusing real life with fiction. Naturally, after all that anxiety, came a feeling of liberation. John Malkovich left, and, miraculously, I succeeded in forgetting both him and Port. The very next day we began the last part of the film, with Kit its only protagonist. I shot it all in a state of trance. It is the "chapter" in which psychology is replaced by something else. The part where the inhuman effort of taking up the tale every day, carrying it forward again and again, is replaced by something new and unexpected. All of a sudden there is the sensation of relief as if you are being drawn along by the adventure of the film, and that by now it is travelling on its own legs — slender but indefatigable, like those of a camel.

It is also the moment in which the film starts to betray the book.

B B : Yes, my great "betrayal" took place just before filming the first night that Kit and Belqassim spend together in the desert. I was standing there next to the dunes, under the moon, looking at the camels and the Tuaregs in the camp site, listening to the flutes, and all of a sudden, I had this feeling of falsehood. At any rate, there was this strong sensation that the last part of the film risked being crushed beneath the weight of cliché. Then, discussing with the Tuaregs I learnt they deny that rape, or any form of carnal violence, exists in their culture. Theirs is a matriarchal society. So it occurred to me perhaps the end of the book was a kind of fantasy on Bowles' part. It was not to be taken too seriously.

If suddenly changing the screenplay means taking a risk, then it also means the ecstasy of improvisation. In any case, there was nothing else to be done. This is why there is no explicit violence in the film. In this sense the film is different from the book. The rapport between Belqassim and Kit is delicate, almost like something between a little boy and a woman. What I was trying to capture in the young man Belqassim was the same slightly "obscene" innocence we see in the child who spies on them as they make love in the mud room.

The moment the caravan arrives, you feel like you are watching another film.

B B : Only later did I realize that the narrative change implied an important change of style as well. Once in Niger, immersed in the vast African crowd, I began to "record" this reality—and Debra hurled into the midst of it—with the "natural" documentary eye of a Rossellini or a Jean Rouch. And so I discovered, in that January afternoon, in Agadez market, that the reality, when it is desired, courted, provoked, in a few seconds is able to transform itself into pure fiction.

And sometimes into dreams as well. But as described by Bowles, Kit's long delirium is usually associated more with "madness" than "dreaming."

B B : In the novel, Kit is the victim of a painful loss of identity. Immediately following Port's death, there is a strange fusion of the two of them. Kit "metabolizes" or absorbs all that Port was and she brings his dream to its extreme consequence. By yielding to the temptation of losing herself in exotic adventures, she imitates him. She prolongs Port's obsession to annihilate himself in risk. Thus Port continues to live on in Kit, just as on the screen Jane Bowles continues to live in Debra. So that at the end everyone involved seems to flow together into the gaze of Bowles. They have understood that in those eyes is their only salvation: nothingness, the absolute night.

The Earth Is My Witness: An Interview with Bernardo Bertolucci on *Little Buddha*

FABIEN GERARD AND
T. JEFFERSON KLINE/1993

BERNARDO BERTOLUCCI GRACIOUSLY WELCOMED us to the London townhouse he shares with Clare Peploe (who was away in Latin America preparing a new film). We had spent the previous afternoon viewing an early version of his new film *Little Buddha*. Certainly there are affinities in this new work with many of his previous films. Bertolucci once said, "I am always making the same film," and certainly one can see in his evolution from *Before the Revolution* to *The Sheltering Sky* many common elements and themes. Each tells a story of a transformation; each is heavily inflected by Bertolucci's own experience with psychoanalysis, and each in some way involves a son's confrontation with the mythic roles of his parents. More recently, Bertolucci has alternated his efforts between epic films (*1900*, *The Last Emperor* and now *Little Buddha*) and more personal stories (*Luna*, *The Tragedy of a Ridiculous Man*, *The Sheltering Sky*) without ever abandoning the qualities of one genre in the other. If his "epics" can be seen to elaborate highly personal themes (for example the oedipal struggles of Olmo and Alfredo in *1900* or the psychoanalysis of Pu Yi set against the backdrop of Imperial China in *The Last Emperor*), his more "intimate" films are often set in spectacular decors (for example the operatic sets of the Caracalla ruins in *Luna* and the grandeur of the African desert in *The Sheltering Sky*).

If *Little Buddha* reevokes many of Bertolucci's most insistent themes, the film nevertheless feels like an important departure from his previous work.

From *I film di Bernardo Bertolucci* (Rome: Gremese editore), 1993. © T. Jefferson Kline. Reprinted by permission.

One of the most intriguing aspects of his work has certainly centered in his ability to weave oneiric elements into an otherwise entirely realistic topos in a way that challenges and unsettles his viewer. In *Little Buddha* the realistic and oneiric levels have been separated into two distinct topoi: nine-year-old Jesse's discovery of Tibetan Buddhism in Seattle, vs. the highly stylized intercuts of the life of Siddhartha. For the first time in his work, Bertolucci has chosen to isolate dream from the diegetic level of his film and to venture into the realm of the fantastic. The film moves in a most unsettling fashion between rather barren scenes of contemporary Seattle and richly mellow sequences of the Buddha's life in Nepal five centuries before Christ. The success of the film depends on bringing these two styles together in the film's final scenes to create a kind of synthesis of these two worlds.

G & K :   *This is, to say the least, an unusual film for you. Where does your interest in Buddhism come from?*

B B :   It started a long time ago when Elsa Morante, Moravia's wife, gave me copy of the *Life of Milarepa* in 1963. We were filming *Before the Revolution*, and in the film there is a scene in which Gina even says: "I know that time doesn't exist. . . . I know a story which goes, once upon a time there was an old guru . . . like you (she nods toward Cesare), who had a young disciple like you (she nods towards Fabrizio), and both were walking through a rocky mountains countryside. One day the old man said to the young man, "I am very thirsty. Would you get me a glass of water?" The disciple said yes, and set out on a road that led down to a fountain, in the valley. And behind the fountain he saw a marvelous landscape and. . . ." Fabrizio interrupts her: "And in this landscape he saw a mysterious woman, quite extraordinary, like you (he nods toward Gina), and they had many children and lived together for twenty years. Until a terrible epidemic of plague broke out. Everyone died and he was the only one who survived. Meanwhile, he had aged. Suddenly he remembered the old guru. Desperate, he set off across the country and walked back to the very place he had left his master. The old man was still there and said, 'Oof, what a long time you took to fetch me some water! I've been waiting all afternoon.' " At this point, Gina concludes: "So, you see, time doesn't exist." Well, this story was quoted from the Milarepa book I had just been reading during the making of *Before the Revolution*.

G & K : *So we can see it as a metaphor of the delay between your first hearing about Buddhism (the need for the glass of water) and your latest film,* Little Buddha *(taking a drink)? By some chronology a space of thirty years but in Buddhist terms no delay at all.*

B B : That's very Zen! So anyway that was the first encounter; then there was a kind of periodic rapprochement with Buddhism which were either casual or intended through the years. For example, in '83 at Brentwood, I had an initiation to Padmasambhava, who is the saint who introduced Buddhism to Tibet (Milarepa came after him), and I met Tibetan Lamas. Then there were some readings, for example, Borges' book on Buddhism, or even a poem by Borges on metempsychosis or reincarnation, which says, "The fish lives in the ocean, and the man in Agrigento remembers he was once that fish," and goes on like that . . .

G & K : *You're not born under the sign of Pisces by chance?*

B B : Of course I am! (Smiles.) And so is Jesse in *Little Buddha*! Then being in Japan and seeing Japanese movies was another kind of encounter with Buddhism, in the early '8os. (I always see Japan through the cinema, you know. What happened to me with Japan happened to me the first time I went to the States too, when I was completely into American cinema). I have been to Japan three or four times and discovered that everything was mediated by my memory of Ozu or Mizoguchi or Kurosawa or Oshima. Also there's the story of my visit to Ozu's tomb. Katsuka Shibata's mother, Madame Kawakita had told us to look for a tomb with nothing on it. And we were all looking but couldn't find a tomb with nothing written on it. But it turned out that there *was* something written on the tomb which was "Nothing—*Mu.*"

G & K : *"Form is empty, emptiness is form." So why make this film now?*

B B : Well, the occasion was that somebody came to me after *The Last Emperor* with an idea for a film which would be a historical treatment of the Buddha, and I started to dive into it while I was doing *Sheltering Sky.* But the person turned out to be so impossible to work with that I told him I would proceed with the project on my own. "However it won't be the same project as your film," I told him, "so you can do your project." (Actually he had just given me a five page treatment which was kind of too much like a Cecil B. DeMille bio of famous mythological characters. What he wrote was exactly what you find in the Encyclopedia Universalis about the life of Siddhartha, no more). Anyhow, I was feeling a strong need of a connection with today's society, and I remembered some news I'd read years ago regarding western children who had been "recognized," as reincarnations of famous Tibetan Lamas. So I invented the story of little Jesse Conrad, born in Seattle, in which I could tell pieces of the story of Prince Siddhartha, like these fairy tales grandfathers use to tell to their grandchildren. And the story of Siddhartha is introduced as a kind of fairy tale. And so I told him, "You can go on with your Big Buddha and I'm doing my *Little Buddha.*"

G & K : *We've been told some people reacted to this title, for example, one Buddhist monk in Los Angeles who said, "Only in the mindset of white male colonial attitudes would Asia's most esteemed historic religious figure be described as 'Little.'" This is hardly the sense of your title, though.*

B B : Of course there have been reactions! Some Buddhist "integralists"—a contradiction in terms—even tried to stop us shooting in Nepal! Apart from the secret reason I just gave, the title is there because Westerners are very ignorant about Buddhism. In fact we are all like children who can be taught a new philosophical idea. And in the same way that a book on chemicals for children is called *The Little Chemist,* or another on wood-working might be called *The Little Carpenter,* I was thinking it would be a kind of manual on Buddhism in very large terms. So I went to see the Dalai Lama because we were quite worried, and I asked him about that, and he asked, "Why did you call it little Buddha?" and I explained that it is for children of all ages who don't know about Buddhism. And he said, "Oh that's very good." And he said the line which will become famous, which is, "There is a little Buddha in all of us." He was talking about the "Buddha nature" which is in all of us. He's such an extraordinary man. In his eyes I believe I really understood what the word "compassion" means, i.e., both "empathy" and "the understanding of goodness." What a pity he's the only head of state in the world who's dedicating four hours a day to meditating on human nature!

   I have to tell you something. Four days ago, I received a phone call from Brando. He knew that I had finished my film, and he said to me, "I didn't tell you this before, but I've been practicing Buddhist meditation for several years and at least three times I've felt something really special that must resemble ecstasy." He asked me if that had happened to me as well, and I answered that at the moment I was quite anxious about the fact that the film was just being released in Europe. "Is it really important to you whether the film is a success or not?" And I answered, "Is it important?!" Since he didn't understand I had to explain to him that this was the first time that I'd made a film which was addressed specifically to children, and given that I still have a bit of Ego left—whereas he was trying to convince me that this wasn't his case—it seemed to me natural enough to worry about whether kids would be able to get into this universe which they knew nothing about. This Marlon understood, and to show that he'd understood, he quoted the last line of Lama Norbu in my film (which he hadn't seen yet) "Children? We are all children. . . ." It took my breath away. Weird isn't it?

G & K : *But are children really going to get into this film?*
B B : For the time being, I'm still trying to find out based on the first reports that are coming in from all directions. Some woman wrote me from Brussels to tell me that she went to see the film with her three kids who had lost their grandfather six months before. After the screening, that night at home, the youngest one, who's seven or eight, said as he was going to sleep, "You know, mother, if that's death, then I don't think I'm afraid of death." At his age, of course, he doesn't understand all the subtleties of Buddhism, but emotionally this kid reacted better than I ever could have hoped. I think he must be one of those reincarnated Lamas!

G & K : *Through their emotions, as you say, children can begin to ask deeper questions.*
B B : Just before the oracle, I had shot another scene in which Jesse's father was witnessing a kind of "philosophical debate," partly improvised, which wasn't used in the final version. Chris Isaak was asking a monk, "But who's the winner?" Then a young Lama who happened to be our Buddhist consultant on the set, Dzongsar Khyentse Rinpoche, said, "You must be a Christian, sir" (because the duality of the winner and the loser, Good and Evil, life and death, etc., is typically Christian), "You think that God created you and you exist because God created you. Now just try to look at it the other way around too. You invented God and God exists because you invented Him." To make it short, eventually Chris got exasperated and

said, "What's this? You guys only pretend to give up passions." And the young Lama says, "No, no, no, you misunderstood Buddhism. You can keep all the passions you want, the strongest passions, endless passions, as long as you give up your ego." Obviously, I cut almost all these "lessons" of Buddhism from the film because I didn't want an explanatory film, like a classroom on Buddhism, but I think that our "own private Rinpoche" has the flavor of the real thing, not script, not fiction, not cinema, but the real thing.

G & K : *Is there an ethics to Buddhism? Does it teach us how to live?*
B B : This is not a classroom! I can only simplify here. In the religions of the past, which are all theistic religions, we have the gods, and because the gods created us, we exist. If there is a terrible earthquake, it is sign of the wrath of the gods. If the harvest is very abundant, it is the god's doing. Buddha came to cancel the twenty million deities of Hinduism, and that was a revolution! In Tibetan Buddhism what is substituted for this tension toward gods from the people is the mind and its incredible power. That's why they talk about "crazy wisdom." There is this Lama who died in the States, called Trungpa Rinpoche. He really gives you an image of the actual position of Tibetan Buddhism in world culture, which is quite different from the Theravada tradition you have in Ceylon, for example. In the states, he was able to express all the incredible pleasure of paradox that hides in Tibetan Buddhism. This kind of joy of logic and sophistication of dialectic is something that has been developed for more than one thousand years, fifteen thousand feet above the Roof of the World, and "crazy wisdom" strangely blossomed in such a magic place, which had very few contacts with other peoples. A Bodhisattva—i.e., a person who reached Enlightenment—is said to be crazy when he is wise and wise when he is crazy.... Of course, Tibetan masters think that nothing exists: "No eyes, no mouth, no death, no fear...." Remember? These are the words of the "Heart Sutra" we hear in the film, chanted by Lama Norbu's ghost, just after he "passed away." Maybe they are a bit too difficult for the children, but it's a real masterpiece of poetry all the same! They also say: "Imagine you are struck by love and hate at the same time." This is crazy wisdom.

G & K : *There is often a misconception about Buddhism, that it constitutes such a negation of the world that there is no room for ethical positions. But Sogyal*

Rinpoche, the author of The Tibetan Book of Life and Death — *who also has a part in* Little Buddha, *I believe — writes, "What is the point of realizing there is life after death? In a sense it will make you more responsible, make you realize that your thoughts, words and actions have consequences in this life and in the future. You realize, as Buddha said, that what we are now is what we have been. What will be is what we do now. As Padmasambhava further clarifies, if you want to know your past, look to your present form and condition. If you want to know your future, look into your present actions. See, being responsible for your actions is, I think, the most important part."*

BB: Sogyal is talking about Karma.

G & K: *In the sense that Karma and responsibility are exactly the same thing. But in the sense that Karma is tied to the notion of reincarnation too. What can reincarnation mean in your film?*

BB: Of course, since reincarnation is the subject and the theme of the film, I started to ask myself that and to wonder what the hell do I think about that. Because you know it's impossible to keep yourself outside your work. By the way, I think a very common form of "reincarnation" we can see in our society between grandparents and grandchildren: still today in Italy, but not only in Italy, the grandchildren are often called by the name of their grandparents. I mean, my own grandfather's name, for example, was Bernardo Bertolucci, so my attitude is very simply the following: let's say I do believe very much in reincarnation in the large sense of the term. I can't accept the idea that everything we are and everything we have done is lost after our death. The thoughts we have had, the work we did is definitely not lost. The Western reaction to reincarnation is completely different from the Hindu and Buddhist relationship to life and death, though. Reincarnation, in the East, is a kind of inevitable *condemnation* of "Samsara" — Samsara is the endless chain of births and deaths which will be interrupted only when someone reaches Enlightenment. Anyhow, in the various Buddhist directions, there are different solutions. For the Theravada school, in Ceylon — and for the other representatives of the Hinayana tradition of Southeast Asia — the goal of life is to reach Enlightenment and Nirvana, and that's all. Tibetan Buddhism is closer to the Mahayana tradition, and more especially the Vajra, i.e., the Tibetan school, which was a fusion between Padmasambhava and the ancient indigenous shamanistic religion which existed in Tibet before Buddhism arrived (there is still a big influence of this preexisting religion on Buddhism). Now, the genius of Tibetan Buddhism is connected to these characters called "bodisattvas," the Enlightened ones, who give up their chance to finally reach Nirvana in order to come back on earth, being reborn a few more times in order to help the others reach the same state of inner peacefulness. That's also why I personally have the feeling that the Tibetans, in their incredible enjoyment of life, invented a way to win over both the curse of Samsara and the pain of being separated from the people we've loved, but then, once they've won, they don't mind coming back at all! In this sense, Nirvana is more symbolic than anything else, it's only a very remote goal.

G & K : *We're interested that in talking somewhere about Buddhism, you said, "Each man is the writer of his own script." Is it possible to think of a lifetime of making movies as a series of reincarnations?*

B B : As Chris Isaak tells Bridget Fonda, in the movie, I just can't believe in reincarnation the way the Tibetans do, where a person with a specific name becomes another with a phone number and everything." This is a bit too much, at least for me! On the other hand, I believe not only in the reincarnation of grandfathers through grandchildren, and also in books and paintings and all kinds of works of art as a form of reincarnation transmitted from one generation to the others, but I do think that we reincarnate during our lives: every time we change, we reincarnate in some way.

G & K : Little Buddha *suggests something very powerful about reincarnation. We have the sense that a child can see this film and say, "Hey, I'm a reincarnation," instead of going home as he does after a Western and pretend to shoot his friends.*

B B : So Jesse goes home and says, "Mom, when you die, will you come back?" I love this relationship between children and death which is so shockingly natural.

G & K : *So what is the place of reincarnation in your film?*
B B : Indeed, what would you say it was?

G & K : *Well, the film certainly seems to be suggesting something very powerful. Take Jesse for example. On the one hand he has some characteristics that are directly borrowed from Lama Dorje. He recognizes Dorje's wooden bowl. He strokes his ear exactly the way we see Dorje touching his ear in the photo on Norbu's desk. So there is a suggestion that he is the direct reincarnation of Dorje.*

B B :   Right, that was on purpose.

G & K :   *But there is something more though. We don't know much about Dorje so that we really can't use him as a pattern for Jesse's behavior. But there is another model in the film who gradually and increasingly does become a model—almost a double of Jesse—and that is Siddhartha himself. The first time you see Jesse he is playing football with his friends in the school yard. And the first time we see the adolescent Siddhartha, he is playing the Kabadi. And then you have the moment in which he's in the bath when he says "Goodbye, Mom," and sinks under the water, a kind of symbolic baptism, much like the one Siddhartha will undergo in the river. Jesse and Siddhartha both have to leave the confines of their families and go out into the world to receive illumination. Both thus symbolically lose their mothers at a certain point in their lives. And, just as Siddhartha finds everyone sleeping when he is ready to leave the palace, on the plane everyone's asleep and Jesse tries to wake them up in a gesture that cannot fail to evoke Siddhartha.*

B B :   Yes, that is a clear reference.

G & K :   *And there's lot's more. There are the mountains: Rainier for Jesse and the Himalayas for Siddhartha. When Siddhartha enters the woods to join the ascetics, he gives his clothes to a beggar. When Jesse arrives in Nepal, he gives his Oakland A's cap to Raju. Both Siddhartha and Jesse do this kind of magic thing with bowls floating on water: Siddhartha makes his rice bowl float upstream and Jesse makes the bowl with Norbu's ashes float on the choppy waters of Puget Sound. When Siddhartha escapes from his procession into the city, he wanders into a square where people are making pottery. Jesse clearly blunders into the same square when he is chasing Raju and his brother shortly after arriving in Katmandu.*

B B :   I'm so glad you noticed about the "pottery square"! I think it's nice when you see the repetition of that scene. The place is almost exactly the same after some 2,500 years. The "circular" movement of the potters is of course very important too as soon as you deal with Buddhism.

G & K :   *So, since Maitreya—the next Buddha figure in history—is supposed to be ultimately reborn in the West, the question then arises is Jesse more than just*

the reincarnation of Lama Dorje? In other words, isn't he the reincarnation of
Siddhartha himself?
B B :   The answer is in the film! Who said the next Buddha would be born
in the West?

G & K :   *We've been told they say so in the Indian tradition. Now, what about the*
choice of Keanu Reeves who is not only a Westerner playing an eastern figure but
whose look and make-up in the film seem almost androgynous.
B B :   I first had the casting director looking for a possible Indian Siddhartha. I couldn't find anybody, but even if I had found somebody, I was
already very much thinking of Keanu Reeves because . . . It's strange but the
whole thing for me is the incredible innocence in his face, his look, what
is in his eyes. Even in roles where he is a little gay hustler, as in *My Own*
Private Idaho, I've always been impressed by his innocence. So also his
origin — he's half Canadian, half Chinese/Hawaiian — makes him look different. So there is a feeling of another race in his blood and his features,
which is what I was looking for.

G & K :   *What were the reactions of the Nepalese to him?*
B B :   They said he was extremely handsome, although they probably
thought he was too thin. You know, rich people in the East have to be fat.
When somebody fat walks in the street, they are all bowing and respectful.
Being thin means you are poor: the opposite of what happens in the West,
where the rich are thin and the fat belong to the junk food addicted lower
middle class.

G & K :   *I heard he lost a lot of weight on the set.*
B B :   Before we did the ascetic part, he fasted for two weeks, just drinking
water and orange juice to become as thin as possible.

G & K :   *So he really got into the part.*
B B :   Oh, yes. He was deeply serious about what he was doing. What I
wanted to create was like the conventions of fairy tales where the prince
charming is very good looking and he has a kind of heroic drive. So I
spoke with him a bit, and I asked him to do this kind of effort. He is so
breathtakingly beautiful in the film. What you said about Siddhartha's
bisexual look is interesting too.

G & K : *If you take the scene of Bridget Fonda washing Jesse in the bathtub*
(which is kind of a reversal of Brando and Maria Schneider in Last Tango*); if*
you consider the androgynous look of Siddhartha as well, and given that Gita—
a girl—is also the reincarnation of Lama Dorje—a man—then it seems that
one of the meanings of the film is that Buddhism has a much wider sense of
gender than we are accustomed to in the West.
B B : When Siddhartha catches sight of the ascetics in the woods and cuts
off his long hair, Keanu has the "look" he had in his earlier films again.
This works only because he's so compassionate.

G & K : *Has this compassion something to do with the kind of maternal role the*
monks have to play—a bit like the eunuchs in Last Emperor*?*
B B : Yes, often there is a kind of weird feminine side in my films. In fact
Siddhartha cuts his hair and goes and says good-bye to his white horse and
to his closest friend, Channa. Someone even said Channa is crying because
they were lovers!

G & K : *So is this confusion of gender in some way connected to Buddhism?*
B B : Actually, when Lama Norbu tells the children about Buddha's thousands of previous lives, he's almost quoting that poem by Borges I told you
about before, the one about reincarnation, which is going on saying the
man in Agrigento not only remembered he once had been a girl, and a
tree, a dolphin, and a monkey, so it is more than being male and female.
Buddhists think that everyone and everything have got minds. Trees have
minds, animals have minds, because the minds you see in the broken tea
cup scene just change containers.

G & K : *This is very much contrasted to the skepticism of Jesse's father?*
B B : Dean Conrad is a cynical material engineer on his own ship.

G & K : *All the glass in this film is wonderful; the Conrads pretend that their*
house is open to the world, and yet what they have really done is to put up invisi-
ble barriers between each other.
B B : An engineer is someone who's supposed to build all kinds of walls. Of
course the mother—Bridget Fonda—is more open. What I wanted was to
portray the movement of the Chris Isaak character, who has to change

completely his attitude and agree that the boy should go to Bhutan. So the film is also about this father's journey, and at the end he is the one who watches fascinated during the Lama's final meditation. But most of the protagonists in recent American films are such tough models that I won't be surprised if this man will seem almost antipathetic in the U.S.

G & K : *Well* Little Buddha *certainly constitutes an antidote to films like* Indiana Jones and the Temple of Doom, *which only creates mistrust about other religions.*
B B : That's the usual inaccurate Hollywood approach to other horizons, other races, other cultures. . . . What I am more worried about is my own approach to the American family because the Conrads don't look at all like these American families in American films where every thirty seconds you get a Jewish joke and where everybody is always hip and funny and we can see a lot of wallpaper on the walls.

G & K : *But you have told a truth about the American family which is immediately seized upon when a Tibetan monk walks into this house and says it is "very empty." What you do best of all is to talk about the lack of values at the center of the American family. And then put within reach of this void something totally unpredictable to hold onto.*
B B : The "emptiness," which for a Buddhist is a basic concept, under Western eyes is not so much a goal to reach as a kind of condemnation for that family. With this family it's like three lonelinesses put together. I see the three of them in this severe house like three people who have been put together in the same place but whose relationships are not allowed by a tension which is a kind of social tension. I thought of Antonioni and Bergman. But the whole thing is still the wallpaper! You know these American family films are all made on a sound stage, and since it is colored like with flowers, it always gives a very fake ambiance.

G & K : *So* Little Buddha *is definitely not another Hollywood film about the American family!*
B B : On the other hand, we have to deal with audiences who are constantly aggressed by news, by reality, by fiction, by everything. I don't want to be above the crowd, because it's wrong. I want to be within the people.

G & K :   *At the end, after Jesse, Gita and Raju emerge as triple reincarnations of*
"Lama Thunderball" there is another level to the magic realism of the film.
B B :   In the enthronement scene there is a wild sense of "barbarity" —
using Pasolini's sense of the word — the monks are so wild, and you feel an
archaic strong solid representation through ceremony which leads to the
moment when the child says, "No eyes, no lips, no nose, no lama, no Jesse,
no death, no fear." It is an initiation, the relationship between the death
and what they say about dying. Norbu's momentary return is one of the
moments when we learn something about Buddhism through emotion
rather than through explanation. In the last part of the film you really
have a kind of cathartic moment where you can see something which is
rare, the way the children have to accept death.

G & K :   *This appeal to the emotions rather than to explanation suggests some-*
thing about the relationship between Buddhism and Western psychology.
B B :   Well, the point which I find the closest to Freud occurs when the
Buddhists say that everything depends on Karma, that you are the author
and the screenwriter of your destiny. In one life you condition the following
life, etc. Freud doesn't talk about the next life, but he says we are responsible for what happens to us. Which is exactly what the Karma idea is.
Buddha comes and says, "Enough with Gods! Human nature is the point."
People used to dedicate their destiny to gods, though. In Islamic culture,
everything is written in the Book. In ancient Greece there was fate, and
the Catholics still say they're in the hands of God. So that Buddha guy
found out twenty-five hundred years ago in the East what Western philoso-
phers will simply "find out" again twenty-four hundred years later. It's
amazing! That's why Buddha's legacy is so important today. The Mahayana
tradition insists more on the power of the mind — with your mind, you
can imagine and destroy and imagine and create. The Hinayana tradition
insists more on the power of love. So a Tibetan, who is much more oriented
toward the exercise of the brain, often talks to you about this incredible
mind power and then to "correct" he will talk about compassion.

G & K :   *You have used the actor, Ryocheng — who plays the part of Lama*
Norbu — in the specific context of The Last Emperor, *where, sitting behind Pu*
Yi in the confession scene, he has the role of a psychoanalyst. So being now kind

of a Buddhist "reeducator" in this film, he seems to offer another link with psy-choanalysis. Could you say more about this?
B B : It's especially in the idea that for Freud we shouldn't blame destiny because crossing the street we are hit by a car, but we should blame our-selves or our unconscious.

G & K : *But what about the Buddhist idea of getting rid of the ego?*
B B : Freud is not talking about getting rid of the ego. He only talks about the fact that there is an ego, and there is a superego—a sort of interior sentinel or superior internal judge who is judging us all the time in every-thing we do and then gives us the sentence about our behavior.

G & K : *So how do you see the correspondence?*
B B : I think that there is a correspondence. What is most amazing is that this abolition of gods and deities by Buddha is the first thing he did. And what he did is very Freudian precisely because it puts man in a kind of central position. So when analyzing the causes of a flood, it is probably because man has also cut too many forests and so on. In other words, there is this relationship between cause and effect which is fundamental to Buddhism, even if for us it may sound a bit prosaic. They say very simply, "Cause and effect? If you eat, you shit." No movement in the universe exists without a cause. So we can find the cause of every effect in our lives and in ourselves. But perhaps I should explain why in my movie Mara is the ego. Last year in Sabaudia when we were working with Rudy Wurlitzer, Dzongsar Khyentse Rinpoche came to stay with us two weeks. And one day we were discussing how Mara should be characterized in the film. And Rinpoche immediately said something that is quite extraordinary for a man from the Himalayas, "You may call him Evil, Devil, Lord of Darkness, etc., but Siddhartha's number one enemy is the ego." Which makes another conjunction between Freud and Buddhism. In the Mara scene it's like the Buddha has won, and his enemy comes out asking, "Will you be my god?" And he says this famous line which I found in Borges, "Architect, you won't build your house again." Which means I won't be reborn. My body won't be rebuilt. And at this point he touches the ground with his hand just like we can see in the best-known Buddhist iconography: and the Earth is his witness, which is the most famous line of Buddha. The moral of this scene is "Who did he beat? He beat his own ego."

G & K: *And what about the Freudian idea of repetition compulsion which is so prevalent in* The Last Emperor *and others of your films.*

BB: The samsara. The cycle of life and death. But the Tibetans find ways of coming back even after reaching illumination.

G & K: *Which suggests that Nirvana is perhaps less interesting than life. Utopias have always been less interesting than ordinary life with all its risks and imperfections. Moreover the palace where Siddhartha is imprisoned is a kind of utopia, but boring.*

BB: Which raises the question of why he has accepted to remain in his palace. "Why did I never want to go out?" he thinks at a certain moment. And Siddhartha says, "Oh father why did you hide from me the existence of old age and death? And the father says, "If I didn't let you go it's because I love you." And Siddhartha answers, "Yes but your love has become a prison for me. How can I live in the palace when I know that so many people are suffering outside." And the father says, "You never wanted to go outside Siddhartha!" So there is this thing that is never mentioned in the Buddhist books which is the complicity of Siddhartha before he wakes up. Because he wakes up when he goes out for his enlightenment. There is something not very different from the Dostoyevskian idiot, when he says, "Suffering? what is suffering?" or when he says, "Old? what do you mean old?" Like somebody who has been kept at the age of six, which is quite amazing.

G & K: *But that is in a sense everyone's story upon discovering life. Isn't that what makes this story powerful since all of us have been "complicitous" with youth before we have to move on to adulthood? Did you read Hesse's* Siddhartha? *Hesse does so much to accentuate the need to leave the father.*

BB: Yes that's very nice, the part about the father. It's also Pu Yi leaving the palace. That's why this film has the potential of a bomb. To wake up people. It has the chance of being something completely new, a spiritual experience that people can completely enter into and end up feeling great.

G & K: *Are you illumined with the spirituality of this film? In the Seattle sequence of the film we see a statue of a great hammer but without the sickle of communism. And you talk of making a "bomb" to wake people up. Twenty years ago you were into Marxism and dialectical materialism. But now China, which used to be the utopia of the left, is the oppressor of Tibet. Thus your "spiritual-*

*ism" undergoes a political reversal. If you have not abandoned the struggle, is it
the nature of the struggle that has changed?*

B B : That's what the Dalai Lama symbolizes. You know there's a region in
East-Tibet where the so-called Kampas tribe lives. After the Chinese invasion in 1959, the Kampas started a guerilla movement. Then they moved
into Mustang, in training camps supported by the CIA. In '87 or '88 the Dalai
Lama said, "No more military attacks, no more blood. It is finished." Many
of them even killed themselves because they'd lost their motivation to
live. Thus evidently the Dalai Lama thinks it's possible to reach practical
and political solutions in another way, without violent resistance. What he
is asking of China is no longer to give the Tibetans political autonomy but
to respect their culture. And the Chinese never answer, acting as if he didn't
exist (for reasons of *Realpolitik*, they wouldn't admit his existence—so in
Freudian terms, they are simply "repressing" the Tibetans). And I think
that, when we faced the problem of deciding whether Ying Ruocheng (a
Chinese actor) could play Lama Norbu, this is why the Dalai Lama told
me, "go ahead, go ahead, use Ying Ruocheng!" So we took a Chinese actor
for a Tibetan part . . . Which was an excellent choice, also because Ying is
such a wonderful man. I just hope the Chinese won't cut his heart out
afterwards!

G & K : *Speaking of Ying Ruocheng, who, as we mentioned played Pu Yi's "reeducator" in* The Last Emperor—*there seem to be so many references to your earlier
films. For example, when the monks surround the kids in the monastery's courtyard were you thinking of the end of the ballroom scene in* The Conformist?

B B : You are incredibly good at seeing this kind of things I personally never
see at all when I made my films! For me it's merely the obsession of being
surrounded by people who are, unfortunately, somewhat interchangeable.
Just the feeling of people around me. Maybe there is the usual desire of
something and the usual fear of being cornered?

G & K : *Then the bodies in the river reminded me of those scenes of drowning in*
The Grim Reaper *and* Before the Revolution. *What I'm feeling with all these
references to your earlier work . . . which you have called an obsession in Freudian
terms, might also have a Buddhist meaning?*

B B : The river seems to serve as a container for different bodies. Yes, it's an
old story—the convent gives you the same soup in different bowls, as we

say in Italy! The bowls contain ashes of course, but when Siddhartha puts the bowl in the river it's the beginning of a new life. So it is the locus of contradiction and continuity.

G & K : *Like the "Mandala" at the very end of the credits . . .*
B B : The Mandala is my film. My film is a sand Mandala. I can make a gesture and it is all. . . . poof!

G & K : *Your film remains though.*
B B : Films don't last more than thirty years, you know! Now they put them on Laser Disks, but the film still doesn't last.

G & K : *Films are made of the same stuff dreams are made of. This is the first time you have actually represented dreams . . .*
B B : My films have always have dream qualities, but the loom is the prison of the dream. In general the dreams remain in the loom. This time two dreams have escaped and gone into the movie. When you do a dream, for the dreamer there's not a lot of difference between the dream and daily life. So dreams in movies are not very different from reality. That's why I had to put a close-up of the queen dancing with the elephant in order to say, "Careful, this is a dream!"

G & K : *Is the dance scene in Maya's dream important in the way it was in your other films?*
B B : No, it is not like the dances that I had in *Spider's Stratagem* or *The Conformist*, for example, which in general are a kind of moment of catharsis of the character into a social life. In this case everybody's asleep and it's just the queen and the elephant.

G & K : *Are you the elephant?*
B B : It's a baby elephant. I'm an old elephant.

G & K : *J-L. Borges writes, "In Buddhism, every man is an illusion, resulting from the vertiginous projection of a long series of momentary and solitary men. The appearance of continuity that a succession of images produces on the cinema screen can help us understand this somewhat disconcerting idea." Do you sense this same thing in your relationship to cinema and to Buddhism?*

B B :   Our lives are made of sequences, like sequences are made of shots. So cinema is like life.

G & K :   *It reminds me of the moment in* Partner *when Clémenti says, "Theater, theater, theater." And Bertolucci's voice can be heard adding, "Cinema!"*
B B :   So here it is Buddhism, Buddhism, Buddhism . . . Cinema!

A Young Bull Has Infiltrated
the Film Industry

STEFANO CONSIGLIO AND
FRANCESCO DAL BOSCO/1995

Q : *The cinema is basically an industry. As opposed to the painter or the writer, the artist who expresses himself through cinema, from the minute he conceives of his film, works in a system which is controlled by the rules of the market. The concept of the* auteur *in the film world seems to assume for this reason a very different meaning from the one usually used in other artistic fields. How would you define this concept and how has it evolved over time?*

A : When I began to make films in the early '60s, the concept of *auteur* first and foremost was used to define a cinema which placed itself in violent opposition to what was called at that time *le cinéma de papa* (old man's film). Leading this movement were a small group of French filmmakers, the New Wave, but immediately, other filmmakers throughout the world saw themselves included in this concept. *Auteur* films have always existed, of course, but at that time for precise historical reasons there was a collective movement and the birth of a new cultural politics of the cinema.

Q : *Wasn't it a bit what we would call today* le cinéma de qualité *(Quality Cinema)?*

A : It's difficult to say. It was very different because within the system of filmmaking there was enough space for a "cinema of quality." At that time they were making many more films than are made today, and the average

---

From *Script*, Nos. 7/8 (Rome), January 1995. Reprinted by permission. Translated by Fabien Gerard and T. Jefferson Kline.

quality was quite high. There wasn't the great gap that exists today between the film industry and *auteur* cinema. There was an intermediate group of successful films that simply doesn't exist today—or hardly. The idea of *auteur* cinema, like everything else in the '6os, was rather extremist and radical, with a heavy political connotation, which went along with a search for a new aesthetics. As for me, I was totally opposed to the Italian film industry; I couldn't identify with it or find any place for myself in it. They were making mostly comedies which I saw as a kind of degradation and betrayal of neorealism. Often these so-called "Italian comedies" made a pretense of including social criticism, but in my opinion, they seemed to be in bad faith. If a "political" film didn't wrestle with aesthetic problems it was a failure. Afterwards in the '70s a type of film that I could identify with was accepted and appreciated by French critics in the *Cahiers du cinéma* and *Positif*. For the entire decade of the '6os, my work was extremely idealistic, based on constant research on Bazin's question, "What is cinema?" The cinema was for me a kind of philosopher's stone which was to allow me to understand the world. At once a magnifying glass and a microscope, the instrument which would allow me to analyze reality and transform it exactly in the way I idealized things in the moments of my greatest and most extreme political passions. Before I discovered psychoanalysis, I saw it as a magical instrument that would allow me to survive. The cinema was everything to me. For one of Godard's shots I would have done anything. It was a question of life and death. Then a number of years went by, and the concept of the *auteur* changed, like a landscape, like our ideas, like our own faces.

Q : *A lot of cinema* auteurs *especially in Hollywood have managed to work in harmony with the industry, contributing in a significant way to its expansion. The work of some of these, from Chaplin to Spielberg, could be cited as a model of identification with the very concept of cinema as an "industrial art." These directors seem to have succeeded without apparent trauma in harmonizing in a perfectly feasible way their individual expression with the industry's programmed research on audience reactions. You yourself, for some time, seem to have worked easily enough in this context. Leaving aside the talent and motivation of any single director, it may be the consciousness of the limitations imposed by the medium of cinema and the capacity to transform these limitations into creative elements that really define the specific identity of the film* auteur.

A : The question of limits is much more pertinent to the cinema than to painting, music or the other arts. Cinema gives the appearance of being limitless precisely because it adheres so close to reality, which also gives the appearance of being limitless. In my case, I have undertaken an almost systematic search of the limits of film. I always try when possible to avoid shooting my films in studios, but instead on location in real decors, because they create obstacles. In the studio, in theory at least, there are no limits. To give you an example, if you want to film an interior from far away, if you're in Studio #5 at Cinecittà, all you have to do is knock down a fake wall and you can do it. In a real setting, on location, on the other hand, the physical limits of the walls are insurmountable. But it is these limitations that become a kind of propeller, platform, springboard, or stimulation. In this way my camera is constrained to go beyond these limitations with more creative solutions which do not rely on simply knocking down a fake wall. Let's take Spielberg. I don't think he considers the rules of the American film industry as obstacles. Looking at that world from this European perspective, Hollywood seems to us like a labyrinth of limits. But from Spielberg's and other American directors' point of view this simply isn't the case. For them, it's just a matter of making film according to rules. Now if we take a step backward, I don't know why I'm suddenly thinking about the films I saw as a child. I remember some movie houses in a mist-shrouded town in the provinces which were always full up on Sundays, the bodies of the spectators enveloped in the rough, badly fitting, smoke enshrouded jackets of post-war Italy.

The enormous physicality of this audience packed into the hall becomes a gestalt in which you pay a few lira to get in, lose yourself in the collective dream, the ecstasy of participating in the rite of the film, to feel yourself carried away in the mass identification of the audience with the film.

Gianni Amico, Glauber Rocha and I called our films "Miuras" or "Young Bulls." The "Miura" is the Spanish name given in bull fights to the most dangerous, strongest and lithest bulls. We told ourselves: even a mosquito couldn't penetrate his asshole, and we'd laugh. "I've made a 'Miura' film; not a single spectator will enter the theater," and we'd go on laughing to keep from crying.

I was deliberately trying to create such "Miuras," and yet I suffered a lot when I thought of these packed movie houses of my childhood. I often wondered what I understood back then by the word "rigor," and I think I can say that it was principally a refusal to have anything to do with my audience, fearing to be seen or judged, a refusal to seek out an audience coupled with the fear of being ignored by them. It's like when you fall in love and you fear being rejected by the object of your love. I only understood later when I read Roland Barthes what was meant by "the pleasure of the text." Because of political moralism we refused ourselves the pleasure of any sensual contact between the author and his audience. This kind of pleasure struck me as belonging absolutely to right wing filmmakers.

And so, little by little, I began to give up this idea of "rigor." I wanted to have contact, to embrace my audience.

Q : *"Fear of the audience," you said. What would this have meant to you at the time if your audience, as the object of your love, had rejected you?*
A : To speak less metaphorically, I'd say the fear of my audience was really the fear of not being strong enough to maintain my integrity; the fear of lowering myself to make compromises which would seem unacceptable to me. During the period 1964–68 I refused several projects, spaghetti westerns, or comedies. Four long years of frustration, in order to remain faithful to "my idea of the cinema." It was my inability to see the positive side of the word "compromise," despite the fact that there was a famous phrase in one of Godard's films, "Compromise is one of the highest forms of intelligence."

In this regard, I remember that Godard, when he won the Lion (Prize) in Venice in 1983 (a prize awarded to him by a jury I was chairing and which I would call a kind of "noble mafia" since it was entirely composed of ex-new wave directors), during his acceptance speech, said that *auteur* cinema was fine, but without Universal Studios, there would never have been any Hitchcock and without Carlo Ponti and De Laurentis, *La Strada* would never have been made. (At which point, Fellini, who was seated in the audience shouted, *"La Strada* was made *in spite of* Ponti and De Laurentis!")* At the end of the '60s, however, I could no longer accept the idea that the enormous amount of work, the incredible emotional investment that goes into making a film should go up in smoke and burn to ashes in a few seconds right before our eyes.

In a sense I think there is something slightly guilty in the maintenance of this quasi-aristocratic position. On the other hand I have enormous respect for the directors of my generation who chose to continue their risky work against the grain, as eternal "Miuras." As for me, after a certain point, this simply wasn't possible any more.

Q : *Some directors have paid dearly for the attempt to adapt their creative demands to the logic of the film industry. I'm thinking in particular of Orson Welles, who fought his entire life a continuous battle causing an enormous loss of time and energy, to affirm his independence as an* auteur. *Certainly he left us a series of memorable films, but one has the impression (confirmed more or less directly by Welles himself in numerous interviews) that his oeuvre would have been even more radical and innovative if the industry had allowed him the freedom that, given its very nature, it was unable to grant him. In any case, despite everything films continue to get made. But what happens, from your experience, when a strongly creative personality with a lively sense of independence stands up to the commercialism of the American film industry?*

A : It's very difficult to get inside the secret desires of a personality like Orson Welles. Ultimately though, don't I also belong to the family of those who seem definitively indigestible to the Hollywood system?

For some mysterious reason, though perhaps not really so mysterious, some of my films have enjoyed some commercial success; the audiences could identify with them, even American audiences. But those are the exceptions. It seems to me that my films, after 1969, beginning with *The Spider's Stratagem,* entered a different phase. I began a game of seduction with my audience. This despite the fact that the more time passes the more this idea of the audience seems mysterious, incomprehensible, undefinable. Ultimately the audience becomes a number, the box office. The only definition we can arrive at is this mathematical one.

In any case, ever since this period, all my efforts have been to bring my films (which have remained the same from the beginning, despite all the developments ascribable to my age and the social changes going on around me) into the heart of the film industry's empire, Hollywood. I intend to bring to Hollywood this idea of cinema I've always loved and identify with, by means of a technique not unlike terrorist infiltration.

My idea hasn't been to copy the great American successes, to imitate Hollywood cinema, on the contrary.... *The Last Emperor, The Sheltering Sky, Little Buddha* are films that could never have been conceived or made in Hollywood. So there is always an element of defiance which today, after *Little Buddha,* I have to admit is beginning to lose its fascination for me.

In fact, except for *Last Tango in Paris* and *The Last Emperor,* which are the two most successful films, my films are very hard to accept for American audiences.

What happens every time? For the last ten years I've been making independent films, independent of the major American studios. Let's say *Luna* and *Tragedy of a Ridiculous Man* were two films with major American backing, so in some sense, I should have accounted for this reality of production. And yet I don't understand how or why I always succeeded in preserving this outsider's position for which miraculously I never had any serious blowups with the major studios. And so because of a strange form of respect accorded me by the producers, I've always been able to maintain a certain liberty and independence. What I mean is, except for *Last Tango* and *Last Emperor,* which are special cases in which you discover yourself at one with your times because you've succeeded in saying things that mesh with the general consciousness, in a way that people can immediately identify with them. . . . So, apart from these two exceptions, I've made films which were a constant challenge, films which the American public didn't know how to react to . . . independent European films put together by Jeremy Thomas and me, a bit miraculously. As if to say, "Look! In Europe we also know how to make big films. We too, as independent Europeans, can challenge the American blockbusters with a completely European aesthetic tension and morality."

Up until now in America there have always been people who liked my films. Probably they like the ambition they can see in my films. I remember very well that after the first Hollywood screening of *The Last Emperor* some of the CEO's of the major studios came up and said, "Thank you! This film reminds us of why we wanted to make films in the first place." The next day they probably forgot what they'd said.

So these films found distributors, they made money, and a lot of money, after which the American distributors don't understand them, don't know what to do with them and get scared. So they end up marginalized.

By some perverse mechanism, which is currently in operation, distributing films in the U.S. means investing a minimum of three to four million dollars on publicity. For some films they'll spend up to fifteen to twenty million dollars. This means they take an enormous risk. For this reason, given the difficulties they have managing my films, the directors of marketing tend to make up their investments through home video and cable, which means they pull the film out of distribution in theaters after a very short time, and what's more frustrating, even in the major cities. So they prevent the film from reaching the larger American public outside of the major markets. The same thing happens for all European films, except, in some cases, for British films which are considered cousins, or relatives, of American films.

Q: *There are also certain American films which are treated in this way. For example the films of Robert Altman.*

A: Of course. And then what happens is that over time the American public is losing its taste for non-American films. In this sense today I am wondering why I should distribute my films in the U.S. The answer is quite simple: because the major portion of the financing for films depends on American distribution. And yet in theory, I'd like to say that I shouldn't even consider that the American market exists. With my last three films I realized that at this time, it's practically impossible to reach the mid-west. Even if *The Last Emperor* enjoyed a somewhat different fate, maybe it was only due to a passing moment. The last possible moment when there was still a place, which may have disappeared even for some American directors. At last year's GATT meetings, I talked about how much European film had influenced American film and about what might happen to American film if European film were to become an endangered species.

The power of the major studios has become so total that even directors like Scorsese, Altman, Woody Allen, or David Lynch, who often work outside the Hollywood rules, would become like Europeans in America, and their films would end up nowhere. In my view, what's happening now is very worrisome. Because not only in the U.S. but throughout the world there is an excessive power in Hollywood that monopolizes the market to the detriment of national cinemas creating a kind of sclerosis. I have tried in my own way to invent through my films a different direction for popular cinema.

I think, in some ways, I've failed, at least in maintaining a relationship with the major American market. The fact is that behind my films there is no premeditated project. I am always working instinctively. As for market considerations, I always think about them afterwards, never before making a film. I wonder very seriously if I've made a mistake in some way, vis a vis myself, in attempting to get my films widely distributed. But I don't think so. I wonder about this because I'm on the verge of making a low budget film, definitely less expensive than my last three films. And so I wonder if this phase I've just completed with *Little Buddha* was a failure or not. It's a very difficult question to answer given that I'm still so close to the experience and still haven't really emerged from it in some sense.

Q : *Wim Wenders has said: "Murnau was a pioneer, and he would still be one today. If he were living today he'd be working with video and computer imaging." What do you think about the idea that in cinema (in the etymological sense of the term) the only territory physically favorable to research and experimentation is video, given its status as a flexible medium, especially one that is less expensive (thanks to the vertiginous development of computerized systems) which allows one to work in a style much more closely aligned with the solitary practice of writers or painters who have complete control over their work?*

A : I think that this hypothesis contains an enormous contradiction. It's true, given its nature and manipulability, that video permits us to work alone with the instrument of expression in the same way a writer works with his pen and paper and a painter works with his brushes and colors. I think, however, that electronics and chemistry (since film is a chemical process) are two worlds very distinct from each other. What is especially different is the way the two are consumed: no need to repeat the differences between what I would call the "ecstatic" experience of watching a film in the "temple" of the movie theater, and the experience at home watching TV. But the contradiction I was talking about lies, in my mind, in the fact that electronics, for the few people who understand it, becomes extremely interesting the moment one considers it as an unknown and unexplored universe. I think of electronics as an instrument, a world all the more stimulating for its mystery. Today it is possible, for example, to do what Godard is trying to do, using electronics exactly as a painter uses a canvas, or better yet as an Irish miniaturist used pages of the Bible.

Q : *In any case, electronics and video technologies are not cinema.*

A : No, it's an entirely different world. I think we have to accept this difference. To sum up this discussion of the cinema, I'm thinking of the writings of the greatest Chinese writer of the first half of this century, Lu

Hsun, who tells of an evening at the movies, this incredible novelty in China in the '20s. He sits down in the first row and turns around to watch all the faces of the Chinese in the audience waiting for the film to begin. He watches their drooping chins, their stupefied eyes and their anguish at waiting. "It's very beautiful," he says. Then, unfortunately, the lights dim, the film begins and the audience's eyes disappear in the darkness.

Toptoeing in Tuscany

ALLEN OLENSKY/1996

A O : *When we last met on the set of* Stealing Beauty, *you were just shooting a scene in which Osvaldo, the boy who is secretly in love with Lucy (Liv Tyler), was telling her about how his father had to flee to Santo Domingo in order to escape jail. You suggested that this line was a key to understanding your return to Italy after more than ten years of working outside the country.*

B B : I remember that day. It was in late August; the whole crew was scattered out over a hay field and it was very very hot . . . It's true, a triumphant cynicism characterized Italian society in the 80's which convinced me to leave in search of horizons uncontaminated by consumerist values. At the beginning of the 90's when I was doing *Little Buddha,* this terrible stink of corruption exploded full scale. That's why the famous inquest known as operation "Clean Hands" seemed to be a kind of collective catharsis, a metaphorical remorse operating at a more general level. In fact, you know, it was the Italian people themselves who had elected all those politicians accused of bringing the country to the brink of chaos. Since then, the resistible rise of a "providential man" like the *cavaliere* Berlusconi has evidently shaken up all the givens of what is known as democracy, but at least it also had the merit of reawakening the old anti fascist Resistance as you can see from the last elections.

In short, the situation sparked my own desire to become reengaged politically, as I had been in the 60's and in the 70's, even if now it has

Previously unpublished interview. © 1996 Allen Olensky and Bernardo Bertolucci. Reprinted by permission. Translated by T. Jefferson Kline.

taken another form; the absence of any desire to film the Italian scene, which provoked a kind of divorce between me and my country ten years ago, seems to have come full circle. And yet, after such a long absence, faced with this new situation in Italy, I felt the need to rediscover my country through the eyes of a foreigner. Whence the story of Lucy, this young American girl who comes to spend her vacation in a Tuscan villa. Her pretext for being there is to have her portrait done by an artist friend of her parents, but her secret goal is to discover the identity of her real father. Like me, the people who make up this cosmopolitan community she enters had been very politically engaged twenty or thirty years previously; but, out of despair, they decided to abandon their political dreams at a certain moment and seek refuge far from the vulgar crowd, at the top of a hill, overlooking a unique landscape whose incredible beauty inspired the Tuscan painters of the 14th and 15th centuries.

A O : *Why did you choose Tuscany and not the countryside around Parma?*
B B : For the same reasons that led me to see Italy through the eyes of this family of English bohemians settled in the heart of Italy: I needed to get some distance on my birthplace. In other words, I needed to come home but only on tiptoe and through the back door! It was a calculated choice, as was the selection of a new director of photography, Darius Khondji, whose work I'd really liked in *Delikatessen*, in *Before the Rain* and *Seven*. Darius is a young French DP of Iranian origin, and while watching him on the set, I sometimes had the impression of jumping twenty-five years into the past, because he looked so much Storaro did when he was working on *Spider's Stratagem*. (I even ended up calling Vittorio my "Persian prince" because of his Arab profile and olive skin!). Maybe for me it was also a way of regaining my virginity, to help me turn a page and forget the terrible weight of the epic frescoes of the "oriental trilogy" in favor of something which felt much more like chamber music. There is an almost Mozart-like lightness in *Stealing Beauty* although the film addresses more serious and even perturbing issues as well, like the imminent death of the playwright played by Jeremy Irons. As we were beginning to shoot, I remember saying that my dream was to make a film that would only weight a few grams.

Behind all that, there was also my personal memory of vacations spent in the Chianti region at the home of some English friends—there's actually a whole tradition of English expatriates who settled in the so-called "Chianti-shire" — who were troubled by the arrival of a girl whose virginity became the big question mark of the summer. That was the point of departure for the film; the sculptures of this family friend, Matthew Spender, have been imported into *Stealing Beauty* and people the gardens of the villa Grayson.

A O : Little Buddha *was a film filled with kids and which was addressed to kids.* Stealing Beauty *is a film filled with older kids who are very rooted in today's reality, and who are wrestling with the difficult choices that confront them as they enter adulthood. Your two most recent films project a kind of desire to reach out to a new generation.*

B B : What interested me was to bring together two worlds whose points of reference seem even more divergent today than they did in the past. For starters, there's this little circle of "veterans" of the '60s, who feel revitalized by the sensual presence of a sort of "Lucy-in-the-sky," who has literally parachuted into their midst, a bit like the character of Terence Stamp in Pasolini's *Theorem.* I've never had much of a relationship with young people. Even when I was young myself I made films that brought me immediately into contact with people older than I was. Then in 1968 I joined the Communist Party as a reaction against the pro-Chinese positions of a large number of people of my generation! Now with this film, for the first time I have the sense of discovering young people. In fact, my mistrust of them came from my sense that they no longer read any books, that they no longer thought seriously about things, that they were completely ignorant of the past and of history and that they were content to let themselves be brainwashed by watching TV. But these kids I worked with made me give up many of my prejudices and pretty much won me over. That's why I'm now thinking of dedicating the third part of *1900* to them. It's a story that could take place between Berkeley, Paris, and Rome in which, through a kind of time machine, today's young people could confront the ideals of the youth of 1968 — their own parents . . .

A O : *Lucy seems like a kind of older sister of Jesse, especially when we see her sitting in the lotus position when she's posing under the tree for the sculptor . . .*

B B : There's no doubt that the experience of making *Little Buddha* transformed me. On the one hand, being around all those Tibetan sages taught me a new lightheartedness; thanks to them I discovered that I'm now saving a bundle on the tons of prescriptions I used to take! And they also helped me understand that it was even possible for an old Italian filmmaker like me to reincarnate himself as a young 19-year-old American girl! What's more, Liv Tyler had this kind of mystery and vitality that were really exciting to someone who habitually sees the world through a camera. When she showed up for the casting auditions, she was only seventeen, but at certain moments she appeared to be fourteen and at others twenty or twenty-five. This was exactly what I was looking for. After having read the screenplay, she came and told me that when she was nine she had discovered that the man she thought was her father was not her real father—it was Lucy's story! I understood that I hadn't made a bad choice.

AO: *The way you talk about your relationship to the camera sounds almost like a kind of voyeurism!*
BB: Well, that's the sense of the entire opening sequence of the film—the trip which brings Lucy to the station in Siena, and which I personally shot in Video 8.

AO: *Which creates a kind of shadowy zone in the film, since not everyone understands who this person is who is secretly filming Lucy in the plane and in the train.*
BB: As a matter of fact, while we were doing the editing, I showed a work in progress to about a hundred spectators, and many failed to associate the African bracelet on the man with the camera with the Carlo Lisca character, the war reporter who was one of the lovers of Lucy's mother, and who resurfaces later in the film. But you're right: these details may be formally present, but the viewers—and I myself sometimes—get so caught up in the emotional level of the film that they miss them. It also happens that I eliminated a scene which would doubtless have furnished additional clues to understanding this identity. When everyone was leaving to go to the party at the neighboring villa, Daisy, the little girl, was going through people's things and stole the cassette that Lucy had been given by the stranger at the station. She inserts it in the VCR and we see the very first images of the film (Lucy in the plane, Lucy in the train...) replayed on the TV screen. Then suddenly out of the blue, they are followed by some terrifying images of Sarajevo, as if Carlo Lisca had reused a cassette that had been recorded

during his last news report from Bosnia. And Daisy goes on watching this bloodshed like kids watch TV today, which is to say without a trace of emotion. I have to say that these unedited images were so frightful that they were rejected by Italian television, so at the last minute I decided to scratch the entire sequence out of pure *pietà*, since I didn't want to exploit anything so tragic. From another point of view, it's certain that this scene would have clarified for the audience the voyeurism of the character of the journalist. But it's no surprise to anyone that I've never liked to be too explicit in my films.

A O :   *If Liv Tyler is Beauty in the film, is Jean Marais the Beast?*
B B :   He's also very enigmatic. For a long time I've wanted to pay homage to Cocteau (and Jean Marais, by the way, quotes something very beautiful about love that I borrowed from the screenplay of *Les Dames du Bois de Boulogne* which Cocteau wrote for Bresson). At eighty-five Marais is obviously a historical monument. His role in the film is to incarnate the whole era of film of my parents' generation, the way Alida Valli did in *The Spider's Stratagem* or the way Massimo Girotti, Maria Michi, and Giovanna Galletti did in *Tango:* for film lovers they represent the great ghosts of neo-realism. I always experience their presence on the set as something very reassuring—like a benevolent, protective aura arising from the past, which sustains me as I venture into the forbidden zones that compose the canvas of unconscious forces driving me every time I try to represent the unrepresentable.

A O :   *The actor who plays the role of the sulptor bears a remarkable resemblance to you...*
B B :   It's true. Someone handed me a photo in the Press Kit that shows us side by side and we really look like two brothers—but honestly I'd never thought about this before! Maybe this is also due to the fact that Donal McCann is Irish (he plays the husband of Anjelica Huston in *The Dead*) and I'm one quarter Irish myself! In fact this was the hardest role to cast. My main concern was to avoid falling into clichés and I had begun to despair of ever finding the ideal actor. But then I went to see *The Steward of Christendom* on the London stage, and I was immediately struck by Donal's very threatening manner. And for me, that's what defines an artist or a creator. Someone who is at once mysterious and dangerous.

A O : *Don't I remember that the collection of poetry you published at age twenty was called* In Search of Mystery?

B B : Lucy also writes poems which are supposed to express the unspeakable. And since she's searching for her father, I took the liberty of "stealing" from my own father an episode from his youth—the one where Lucy tosses to the winds little scraps of paper on which she has written some verses, just like messages in bottles cast into the sea. This happened while my father was studying in boarding school; he was dying to show his poetry to one of his teachers but didn't dare give them directly to him so he scattered the sheets of paper on the window sill of the teacher's room to give the impression the wind had blown them there! When he watched *Stealing Beauty* for the first time a few weeks ago, my father said that he had the impression he was watching my "first film!" So you see, instead of killing the father, in the manner of Oedipus, as in most of my films, a strange harmony has developed in our relationship through this "portrait of a lady," so youthful that I'm still surprised that I have made it myself.

A O : *"Didn't anyone ever tell you the artist always depicts himself?"*

B B : To this I would reply with another quote (but it's up to you to find out who authored it!): "We all work in the dark, we do what we can, we give what we have. Our doubt is our passion and our passion is our task. The rest is the madness of art."

Interview with Bernardo Bertolucci

GEOFFREY NOWELL-SMITH AND
ILONA HALBERSTADT/1997

G N - S : *Can you tell us something about your current project?*

B B : I'm working with Susan Minot on a contemporary subject, medium budget, to be shot in late spring or early summer in Tuscany, with the provisional title "I dance alone" [To be released as *Stealing Beauty*]. We're doing a revision of the script right now.

G N - S : *Who will produce it?*

B B : Jeremy Thomas, as usual.

G N - S : *Does the fact that you're working with Jeremy Thomas again mean that you feel you've definitely found a producer who's not going to give you anguish of one kind or another?*

B B : We've been working together for ten years, which I think means there's a kind of affinity. Looking for a producer is like looking for an ideal figure and all my life this has not been satisfied. It may sound banal, but every time I thought I'd found the right one, dramatic problems would appear. With Jeremy, I have rediscovered a kind of playful, joyful side, perhaps a bit childish, working *à deux* on the building of a project—from the first seed, through the battle of the shooting, to the completion of the mixing.

G N - S : *What about distribution? Do you feel that with your current set-up your interests are being well looked after, that you won't any longer get the sort of problems you had with 1900?*

From *Pix*, January 1997. © 1997 by PIX. Reprinted by permission.

B B : Distribution is the most painful phase, because it's completely out of our control. We can decide what movie to shoot, where to shoot it, what cast to have, and nobody can interfere because, for the last ten years, we have been making independent movies. I insist on this because many people think that they are, in some ways, American movies. In fact they are a demonstration that even in Europe you can challenge big, spectacular, ambitious Hollywood productions. We then sell them to an American distributor in the same way as to distributors in Italy, France, Japan, etc. But they remain independent movies in which pre-production, casting, the script, shooting, everything, is under our control. When we enter the distribution phase, we lose control, particularly in the United States. I'm referring here to the three "oriental" movies, which for me represented a challenge—to achieve a very wide response, to attract a very big audience, even in the U.S. with a European movie. In the United States, especially recently, the audience has forgotten that other cinemas exist. European cinema has more or less disappeared from American screens, except for a very few films, which tend to be British ones, shot in English and so on. I've had two films which were very successful in the States—*Last Tango* and *The Last Emperor*. But even with *The Last Emperor*, in spite of all its Oscars, the experience was only half a success, since the film could have been released in a better way. When I go to the States, American distributors are always very keen to buy my movies, there's something about them which excites these young Hollywood execs. I remember one of them saying, at the première of *The Last Emperor*, that it was a film which reminded him of why he decided to go into movies. So they buy the movies, but when in fact they have to release them they realise that they are very different from American movies. And increasingly the American audience, as I said, only watches American movies, and so, I'm afraid, do Italian audiences, French audiences, audiences everywhere. To get real distribution in the United States you need to spend four or five million dollars on P & A, that is prints and advertising. And at that point the American distributors say, Oh my God, should I risk all this extra money? Couldn't we just recoup the money we spend to buy the movie from video and cable and syndication and all that? And in the end they decide to spend a bit, but not enough. So on the one hand you have the distributors who are terrified by the risk of that investment and on the other hand you have the audience which is less and less able to sit and watch a movie which is not

American. This means we have to create a distribution set-up in the United States, owned by the European Community, which would have a solid economic foundation and could engage in serious long-term work to re-educate American audiences to see non-American movies. I was talking about these issues with Martin Scorsese, at the time of the discussion about the GATT agreement. In general, Americans in Hollywood couldn't understand what the *exception culturelle* meant, which was the French formula. GATT is against any form of protectionism and the Americans would ask, Why should movies be treated any different from cars? And if you ask a question like that it's clear that you think a movie is like a factory product.

G N - S : *This has always been the American position. For example, for a long time films were not protected by the Constitution as embodying a right to free speech because they were seen as a commercial product like any other. There is a complete cultural gap between the French, who regard films as the work of an author, and the Americans who just see them as products.*

B B : Exactly. And yet — and this is what I was talking to Scorsese about — you have to be vigilant. American cinema has been influenced by European movies in its cinematic language for a long time now and vice versa. Also, a lot of big American hits are remakes of European films. Cinema is inter-active in that way. It's extraordinary to find that John Ford, in *Seven Women*, which is one of his last movies, uses jump cuts, which wouldn't have been possible without Godard. I think that Ford was allowing himself some naughty tricks. There have always been fantastic waves of influence be-tween filmmakers. It would be a terrible impoverishment for American cinema if it was only influenced by itself and ceased to be influenced by films from elsewhere in the world. So I said to Martin, help us to help yourself. People like you, or Altman, or Woody Allen, or David Lynch, or any of the interesting directors, could become kind of European figures lost in the United States, and your space would be reduced and reduced and reduced, if the Majors are allowed to become even more powerful.

What interests me is to have a great love affair with a huge audience. This is the direction I've taken since the end of the '60s. Throughout the '60s I was making movies alongside Glauber Rocha and Gianni Amico and we had this joke about the *Miura*. You know what the *Miura* is? He is the bull in the bullfight, the most aggressive of all the bulls, the one who is so tight-arsed that not even a mosquito can get up there. And we would say to each other, laughing, "I've just made another *Miura*," meaning a film nobody could get into. But then at the end of the '60s I began to suffer from the sterility of this, the lack of communication. I needed an interlocutor, someone to talk to. I was fed up with just hearing my own voice, without hearing any response. So that's why I went on to make *The Conformist* and *Last Tango in Paris*. I always thought that what we called "rigour" in the '60s was like when you love someone and don't have the courage to express yourself, because you are afraid of being refused. Maybe we really wanted very much to communicate with an audience, but were afraid to make a move and not get a reaction.

I think, though, that there was more to it than that, and looking back I see a clear itinerary. The '60s was a time when I felt I belonged to a movement which was changing the cinema. It began with the French *nouvelle vague* and spread outwards. In every country there was one, or two, or three young filmmakers who felt a togetherness of intention, going against the old cinema, the *cinéma de papa,* but also seeing the political side of that revolution, which was a revolution of style and of cinematic vision. With our movies then we wanted to understand the nature and meaning of cinema. Our movies were reflections on the cinema, and this led us in a direction where not everybody could follow us, especially audiences.

GN-S: *You want to get an audience to follow you.*

BB: I want to have a reaction, an answer to my questions, my voice, my cries.

GN-S: *There is a middle way between something that is addressed to the Happy Few and something that goes out into the world at large and may or may not be successful in a small town in America—if you were ever to find out, which you might not.*

BB: Of course. Also it's all a big illusion, a projection which goes on in your fantasy, in your head. Because, what is the audience, big question mark. Unfortunately today it seems that the only way to know if you are an artist or not is to look at the figures at the box-office. Glauber Rocha used to say—as a provocation, with apparent cynicism—that a film director is someone who is able to find the money to make his movie. That is the structural level of cinema, money. Fortunately ninety percent of the movies we love are proof of the opposite.

Can I open a little parenthesis here, thinking of Glauber, and Brazil. I was at the Festival of Brasilia in December for a homage to Gianni Amico, who died in November 1990. We wrote scripts together including *Before the Revolution* and *Partner,* and I co-wrote a script which he directed called *L'inchiesta.* He was a great friend of Brazil, and so to speak a co-founder of the Brazilian *cinema nôvo* because in the early '60s, as director of the Sestri Levante Festival, he brought Glauber to Europe and showed his first films, and those of Nelson Pereira dos Santos and the others. The Brazilians felt a fantastic gratitude to him. So they gave him this homage and around this table there were something like ten or fifteen Brazilian filmmakers of my generation, talking about Gianni Amico's cinema and about *cinema nôvo.* *Cinema nôvo* faded out with the death of Glauber, the death of Léon Hirszman and David Neves. We were talking about *cinema nôvo* and then we went as a delegation to see the new President, who is an intellectual and who they call the "elected President" (Presidents before him were imposed, not elected). This "elected President" is Fernando Enrique Cardoso and when he was in exile he spent a lot of time with Hirszman, who was a real intellectual—a sociologist—as well as a filmmaker. Cardoso, when I pressed him, was very, very encouraging. He said he wanted to do a lot for culture and to support the cinema. It would be fantastic if thirty years later Gianni Amico could be the occasion for a revival of Brazilian cinema.

G N - S : *He had a small part in* Before the Revolution *as the cinephile who "cannot live without Rossellini."*
B B : And Brazil couldn't live without Gianni Amico. He made a really fine film in Brazil, called *Tropici*, remember?

G N - S : *I did the English subtitles.*
B B : They showed it in Brasilia in front of twenty-five hundred people, in a big theatre, as the closing event of the festival. The audience was completely captivated by a film made in 1967, in 16mm black and white, about a family of peasants from the Nordeste, very poor, who move to the big city. They all trek to São Paulo. And the movie ends with this guy, the father, who has become a builder and is working on a construction site building the São Paulo Hilton. And some Brazilians who had never seen it before told me: you know, that story could have been written today.

G N - S : *This takes us back to the question of the audience. Every film has got its own audience, or audiences which will take it up differently. A film like* Tragedy of a Ridiculous Man *is addressed to an Italian audience, and other audiences can eavesdrop on it. But* The Sheltering Sky *addresses people in different countries equally, and it's rare for a European director to be able to make films that are not constrained by nationality. Mostly, a European director makes a film for his country's audience, and then looks to sell it abroad. A lot of Italian films barely get any release abroad. Gianni Amelio's* Lamerica *for example doesn't look as if it will be released in Britain, ever.*

B B : Yes, but because of the high cost of movies today, it's very hard to cover the cost of your movie on the national market alone. It only works if you have a big hit, like with Benigni in Italy or some French comedies. My idea, starting with *1900*, was to go beyond national borders. *1900* was a kind of complete dream because at the beginning I thought I could use it to create my own kind of "historic compromise." This was the time of the "historic compromise" in Italian politics, when Berlinguer [leader of the Italian Communist Party] and Moro [Christian Democrat Prime Minister, later assassinated by the Red Brigades] were thinking of a fusion between the Communists and Christian Democrats. They were thinking the Communist workers and Catholic workers had the same objectives, so why not get together. And I was thinking that with *1900* I could make a bridge between the Soviet Union and the United States, being in the middle. Which was the most extraordinary, naive idea I could have had. This idealism came to grief immediately. I wanted a Russian actor to be the peasant and an American the landowner. But the Russians said to me: First we have to read the script, then we can ask for corrections, and eventually we'll give you a Russian actor. So I said: Forget it. The two countries in which the movie really got punished were the United States and the Soviet Union, since in both of them the movie almost didn't open at all. I think it was for the same reason: too many red flags both for the United States and for the Soviet Union. But to get back to what you were saying, if it's a big, expensive movie you have to cross the borders, otherwise you'll never get your money back. If it's less ambitious, and less expensive, then you can think of only being seen by Italians, but I think that's a bit of a limitation.

I H : *Doesn't this take us back to the question you raised earlier—audiences and reeducation? As a child, in Egypt, I saw* Stromboli. *We went to see a Rossellini*

film because we were reading about Ingrid Bergman in the fan magazines. A
kind of education.

B B : The world is now less and less educated, thanks to television. In
England it may be better, but in Italy and in the United States, television is
just a great repository of non-culture, of sub-cultural values. Look at what
happened in Italy last year when a TV tycoon was able to create a party
and become Prime Minister in three months, by using the power of his
three television channels. Television has this extraordinary impact, and if
it were used differently it could become a fantastic university, a collective
university. What's actually happening is what Pasolini would have called
a genocide, a cultural genocide, in the sense that the murder of Italian
peasant culture was for him a genocide. So when we say re-education, the
question is how? Cinema, by its nature, has to deal with reality. The reality of the societies we are living in is important for our movies. This is one
reason why I didn't do movies in Italy in the '80s. I couldn't stand the
atmosphere of Italy in the '80s. It was a time of economic boom and with
that came the supremacy of sub-culture, of non-culture, which I found
suffocating. I made *Tragedy of a Ridiculous Man* just at the beginning of
the '80s, and it tried to talk about this confusion, the strong unbearable
malaise. And then I left. Twenty years ago I would have been accused of
escapism, but fortunately, not now. I went to China, to get as far away as
possible from Italian reality, which, since my nature is a bit idealistic, I
couldn't deal with. I couldn't take the cynicism of Craxi and company,
although cynicism can be interesting at a certain period, as in the case of
Choderlos de Laclos, a kind of noble cynicism. I needed some oxygen, so I
went to the Far East.

G N - S : *The important thing is whether one has the cultural horizons to make*
something of a situation that is not one's own. Some people can, some people
couldn't. There's no way Fellini, for example, could have stepped out of Italy and
made films somewhere else, because he's very national.
B B : I think *The Last Emperor* is a very Italian film. It's about China, but in
the manner of an Italian opera or melodrama. Like in an opera you have
the Emperor and the Empress, the Cause, the Country, the baddies and the
goodies. It may sound presumptuous, but I'm quite happy with what happened to me in those ten years, especially that I discovered cultures of
which I was previously ignorant. . . . Pasolini in one of his essays talked

about the cinema as the language through which reality expresses itself. To create the language of the cinema, more than with any other form of expression, you first have to put your camera in front of reality, because cinema is made of reality.

G N - S : *It's also a matter of putting reality back together. But one way or another you're always dealing with real things. If you want to create a character you have to do it through an actor, through the actor's body.*

B B : Actors or non-actors. I always think of myself as using these pieces of reality—bodies, faces, objects, lights. And that's what makes it hard to work in a society where reality has become sub-cultural. Everything gets conditioned by this sub-cultural reality. When you put the camera in front of something, that something belongs to reality. You are always filming what is in front of the camera and you cannot lie to the camera—it shows, it's embarrassing. It would be nice if television could also work in that way. A television that respected reality could be a great promoter of culture.

G N - S : *That's what Rossellini wanted.*

B B : That's what Rossellini achieved in the '60s and '70s with his educational, poetic TV films—*The Age of Iron, The Rise to Power of Louis XIV, Socrates* and so on. But I don't think that sort of thing is happening now. However, in England your television performs more of a social function, even when it's private, like Channel Four. Culture became kind of attractive here. Coming from Italy I find it very impressive how very often in this country one can see discussion and analysis on TV.

G N - S : *I once had an argument with Pier Paolo—with Pasolini—as to whose middle class was worse. He said that the Italian middle class was the stupidest, most philistine one in the world, and the British middle class was wonderful and very intellectual. I said, nonsense, it was the other way round, but in a sense he was proved right because the middle-class intelligentsia in Britain at least proved capable of preserving its television which, unlike anywhere else, even when it is privatised, retains a role as a form of public service.*

B B : It was privatised much earlier than in other European countries, before Italy, before France. Privatisation in Italy happened only in the mid-'70s and in France not until the '80s. In Italy it was a disaster. It was chaotic, completely deregulated. In France they liberalised TV, allowing private channels but with rules of the game which protected cinema. We called it the network jungle. It was bad for the cinema because all the big, new movies kept cropping up on TV during the hours when people go to the movies. This was the time of terrorism and people weren't eager to go out, so they stayed in and watched movies on TV and lost the habit of going to the movies. There's a beautiful anecdote about Eduardo de Filippo, you know the great Neapolitan playwright, actor and director. Once in the '60s, a senior TV official phoned him and said "Is that de Filippo?" "Yes." "Television here." And de Filippo said, "One moment, I'll pass you the fridge."

GN-S: *The lack of regulation was partly the politicians' fault, especially Craxi and the so-called Socialist Party.*

BB: Yes, Craxi was close to Berlusconi and protected him, so that whenever a judge ruled against him and had his network closed down for breaches of the law, Craxi promptly had it reopened. Berlusconi also ran up huge losses and had to turn himself into a politician to protect himself and his empire.

IH: *How can the Italians put up with such a TV system? Isn't Italy a country where art is very important to people, unlike England, where there is a suspicion of art?*

BB: You think so? But in a way there is a suspicion of art in Italy too. I remember when Pier Paolo used the term poetry, poetic, all the time, and people were very suspicious. But thank God he had the courage to go on using it. I think the problem in England is embarrassment. People in England keep using the term embarrassment. It's part of English reticence, and the famous English understatement. You find art embarrassing. This is quite unlike the French who have no sense of embarrassment, otherwise they wouldn't use words like *sublime* and *sublimissime*.

GN-S: *A suspicion of anything that smacks too much of art is a big problem for filmmakers.*

BB: In what way?

GN-S: *Because it's so difficult to make films which have got some kind of cultural depth to them and still find an audience. How many filmmakers are there out there at the moment making popular films with any cultural depth?*

BB: But that's precisely the challenge. I'm still very much the same person who was doing movies in the '60s. Some are more successful than others, but all of them in some sense are infiltrators. They smuggle in something. Somebody said that *Little Buddha* is Spielbergian. I think it's more Michael Powell than Spielberg.

IH: *It reminds me of* The Thief of Baghdad.
BB: Whatever people may say, the fact is none of my movies could ever have been made in Hollywood. That's why they encounter problems with getting distributed in the U.S.

GN-S: *Can you pinpoint the difference? What is it about them that makes the distributors feel they don't have the same audience appeal as American movies?*
BB: It's the attitude towards reality. It's point of view. Optical point of view. Moral point of view. Philosophical point of view. Style. That's what makes my movies mysterious objects to them. They say the movies are difficult. I don't think they are, but this is the way things are going at the moment. The problem is that nowadays films are basically talked about only if they are successful. This is the terrible injustice of our time. Half of the great masterpieces in film history wouldn't exist if this had always been the case. I love *Pulp Fiction* but I also love Kieślowski's *Three Colours*. But nobody wants to talk about *Rouge* and the others in the *Three Colours* trilogy. They only want to talk about *Pulp Fiction*. It's the supremacy of Pop, of instant culture. *Three Colours* isn't Pop.

GN-S: *It's a problem of journalism, of journalists only writing about what's hot, and if a thing ceases to be hot it's no longer talked about. They'll stop talking about* Pulp Fiction, *but at least they did talk about it, whereas very little was said about* Rouge *even when it came out.*
BB: *Rouge* is a beautiful film. Someone said to me that it was too precious and I replied that it's mannerist, seeking perfection, a jewel. But *Pulp Fiction* is an incredible mannerist film too. In spite of the cheeseburger look, it's actually completely influenced by Godard's gangster films. Godard's films are already mannerist, and here we have an American mannerist, influenced by a divine French mannerist. It is very unjust that *Rouge* has been neglected. Think of the great movies of the past, entire schools of cinema, neo-realism. Dreyer, *La Règle du jeu*, you name it. Today they would be

completely ignored. Something has to be done, but I don't know quite what.

As far as my own projects are concerned, I'm entering a phase when I first want to withdraw a little bit. The movie I am making now is a kind of chamber music work. Then after that? There are two big projects I am considering. One is to make a film of Malraux's *Man's Estate* which I would shoot in Shanghai. This would mean going back to China, which I'd like to do, to see what's been happening there over the last ten years. And then I'd like to do a kind of sequel to *1900*. I have to thank Berlusconi for that. His attitude has been so offensive it has woken Italy up. Words like resistance have come back into use. Italy is now a country where Fascists have been democratically elected to the government. Imagine that! It's especially the young voters who brought the Fascists to power. You can see this from the fact that the Chamber of Deputies, which you can vote for at eighteen, is full of Fascists from the Alleanza Nazionale, whereas the Senate, which you can't vote for until you're twenty-one, has fewer. It's not the young people's fault. They don't know what they're doing because the school system has totally failed to give them any background. So I would want to make a film which took up the story where *1900* left off, in 1945, in order to restore a certain sense of historical memory. Young people today don't know what happened even fifteen, twenty years ago. You remember the documentary made in France by Bertrand Blier called *Hitler, connais pas!* That sort of ignorance is scary.

GN-S: *So you see your film as political intervention?*

BB: And *Man's Estate* as well. When I first went to China in 1984 it was with two projects. *The Last Emperor* and *Man's Estate*. Well, at the time the Chinese didn't even want to discuss *Man's Estate*. They were afraid of it — in spite of the fact that it was the novel that made the Chinese Revolution and the Chinese Communist Party loved all over the world. It was a novel that brought together Revolution and Love, collective mystery and the personal story of the characters in a burning flame. You know the story of the Shanghai uprising? It was led by Chou En-lai, which is perhaps why they were afraid of the story. The Communists were in alliance with Chiang Kai-shek and the Kuomintang, but when the uprising came Chiang betrayed them. Shanghai was in the hands of the Communists and Chiang was outside the city, waiting in his armoured train, and the foreign legations and the big landowners and industrialists came to him and offered him $50 million to change sides. Which he did, and at that point the train started off and the Communists were massacred. This betrayal will be the key to the film.

As for the sequel to *1900*, I don't yet know how to structure it, but the idea excites me because it will talk about the past fifty years of our life.

G N - S : *It will talk about the years of your life. In the '70s you made a number of films about the years immediately before you were born, the years of your parents' lives. There's a particular fascination in that, imagining the world before you were born. But there's a different fascination in talking about one's own times. I want to ask you about something else: the way you work and the importance to you of collaboration, and particular people you like to work with.*

B B : I used to write poems, and when I did my first movie I had just put down my pen and went from the loneliness of writing to the joyful, human chaos of the movie set. At the time I thought the camera was just another pen. What I didn't realise at first was that in the cinema the hand that holds the pen is a collective hand. A movie is not made by just one person. It is made by everybody around the camera, in front of the camera, behind the camera, even by the environment. This was particularly important with *1900*, which was shot as season after season, with particular types of light corresponding to periods of history. It starts in summer, which was youth, and then there were the autumn and winter of Fascism, and finally the spring of Liberation. The film is a big cyclical flashback, beginning and ending with 25 April 1945 and the trial of the landowner. Shooting those scenes, in the spring of 1975, with the people playing the peasants who were experimenting with the fantasy of this trial of the landowner—somehow they took over. The people taking power in the film took power of the film as well. You know how a roll of film has written on it what its sensitivity is, ASA such-and-such. Well, the real sensitivity of a film is not what's written on the box but the sensitivity of people to what they're doing.

The first person who helped me give up the idea of the solitary author was probably my editor, Kim Arcalli. You know who he was? He was in the Resistance when he was fourteen. He was the youngest Political Commissar in the partisan Garibaldi Brigades. He took part in the action in '44 or '45 when the Partisans held up the Teatro Goldoni in Venice with machine-guns and the audience consisted of all these Fascist high-ups and the Partisans threatened them with their guns and made them listen to an anti-Fascist, anti-Nazi manifesto before letting them go—like the beginning of *Senso*. After that he had to go into hiding, in the mountains. Then, after the war, he became a writer and a film editor.

Anyhow, as I was saying.... In the '60s I couldn't swallow the idea of editing. I hated the idea of losing anything I had made, and I was into a kind of cinema of cruelty, making the audience see everything. I considered editing a gesture of law and order, imposing conformity on the beautiful chaos of the rushes. It was very 1960s, the all-powerful author. Well, Kim first became my editor when I was making *The Conformist*, and he showed me how the editing can be very enriching, because in the editing, as well as losing things, you also discover things in the material you weren't aware of. Before that my editor had been Roberto Perpignani, who was a very good editor, but we were too close, there was no dialectic. Kim made me step back from what I was doing, and see things differently.

G N - S : *Was Kim involved in the pre-production, or did he get involved only after the film was shot?*

B B : On *The Conformist* he only came in at the end. He was brought in by the producer, who was my cousin Giovanni. But then he and I wrote *Last Tango* and *1900* together. Then he died. As an editor he had a fantastic kind of relationship with the material, with the print, a very physical approach, manipulating it, touching it.

G N - S : *That doesn't happen nowadays, with video.*

B B : Four years ago, when I was doing the assembly of *The Sheltering Sky*, we started working with this electronic machine. It was much, much faster than working with celluloid. But the image had no body. It was transparent. The electronic image is like the ghost of the film image. It doesn't have the body, the thickness, the weight and resonance. In the end I went back to film and finished the editing of the movie on celluloid. The actual physical quality of film is important to me. Videotape isn't film. Television isn't film either. It's a kind of graveyard of the movies. The movies are a grand, collective, ceremonial experience, which you can't have with television or video. But then, we have Jean-Luc Godard, and his fantastic work with video and electronic images.

GN-S: *When Godard does video work he doesn't pretend he is doing cinema. It isn't television either. He is working with video to see what it can do. The whole mental paradigm shifts.*

BB: You know my idea of Godard's work today? It has become like a fantastic diamond which has an interior light. It's detached, because it doesn't need light from the sun and its own inner light radiates outwards. So it's sublime and far away.

IH: *I wanted you to talk about light, and now you're doing so.*

BB: Light for me means Storaro. He's my age, or a little older. He started working for me on *Before the Revolution* where he was assistant to Aldo Scavarda.

GN-S: *Scavarda had been Di Venanzo's assistant, and then went on to be director of photography on* L'Avventura.

BB: Storaro and I in a sense grew up together. But I didn't see him between 1964 and 1969 when he was taken on for *Spider's Stratagem,* by which time he'd already made a couple of movies as director of photography. He's an inspired person, one of the most interesting DPs anywhere, ever.

GN-S: *If you have the same collaborators regularly, they must get to know each other and be able to think in terms of what each one is going to do. The Last Emperor is so harmonious that you feel it must have been put together by people who understood each other pretty well.*

BB: Yes, but you can have too much of a good thing. You need continuity of focus and so on, but you also have to keep your curiosity and want to make new discoveries which you can only do by admitting newcomers. On my next film I don't necessarily want to have Vittorio, or the extraordinary Jim Acheson who has been doing the costumes for me for ten years. I'll have some other people who've worked for me before, but I also want there to be some surprises.

GN-S: *Where does the music enter the picture? Do you have an idea for the music and who should do it when you are first thinking of the film, or does that only come at the end?*

BB: It depends. Usually I wait to see how the movie looks before deciding what the music should be, or who the musicians should be. But for *Tragedy of a Ridiculous Man* I was moving around in such a fog—because Italy itself was such a fog—that I needed a fixed point, and I asked Morricone to do some music in advance, to provide two or three important pieces for me to work from.

I H : *How does this relate to your love of opera, and your use of Verdi for example?*
B B : There are all sorts of ways music can be used. In *1900*, for example, I asked Morricone to come up with ideas in various styles, either from the Italian musical tradition, ranging from Verdi to folk songs, or from twentieth century music like that of Stravinsky or Schoenberg. But for *Last Emperor* I had three composers and I wanted different things from each of them. From Ryuichi Sakamoto I wanted something epic with an Eastern flavour. Cong Su was brought back from Germany, where he lives, to do Chinese-flavoured court music. And I also had David Byrne. In the end Sakamoto did a kind of western, symphonic music and David Byrne did the chinoiserie because his music is always full of subtle irony. But I always work close to my composers because I'm a frustrated composer myself. I'd like to be able to sing and play an instrument, but I can't. I'd like to be able to dance.

I H : *In every one of your films there is a central dance. They are also, as you say yourself, like operas and the music is integrated with the image. You have said that poetry is a space for freedom and that you wanted to carry that freedom over to your films. Talking about these things should take us back to your origins— your cultural origins and the way they have stayed with you even though you seem to be at home internationally and have become cosmopolitan.*
B B : Ideally the itinerary should be from the provinces to cosmopolitan life and back again. You need to be able to keep in touch with your roots. Maybe you've come too late to ask about my origins, as I forget. My guilt is that I was born with everything in the world. The work was already done before me. Pasolini grew up in quite an uncultured environment—his father was an army officer and his mother taught in an elementary school. My father became a poet but grew up in a house where there were no books. He really surprised his parents when he was fourteen or so by going into a bookshop during a trip to Venice, instead of visiting San Marco, and buying a volume of Proust because he'd heard about him from a teacher at school. I did not have to buy books. Everything was there for me. And I

had an instinctive reaction to this, a rebellion. My parents were always trying to persuade me to stay at home and read instead of going out all the
time but I said, my school is life, my university is the street. In fact, I never
finished my course in Modern Literature at Rome University as I had started
to make movies. On the other hand for two or three years when I was 20,
21, 22, I had dinner almost every night with Pasolini, Moravia and Elsa
Morante, and I consider that my university. It was my great friend Pier
Paolo who introduced me to Moravia and Elsa Morante and they liked my
poems and published my book and became my friends. In 1961 I had the
great chance, as first assistant on *Accattone*, to see Pier Paolo directing his
first film, or I would say, inventing cinema.

I H :   *What did they talk about? Poetry?*
B B :   And politics. Literature and politics. And travel. They were travelling
a lot, to India and Africa. Moravia was doing a lot of travel journalism,
and Pier Paolo did this book, *The Scent of India*. They went there together.
Elsa Morante went with them. She was a great writer too, and still living
with Moravia at the time, though they had terrible rows. She went off to
Mexico—it was the early '60s—and got into *peyotl* and hallucinogenics.
She was very much into absolute values and hated compromise. Her
favourite insult was "petty-bourgeois." And I was there listening, listening
and learning, and that was my education.

I H :   *But you weren't travelling with them?*
B B :   No. I started travelling much later, only because I couldn't stand the
reality of Italy in the '80s. A kind of voluntary exile.

G N - S :   *That's also why Pasolini travelled. Because he couldn't stand the reality
that surrounded him and he hoped to find something else by going to India or
Africa. For him the Third World was a kind of utopia, in contrast to the capitalist West.*
B B :   That was the impulse behind the Trilogy of Life—*The Decameron, The
Canterbury Tales* and especially *The Arabian Nights*. But then he rejected them
and wrote those very bitter articles in the *Corriere della Sera* in '74 and '75.

G N - S :   *Time's running out and there are lots of things we haven't had time for.
I wanted to ask you a couple of things about* The Sheltering Sky *and* Little

Buddha *because it seems to me there's a kind of turning point there. There's a sort of violent desperation in your films up to and including* The Sheltering Sky *which isn't there in* Little Buddha *which is a very tranquil film. But this may be prefigured in* The Sheltering Sky, *depending on how you interpret the ending. Most people describe the Debra Winger character as having gone mad, but to me it seems as if she's quite sane. She's reached a kind of equilibrium, but at a cost. She doesn't want to see anyone because she needs to cling on to the experience that has transformed her.*

BB: She's maybe mad because she can't stand the sadness which is too much for her. It's a sort of refusal. "Are you lost?" the old man, the writer, asks her. I shot two versions, you know — "Yes, I'm lost" and "No, I'm not lost" — I can't remember which one I put in the film.

Interview with Bernardo Bertolucci

BRUCE SKLAREW/1998

B S : *Your new film,* Besieged, *is based on a story by James Lasdun, entitled "The Siege." Where did you come across this short story by an author who is relatively unknown both in Europe and the United States?*

B B : Clare Peploe, my wife and co-screenwriter of the film, wanted to do this film ten years ago. She wrote a screenplay, and they told her that she couldn't develop it into a film because it was such a little story, and so she dropped it. A year ago, a friend who was chairman of Italian television and was very insistent on my doing something for him. I finally said, "Okay, we'll do something for you." Clare came to me and said, "Why don't you do this?" I read it and said, "It's really good." I think that television is like a miniature in comparison with cinema, which is like a big fresco. The TV screen has the same density and dimension of the miniature, while the screen which shows, say, *The Last Emperor,* is like a big dome with a lot of frescos. And I said this minimal story is very, very dense. I loved it. Between Clare and me there is a kind of leitmotiv. When we would talk between the takes, we were exchanging our communal love for cinema. You know, soon after we met in the late '60s, Clare had taken me to see Robert Bresson's *Les Dames du Bois de Boulogne* in which there is a line from Cocteau, "Il n y a pas d'amour, il n'y a que des preuves d'amour." [There is no love, there are only proofs of love.] So Clare was always telling me there is no love, there are proofs of love. I used that in *Stealing Beauty,* where

---

From the world premiere of *Besieged* at the Toronto Film Festival, 15 September 1998. Reprinted by permission.

Jean Marais, who was Jean Cocteau's lover, quotes this same line. If I happen to say, "I love you," but the other person says, "Yeah." Well, it's easy to say "I love you," it's more difficult to give proof, proofs of love, right? *Besieged* is about that.

BS: *Yes.*

BB: So this film is about the most extraordinary proof of love. Kinsky is ready to give up everything in order to help Shandurai in the most discrete way. In theory, she will never know that the husband has been freed because of Kinsky giving up first his little sculptures, then his paintings, then his tapestries, then his furniture [and, finally, his beloved piano]. The house becomes completely naked. But in doing that, I had this idea that came naturally out of the story. The only way of being really happy is making happy the people you love, which is absolutely the opposite of the ideology of the last, let's say, twenty years. It's the opposite of the society which has been in a kind of drunkenness of me, me, me, me, individualism.

BS: *You mean like what Christopher Lasch is saying in* The Culture of Narcissism.

BB: No, narcissism is something else. Individualism is what I mean. But this is really the opposite. In fact, having approached the Tibetans and Buddhism helped me to understand it because I remember what the Dalai Lama told me the first time I met him, which is that compassion in Christian terms means a kind of duty to be good to the loved one. You have to be good. In the Buddhist sense, compassion means before everything else, the understanding with your mind the reasons of the pain of your loved one. So it's a matter of *understanding.* Why do I say that? Because for a Buddhist, there isn't a soul like for the Christians and the Catholics, and even the Moslems, I think. Instead of using the world "soul," the Buddhists say the word "mind." Hence, understanding. Anyway, that was a little digression.

BS: *I was most impressed with the sudden presences and sudden absences in the film. The presences of the question mark on the music paper, the orchid, the ring, in this very delicate courtship, and then the denuding of the objects as they slowly disappeared, the audience of children disappearing, and also the disappeared husband, who arrives at the very end. And it reminded me of Pu Yi in* The Last Emperor *in Manchukuo, when his Japanese audience disappeared. In your foreword to* The Last Emperor: Multiple Takes, *you wondered in a dream about "the secret of this cocoon, The Forbidden City, . . . the essence of my set. . . . Today, the ultimate meaning of The Forbidden City lies in the endless series of repetitions of the absence and presence of the Emperor."*

B B :   The husband is a kind of character from a dream because the movie starts with a dream, a dream which is half a dream and half a flashback, like often dreams can be. In fact, when she cries, when she shouts at the jeeps, the jeeps which are taking away her husband, you can't hear her voice, like in dreams when you can't hear words. In fact, from there we cut to her in bed having a nightmare, shouting and waking up. And the present is the noise of the dumb waiter coming down with a question mark [written on music paper among her clothes]. And later, the objects disappear, sculptures, paintings, tapestry. And then she tells him, when she's Hoovering [vacuuming], that there is not much to dust here; he says, "I know," with a kind of joy, because he's in the fulfillment of his mission. And the mission is to free her husband. The disappearing objects correspond to a great gratification for him. So giving away, he gets something—giving away, he gets this kind of great gratification. You can see it, while at the beginning he was awkward and weird and shy and aggressive, at the end he's kind of growing up. He's more adult.

B S :   *It's a true enjoyment in relinquishment.*
B B :   Yes, a true relinquishment.

B S :   *But you don't see this as a manipulation.*
B B :   It's not a manipulation at all because she doesn't know what he is doing. So he's doing it without even the privilege of being able to say, "You see, I'm doing that for you." So it's the total annihilation of selfishness which gives him an incredible substitute for sex—a very solitary feeling of being able to take this mission to an end. He will free her husband.

B S :   *And there's the theme of getting what one wishes for and then the mystery of what happens after that, which is such a wonderful ending.*
B B :   Oh, the ending. You know, we thought about it, and then I think that the warrior is outside the door. The door is left out in the film—and you see the first passengers, the first people coming out from the metro.

B S : *Warrior? He's not a military man. . . .*

B B : Well, he's a warrior. He's a hero. He's becoming in her mind a memory, a hero. Anyway, he comes back. He's outside of the door. She will let him in, I think. That's why she moves from the bed, with a kind of pain on her face. When she moves, she's like crying, but she can't leave this man, who's been two years in jail. I think she would be a horrible person leaving her husband outside the door. I mean, we don't know what will happen. I don't want to say, because if I knew it, I would have said it. I would like to end with that kind of "question mark" myself, but what I know is that we have her moving to leave the bed and him outside the door.

B S : *So, she's besieged, not just externally, but internally throughout the film both by her desires and her conscience.*

B B : Yes.

B S : *I was struck with the story in which there were so many references to whiteness: the sheets, the black and white tile, the shadows, the suds, the white blossom, his shins, the paper, the steam. You see her as someone who is focused on cleaning and cleansing as though this was part of her internal struggle between her mounting desires for Kinsky and at the same time her conscience that was trying to cleanse her, have her be good, have her be a helpful, healing physician. Or is this more circumstantial?*

B B : It's her job, first of all. She lives there and in exchange for having a nice room, she cleans and irons. The arrangement is that she has the room and maybe some *argent de poche*, some pocket money. But there is a kind of meditation, washing and cleaning. It is a kind of therapy. You can see that when she's in the nightclub pouring a beer; the foam of the beer becomes the foam on the floor and then she wipes the floor with this foam and there is a Beethoven piece and she's in the spiral staircase and it's a little piece I really wanted, where there are no words. And if you noticed that in the first twenty minutes of the film, there are so few words; the beginning is completely silent of words, not of sounds, but of words. Part of the reason for this is that recently I've been struggling with the question: Where is cinema going? How much should cinema try to fuse with new technologies? I think *Besieged* answers these kinds of questions. My feeling was that I had to go back to the cinema of origins, as it was before the advent of sound in 1927 when it succeeded in communicating feelings uniquely through images: in fact the first fifteen to twenty minutes of the film are silent like the cinema of the origins.

BS: *You have instead the beginning spiraling of the music. Tell me about the music in this film.*

BB: Well in *Besieged* there is this struggle between African music and Western classic music, which is of course the confrontation of two different cultures, but it is also the way of communicating or the way of not being able to communicate. Indeed, *Besieged* is a metaphor for the shock between cultures—and it's precisely their differences from the culture of Rome which unite Kinsky and Shandurai. I've always been a partisan of all forms of cultural "contamination" whether on the stylistic level, as an artist, or on the cultural level, as a man. So we see that while he is composing his concerto that he's being influenced by her and it's so underwritten, and he begins playing for her when she's Hoovering. And the more he plays the more he becomes very sensual. She is the muse and he's inspired by her, and because he wouldn't dare put his hand on her, his sexual desire goes into the music and he starts giving shape and form to the music and it's the moment where he seduces her for real. It's not so much the discovery that he has given up everything for her; she's already been seduced by the music.

BS: *And I must say this music is extraordinarily beautiful. Who actually wrote the "Ostinato" piece for the film?*

BB: I asked Alessio Vlad to write it. He is the son of a well-known conductor, Roman Vlad. Alessio also happened to be an actor for me in *Luna*, twenty years ago. Remember the young conductor on the stage during the final sequence in Caracalla?

BS: *What about the project that you're planning on Gesualdo, the great madrigal composer of the Italian Renaissance. Can you comment on your evolving use of music?*

BB: It's always been there; now, it's more direct.

BS: *What's inspired that?*

BB: I always had a great love for music. I always felt that in this huge amount of camera movements that are in my movies, what was driving the camera was musical input. I always thought that my camera moves for musical reasons.

B S : *With music, with a rhythm?*
B B : Yeah, but not the music that you hear.

B S : *Yes, an internal rhythm.*
B B : A kind of internal music you cannot hear. And so, now, it is coming more direct. In this film, to be called *Heaven and Hell*, about Gesualdo a composer that Stravinsky thought was the most incredible case of musical prophesy because in 1591 he was writing music that Stravinsky thought was in anticipation of the music of the twentieth century, with a kind of dissonance. That's why Stravinsky went to Naples in 1951 on his way to Venice for the opening of *The Rakes' Progress*. Stravinsky stopped in Naples because he wanted to know more about Gesualdo, so Stravinsky is in the film because he's the greatest admirer of Gesualdo in recent times.

B S : *To come back to* Besieged, *where did you find that wonderful staircase?*
B B : It was in a little abandoned palace just next to the Spanish steps. It's a unique house, there are no flats. And in working with Clare, I imagined a spiral staircase, and so we found many houses, but never a spiral staircase like this one. The real character of the film is the spiral staircase. Then the piano. Then you have a woman and a man.

B S : *A woman and a man in an empty house, a bit like* Last Tango in Paris!
B B : In fact, it could be considered a kind of post-modern variation on the *Tango* theme, but I believe I have been even more economical here on the minimalist side! You just have a glimpse of the Spanish Steps when Shandurai reads the letter on the terrace, between the drying sheets. You see behind the two towers and the obelisk of the Spanish Steps. I've been very economical with the Spanish Steps because it's so much the image on postcards.

B S : *So obviously, that house was not chosen because of its proximity to the Spanish Steps?*
B B : No, also, as you know, when you were mentioning absence and presence, the same goes with the Spanish Steps because when she opens the

windows there at the beginning of the film, you see the Steps outside. You don't know what Steps they are, but people living in Rome, they would know. The way I show the Spanish Steps is like a game going back to Freud's little grandson who didn't cry when his mother left him. He would throw a wooden spool tied with a string over the edge of his crib and then pull it back. It was like exercising in abandoning, and being abandoned. Freud noticed that the son of his daughter, who died when he was two or three, was doing this thing. He was throwing it away and saying, "Ah, it's disappeared," gone, and then it reappeared. As a way of practicing being abandoned.

B S: *The English analyst, Winnicott, spoke of transitional objects like the comforting security blanket and other inanimate objects that are linked to the mother, and one could speculate that the mouse might have served that function in* The Last Emperor.

B B: It reminds me that, at the time of *The Last Emperor*, Jeremy Thomas' child was calling his blanket, "Mom."

B S: *I was struck in the film that you had Shandurai dusting the nude statues, stroking and making his bed and her student friend saying that you will end up in bed with this man, whom she felt initially repelled by. Can you talk more about the transformation in this besieged woman, from the early repulsion to acceptance?*

B B: I think that there is an evolution. I think that in the beginning he is a real weirdo because he is in love. And he has an awkwardness which is not appealing. He's shy and aggressive. I think that his love declaration is a masterpiece on the verge of becoming ludicrous, because he's so awkward that he's incredibly shy and terribly aggressive. He takes, he grabs her as if he wants to rape her. Then, in fact, he just wants to say, "Marry me." And then, little by little, because of the accomplishment of his mission he becomes appealing, and at the end of the film Kinsky is attractive although Shandurai was first repelled by him.

B S: *You mean because of his "mission" in selling the objects to get husband released from prison.*

B B: No his mission of giving a proof of love by giving up everything he owns just to get her husband out of jail. He becomes attractive and appealing because of this extraordinary proof. I mean what she does eventually is not a mercy (thank you) fuck. It's her life; it's going in that direction now.

B S : *Right. She's fully falling in love with him. So it was important to find an actor who not only was a superb actor but someone who doesn't fit the stereotype of the male movie star.*

B B : No, of course. In the story Kinsky is as mysterious as he is in the film. He was around mid-fifties, fat. Clare and I thought maybe we'd better go with a younger man. I didn't want to see myself in some way having a crush for a young lady, it's a bit pathetic; so I wanted to go for a younger actor. I'd seen David Thewlis in Mike Leigh's *Naked* and loved him. It's a beautiful film, and he is fantastic; he won the best actor in the Cannes Festival.

B S : *What about Thandie Newton?*

B B : In James Lasdun's story the girl was called Marietta and she was from Latin American, but that was fifteen years ago when Latin American countries were in the news because of their dictators. The story happened in London, and I moved it to Rome today where there are political exiles from some not very democratic African countries. So that was a big change. And I was in London looking because I knew I wanted to keep the original idea of this English pianist and this girl who was from one of the Anglophone countries. When first I met Thandie, I found a very well educated English young lady, and I told her I wanted the real thing. And she said, "Well that's my job to learn how an African girl speaks English," and she studied her mother and mother's friends' accents.

B S : *In addition to using actors you've never used before, you used a new director of cinematography. Was this because you were making the film for TV?*

B B : Well, certainly doing a film for TV really freed me up. I found myself on a very low-budget doing a movie in Rome in twenty-eight days with a small crew and also some new people, including this new cinematographer, Fabio Cianchetti, who had already been working for my brother, Giuseppe. Fabio made me feel like I did when I did first started making films. With Vittorio Storaro there was always so much time spent setting up shots. But now I had this great feeling that I was doing a shot, and this shot immediately creates another shot which gives birth to another shot, and so on and so on, which means that at the end of the day we'd been able to do twenty or thirty set-ups, something incredibly stimulating I hadn't experience for many years! I asked him not to think, not to elaborate too much the so-called "ideology" of the lighting. I needed this kind of immediacy so I told him: please don't try to be elegant with the light of this film. We're going back to the origins when the darkness was too dark and the light of the sun was too strong. So often we shot with the 2000 ASA film. And also I did something only five years ago I would have condemned, which was to mix up hand held camera with steadicam with tracking shots — all mixed together without really any concern for continuity. And that gave me such fantastic pleasure. It was like going back to the '60s, to the old times when there wasn't so much pressure. To go back to that feeling was extraordinary. In the last fifteen years this was obviously impossible because the projects were so big. Now to go back to a little budget film was incredibly stimulating.

BS: *Since you're evoking those early years, let me ask you about them. This book of interviews begins with one you did at age eleven and it included a poem that you wrote about a shadow. You may not have looked at these early poems for a long time.*

BB: Well looking at these poems is like reading with detachment something that someone else wrote! How old was I?

BS: *Eleven.*

BB: Eleven. I think that for an eleven-year-old school kid, it's as Pasolini once said, "Together, very sophisticated and very naive."

BS: *But amazingly precocious. In* Besieged *you have, perhaps, a double of the young poet who's playing the piano.*

BB: Little Amadeus. He was exceptional. I discovered he'd given a few concerts. I remember that I think I was writing poetry in order to imitate and eventually beat my father in the Oedipus search, beating the father for conquering the mother. But I think that that's why at the age of twenty, I decided to stop writing poems because I understood that I couldn't beat him on that field. I thought I could beat him only by becoming a film director. But my present feeling is that I think I lost all my struggle with him.

B S : *You lost all your struggle?*

B B : Struggle. Fight. Because there he is now, unable to move in the chair, switching off like a candle, and there she is sitting in front of him, protecting him as she has always done. I mean, it's still the same, the same kind of image and relationship.

B S : *Thank you for finding this time between all your press conferences to share these thoughts with me!*

INDEX